HISTORY
OF
ELEMENTARY EDUCATION
IN INDIA

HISTORY

OF

ELEMENTARY EDUCATION

IN INDIA

J. M. SEN

GYAN

Published by

GYAN

Gyan Publishing House
5, Ansari Road
Daryaganj, New Delhi-110002
Phone: 011-47034999, 9811692060
E-mail: books@gyanbooks.com

Distribution Network
gyanbooks.com
India, USA, Canada, UK, Australia

ISBN:978-93-7097-349-7 (PB)

First Published, 1941

2nd Impression 2025

Printed at: Gyan Press, Delhi.

HISTORY OF ELEMENTARY EDUCATION IN INDIA
Arthur J. M. SEN

HISTORY
OF
ELEMENTARY EDUCATION IN INDIA

BY

J. M. SEN, M.Ed. (Leeds), B Sc (Cal), F.R G S ,

Teacher's Diploma (London), Diploma in Education (Oxford).

Bengal Senior Educational Service

SECOND EDITION

THE BOOK COMPANY LTD.

COLLEGE SQUARE, CALCUTTA

1941.

INTRODUCTION

Nearly a quarter of a century ago late Gopal Krishna Gokhale from his place in the Imperial Legislative Council said to the Governor-General of India, who was presiding over its deliberations —"My Lord, if the history of elementary education throughout the world establishes one fact more clearly than another, it is this, that without a resort to compulsion no State can ensure a general diffusion of education among its people. England, with her strong love of individualism, stood out against the principle of compulsion for as long as she could, but she had to give way in the end all the same."

No comprehensive History of Elementary Education in India has yet been written. The task is not an easy one, for India is a vast country and the problems concerning education are different in different provinces. In this book I have attempted to trace the State's relation to education in India from the earliest times to 1932.* Prior to 1854, the only policy which dominated the educational history of the country was that of creating a limited intelligentsia of the upper classes. Since then the policy had no doubt changed, but the process had been a very slow one extending over a period of more than fifty years. The Government of India had always

* In the second edition this has been traced to 1940 (*vide* Preface).

encouraged voluntary efforts in education and to supplement them had introduced the grant-in-aid system in the latter half of the nineteenth century. But the Government did not undertake the task of formulation of any comprehensive system of education for the masses of India till 1904.

Although a provision in the East India Act of 1813 empowering the Governor-General of India to spend one lakh of rupees each year for the purpose of education was the first legislative admission of the right of education to participate in the public revenues of India, and though the Education Despatch of 1854 issued by the Court of Directors of the East India Company (re-affirmed by Lord Stanley, the first Secretary of State for India, in his Despatch of 1859) was the first basis for a state educational programme in India, it is in the Indian Educational Policy of 1904 that we find for the first time the Government of India declaring that the rapid spread of primary education is one of the foremost duties of the State.

The reluctance of the Government of India to interfere in education was more or less due to the controversy that had been raging in the West, especially in England, regarding the right of the State to intervene in education. The British public tried for a long time to uphold individual liberty in education and we find that it was not till 1870, that Parliament became successful in formulating a state system of elementary education for England. In all countries in Europe and America the State slowly intervened in education. At the present age State-consciousness in education is visible everywhere. Each nation is now trying to give its people opportunities for realizing their citizenship to the fullest extent. The State now realizes that if a child is to become with increasing years a more efficient citizen and man, if he is to render more and more aid to the State, he needs to be trained properly so that all his powers, physical, mental, moral and religious may be developed to the best advantage. The process of realization of this responsibility on the part of the State has been a slow one. But we find that all nations sufficiently raised above barbarism to exist as States have in all ages—after making due provision for comfortable physical subsistence—afforded a moderate and increasing share of instruction to the people. In India, however, so completely, so desperately, had the whole popular body been pervaded by the stupefying power of a long reign of ignorance, that we still have before us a melancholy spectacle.

In Chapter I, I have tried to show what the Hindu and Muhammadan kings did for the spread of education. Sufficient materials are not available even now to write any exhaustive account of what the Hindu kings did in that direction. As regards the Muhammadan period a very valuable book, 'Promotion of Learning in India by Muhammadans', has been written by Mr. Narendra Nath Law. For the materials of this period I have drawn largely on his book and supplemented them by other works. A great part of the facts related in Chapters II, III and IV was obtained from the Proceedings of Parliamentry Debates, Reports of the Indian Education Commission of 1882-83 and "Selections from Educational Records", Parts I and II (1781 to 1839 and 1840 to 1859), published by the Bureau of Education, India. So far as vernacular education in Bengal is concerned I have received considerable help from the materials contained in a history of it, from 1813 to 1912, written by Mr. H A. Stark, a retired Inspector of Schools in Bengal. In Chapters I, II and III, elementary education could not be separated from secondary and collegiate education. In those chapters an attempt has been made to show why and how the Government of the country tried to give more encouragement to secondary and collegiate education than to elementary education. And for this reason the first three chapters of the book can be considered as History of Education in India from the earliest times to 1859. In Chapters IV, V and VI, an attempt has been made to show clearly the development of the policy of Government concerning elementary education in India culminating in the passing of compulsory Education Acts in different provinces of the country.

The facts given in the book have been drawn mainly from official records and personal experience gained by visiting a large number of educational institutions in several provinces of India. Arguments and illustrations I have not hesitated to draw from more gifted writers, and I have acknowledged them throughout the book in foot-notes. If this book can assist the general public, particularly those interested in popular education, in understanding what has already been done and what still remains to be done in regard to introduction of compulsory education in India, its purpose will have been fulfilled.

CALCUTTA,
June, 1933. J. M. SEN.

PREFACE TO THE SECOND EDITION.

Eight years have elapsed since the first edition of the book was published. The intervening period had witnessed a lot of political unrest and constitutional changes in India. Since 1935, the social and educational ideas of the people had also undergone considerable modification in the light of the changes made in the administration of the country. A new orientation in educational policy was attempted in all the provinces of India. But the present European War which has also spread to Asia has caused a set back as regards progressive development of the policy. It is all the more necessary that the History of Elementary Education in India should be brought up to date. For this purpose the last chapter (viz. Chapter VI) of the first edition of the book has been revised by incorporation of fresh materials and a new chapter (viz. Chapter VII) on *Education under the new Constitution* has been added. The contents of Sections IX and X of Chapter VI of the first edition of the book have now after revision been included in relevant sections of Chapter VII. A new section on "the Control and Administration of Primary Education in different provinces" has been inserted. It deals with the problem of dual control over education by the provincial governments and the local authorities which have been set up under the various Local Self-Government Acts and the Education Acts. The Wardha Scheme of Education as an important contribution towards a curriculum for a Basic National Education has also been given in the last chapter. It is hoped that all these will add to the usefulness of the book.

KRISHNAGAR,
June, 1941.

J. M. SEN.

CONTENTS

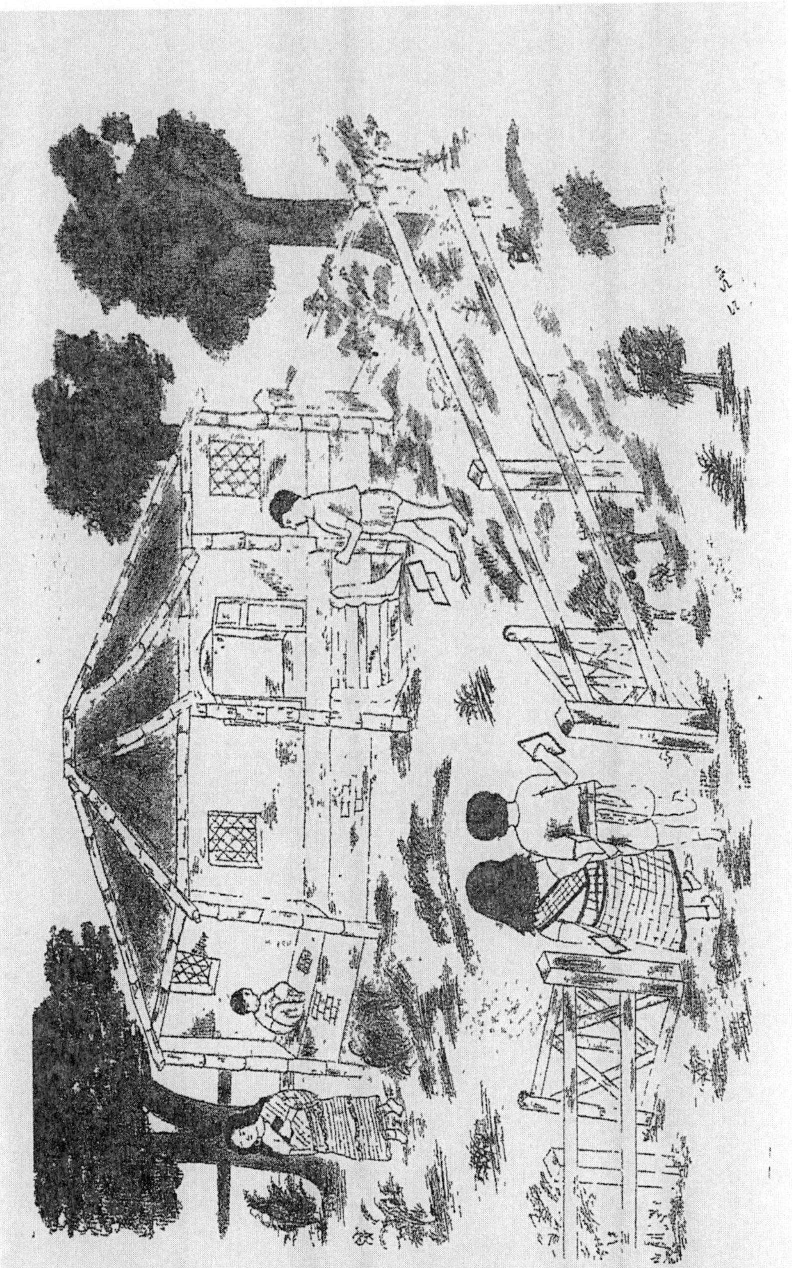

CHAPTER I

HINDU AND MUHAMMADAN PERIOD

SECTION I—INDIGENOUS EDUCATION

For centuries India had been famous for her philosophy, literature, and ancient schools of learning. They were inseparably associated with the religion which dominated her people and have profoundly affected the course and progress of education. In any society, however advanced or however primitive, education may be regarded as a process of adjustment to environment. Its nature is determined by the inherited powers and capabilities of the recipients as well as by the environment in which they grow up. It is a known fact now that the Aryans were not the original inhabitants of India. They entered India by some passes and gorges between the mountains lying on the north west of India. Those who first entered India were highly intellectual people and were remarkable for their manly virtues. The Aryans came not in one batch but in a number of waves of invasion spreading over several centuries. With each invasion the older tribes were pushed farther east or south by the new tribe. The ancient sages of India not only composed Vedic hymns and performed religious sacrifices but cultivated their agricultural lands and when occasion arose fought wars with the aggressive tribes. These wars kept up their fighting spirit for a long time. But when they settled down in the vast plains of Northern India very little scope was left for developing their martial spirit and manly virtues. The tropical climate and highly fertile soil enabled the people to get their food and clothing without much effort. Hence the struggle for existence in India in ancient times was an easy one. Moreover, after the several waves of Aryan invasion the country remained absolutely shut off from any outside influence by the lofty mountains on the north and the north-west, and by the seas on the other sides. This gave the Hindu culture a unique character.

The peculiar environmental conditions lasted for generations and helped to make the people of India more passive, meditative and philosophical than the people of any other country in the world. In the earliest stages, when the Aryans settled down in different parts of the country and formed groups, both the individual and the social forces worked more or less unconsciously. In ancient India there had been no deliberate effort on the part of the individual to assert his individuality, nor had society attempted to subordinate that individuality to public interests. Yet each tendency had continually been at work. By the mere fact of living in a society the individual had then been moulded to the needs of that society. There was, of course, no deliberate attempt to check the growth of his individuality, but some check constantly acted on him. No doubt the individual reacted upon society and did his best to modify it; but the society's influence on the individual was undoubtedly greater than his influence on it. However independent the individual might have felt himself to be, almost all his activities were carried on in such a way as to meet the approval of the society in which he had been living.

History tells us that from very early times men lived in India in some form or other of organised society. Even the pre-Aryan races had a system of public administration. Family was the basis of the primitive Aryan state. Several families coalesced in the process of evolution and grew into the clan, the clan in the course of time expanded into the tribe and ultimately the tribe was merged in the state. "The head of the family became the chief of the clan, then the leader of the tribe, and ultimately the ruler of the state. . . . In the course of time the state outgrew its original limitations and became national."[1]

In an ancient Indian state the ruler was never regarded as the head of the religion; the primary duty of the ruler was to look after the social well-being of the people. Religious ministrations were

---

[1] P. N. Banerjea—'Public Administration in Ancient India', page 38. This paragraph and the one following are based upon Chapter IV, 'The Origin and Nature of the State', of P. N. Banerjea's book.

left in the hands of the priests. This led to the position that "the political status of individuals was independent of their religious beliefs and convictions."[1] As regards the sphere of state action we find that it was originally confined simply to the maintenance of internal order, then it assumed the administration of justice. With the progress of civilization the society became more and more complex and the sphere of state action gradually widened and enveloped almost the entire life of the people with a view to securing for them the maximum well-being in every department of life. During the earlier stages of political growth there had been hardly any differentiation of functions—the same persons used to exercise various powers. But as the sphere of state action gradually extended, and the authority of the state also increased it was found necessary to have division of functions. This division and sub-division, although necessary, was carried to such an elaborate extent in India that each individual was obliged only to work in his particular line without having anything to do with the work of other people. This led to the formation of a rigid caste system which marked off Hindu society from the rest of the world. "The great drawback of the State in ancient India was that the rights of man as man were not fully recognised. Individuals had rights and duties not

[1] Banerjea—'Public Administration in Ancient India', page 39.

as component parts of the body politic but as members of estates or classes in society; and consequently, as we have already seen, the rights and obligations varied according to the class to which the individuals belonged."[1]

There is hardly any record of what the Hindu and Buddhist kings did for education before the third century B.C. There was, of course, the old Brahmanical system of education prevailing in the country. *According to this system the pupils were required to spend a good many years, from the age of six to twenty-one, in the house of their preceptors.* In some institutions they were not even allowed to come back to their parents or guardians during the period of their instruction. The pupils used to do all the work of their preceptors, including the cultivation of their lands. They also used to go out begging for the needs of the institution. The pupils were looked upon as young mendicants and people used to give money and food for their maintenance. They occasionally used to get special grants from the kings and landholders. But every citizen thought it was his duty to help towards the upkeep of such institutions. It was as much a duty of the rich, as of the poor. And very few shirked their responsibilities. It need not be discussed here what was the nature of the education they received

---

[1] P. N. Banerjea—'Public Administration in Ancient India', page 40.

in such schools and colleges. But it must be noted that education was not universal; it was confined to particular classes.

There were three types of institutions viz., the 'parishads', the 'tols', and the 'pathsalas.' The *parishads* were assemblies of the elders—almost exclusively Brahmins—of the community. Their function was primarily to assist the kings in the interpretation of the law and usages. As such they might be compared to the judicial assemblies. But they used to take in a number of students in philosophy, logic and law for advanced work. Hence they also can be compared to the association of teachers in Europe in the middle ages which developed later into universities.

The *tols* were the second type of these institutions for imparting education, and they had residential quarters attached to them. In the early Hindu period the word 'Matha' meant a residence of pupils and ascetics. The *mathas* which used to take in only students gradually came to be called *tols*. The *tol* as a rule admitted only the Brahmin students. A student remained at the *tol* for eight to twelve years from the age of about ten years. The years of residence depended on the subjects which he used to study and specialize in. The students used to live in the simplest manner in huts built and repaired at the expense of the pandit (teacher). In a few *tols* the teacher did not live with the pupils but came every day early in the morning and stayed till sunset. The senior students used to act as guardians of the juniors in his absence. Not only were no fees charged in the tols, but the teacher also provided the pupils with food and clothing. Each tol used to take in about twenty-five students, and that was possibly the number which one teacher could manage. As regards financial help the teacher depended entirely on the generosity of the public. The more famous a teacher became, the more he used to get grants and presents from the benevolent rulers, and citizens.

These institutions also showed the corporate life of ancient India. "We read in Losaka Jataka how the villagers appointed a teacher by paying his expenses and giving him a hut to live in. . . . In those times the Benares folk used to give day by day food to poor lads and had them taught free. A very good example of the public co-operation as well as the corporate character of the institution itself is furnished by Tittira Jataka. We read that a renowned professor at Benares gave instruction in sciences to five hundred young Brahmins. One day he thought, 'So long as I dwell here, I meet with hindrances to the religious life and my pupils are not perfected in their studies. I will retire into a forest home on the slopes of the Himalayas and carry on my teachings there.' He told his pupils, and bidding them bring sesame, husked rice, oil, garments and such like, he went into the forest and building a hut of leaves took up his abode close by the highway. His pupils too each built a hut for himself. Their kinsfolk sent rice and the like, and the natives of the country saying 'a famous professor is living in such and such a place in the forest, and giving lessons in science,' brought presents of rice, and foresters also offered their gifts, while a certain man gave a milch cow and a calf to supply them with milk. Similar corporate educational institutions are frequently referred to in the Jatakas."[1] A few instances therein clearly prove that the students had a common mess and lived as an organised corporate body under the teacher. While other instances show that some such institutions were partly maintained by honorariums paid by the sons of wealthy members of the society. It is particularly interesting to note that not only religious treatises like the Vedas, but various secular arts and sciences were also taught in these centres of learning.

Section II—Hindu and Buddhist Education

In early times Hindu civilisation remained confined to the north-western part of India. Hence we notice that Kashmere and Badarikasram for a long time enjoyed the reputation of being the cradle of Hindu civilisation. In the sixth century B.C. Takshasila (modern Taxilla near Peshwar) became the chief centre of learning.

---

[1] R. C. Majumdar—'Corporate Life in Ancient India', p. 173.

The king Bimbisara (582 to 554 B.C.) helped the institution with grants, because it is said that he was once cured of some painful diseases by the physician of repute, Jivaka, who was attached to the school of Medicine at Takshasila.

Nothing further is known as to the educational history of the country till we come to the reign of Asoka (269 to 229 B.C.) and we get a very interesting account of what Asoka did for education in Vincent Smith's book, 'Asoka, the Buddhist Emperor of India':—

"The care taken to publish the Imperial edicts and commemorative records by incising them in imperishable characters, most skilfully executed, on rocks and pillars situated in great cities, on main lines of communication, or at sacred spots frequented by pilgrims, implies that a knowledge of reading and writing was widely diffused, and that many people must have been able to read the documents. The same inference may be drawn from the fact that the inscriptions are composed not in any learned scholastic tongue, but in vernacular dialects intelligible to the common people, and modified when necessary to suit local needs. It is probable that learning was fostered by the numerous monasteries, and that the boys and girls in hundreds of villages learned their lessons from the monks and nuns, as they do now in Burma from the monks. Asoka it should be noted, encouraged nunneries, and makes particular reference more than once to female lay disciples as well as to nuns. I think it likely that the percentage of literacy among the Buddhist population in Asoka's time was higher than it is now in many provinces of British India. The returns of 1901 show that in the United Provinces of Agra and Oudh, which include many great cities and ancient capitals, the number of persons per 1000 able to read and write amounts to only 57 males and 2 females. In Burma, where the Buddhist monasteries flourish, the corresponding figures are 378 and 45. I believe that Buddhist monasteries and nunneries in the days of their glory must have been, on the whole, powerful agencies for good in India, and that the disappearance of Buddhism was a great loss to the country."[1]

The ancient university of Nalanda, which was a great seat of learning, for many centuries received state endowments from successive kings from the time of Buddha. The genuinely historical period of the institution, however, begins with the time of Bälâditya who flourished in the middle of the fifth century A.D. The Chinese traveller, Hieuen Tsiang, who visited India in the seventh century A D. found the institution at the height of its glory and the resort of a number of foreign students and scholars.

A very interesting account of the growth of the institution at Nalanda is given in "the life

---

[1] Vincent Smith—'Asoka', (Oxford Clarendon Press, 1920), p. 138 f.

of Hieuen Tsiang" by Shamans Hwui and Yen-tsung, translated from Chinese by Samuel Beal. The account is so interesting that I am constrained to give lengthy extracts from it.

"The Nalanda monastery is the same as the 'charity without intermission' monastery. The tradition of the old people is this:—To the south of the convent in the middle of an Âmra garden is a pool. In this pool is a Nâga (serpent) called Nâlanda, and the convent built by the side of the pool is therefore called after his name. Again there is a saying that Tathägata whilst a Bôdhisattva was the king of a great country and built his capital in this place. He was deeply affected towards the orphans and destitute, and ever moved by this principle gave away all he had for their good. In memory of this goodness they named the place 'doing charitable acts without intermission.' The place was originally the garden of the Lord (Shreshtin) Âmra (or Âmara). Five hundred merchants bought it for ten lacs of gold pieces and presented it to Buddha. Here Buddha preached the law for three months, and most of the merchants obtained the fruit of *Arhatship* in consequence. After the Nirvana of Buddha an old king of this country called Sakrâditya, from a principle of loving obedience to Buddha, built this convent. After his decease his son Buddhagupta-râja seized the throne, and continued the vast undertaking; he built, towards the south, another sânghârâma (or monastery).

Then his son (successor) Tathâgata-rajá built a sangharama to the eastward. Next his son (or direct descendant) Baladitya built a sangharâma to the north-east. Afterwards the king seeing some priests who came from the country of China to receive his religious offerings, was filled with gladness and he gave up his royal estate and became a recluse. His son Vajra succeeded and built another sangharâma to the north. After him a king of mid-India built by the side of this another sangharâma. Thus six kings in connected succession added to these structures.

"Moreover, the whole establishment is surrounded by a brick wall, which encloses the entire convent from without. One gate opens into the great college, from which are separated eight other halls, standing in the middle (of the Sangharama). The richly adorned towers, and the fairy-like turrets, like pointed hill tops, are congregated together. The observatories seem to be lost in the vapours (of the morning), and the upper rooms tower above the clouds. From the windows one may see how the winds and the clouds (produce new forms), and above the soaring eaves the conjunctions of the sun and moon (may be observed). And then we may add how the deep, translucent ponds, bear on their surface the blue lotus, intermingled with the Kieni (kanaka) flower of deep red colour, and at intervals the Âmra groves spread over all, their shade. All the outside courts, in which are the priests' chambers, are of four stages. The stages have dragon projections and coloured eaves, the pearl-red pillars carved and ornamented, the richly adorned balustrades, and the roofs covered with tiles that reflect the light in a thousand shades, these things add to the beauty of the scene.

"The Sangharamas of India are counted by myriads, but this is the most remarkable for grandeur and height. The priests, belonging to the convent, or strangers (residing therein) always reach to the number of 10,000, who all study 'The Great Vehicle' and also (the works belonging to) the eighteen sects, and not only so, but even ordinary works such as the Vedas and other books, the Hetuvidyâ (Logic), Sabdavidya (Phonetics) the Chikitsâvidya (Medicine), the works on Magic (Atharvavidya or pharmacology), the Sankhya (a system of philosophy); besides these they thoroughly investigate the miscellaneous works. There are 1000 men who can explain twenty collections of Sutrâs and Sãstras; 500 who can explain thirty collections, and perhaps ten men, including the Master of the Law, who can explain fifty collections. Silabhadra alone has studied and understood the whole number. His eminent virtue and advanced age have caused him to be regarded as the chief member of the community. Within the temple they arrange every day about 100 pulpits for preaching and the students attend these discourses without any fail, even for a minute (an inch shadow on the dial).

The priests dwelling here, are as a body naturally (or spontaneously) dignified and grave, so that during the 700 years since the foundation of the establishment, there has been no single case of guilty rebellion against the rules. The king of the country respects and honours the priests, and has remitted the revenues of about 100 villages for the endowment of the convent. Two hundred householders in these villages, day by day contribute several hundred piculs (one picul= 133⅓ lbs.) of ordinary rice, and several hundred catties (one catty=160 lbs.) in weight of butter and milk. *Hence the students here, being so abundantly supplied, do not require to ask for the four requisites (clothes, food, bedding and medicine)*. This is the source of the perfection of their studies, to which they have arrived."[1]

Education evidently was diffused widely, especially among the Brahmins and numerous Buddhist monks; and learning was honoured by the government. King Harsha (606 to 647 A.D.) was not only a liberal patron of literary merit, but was himself an accomplished calligraphist and an author of reputation. About the middle of the eighth century A.D., Gopala, who was then king of Bengal founded schools attached to the monastery of Odantapuri, or Uddandapura. At the close of the eighth century A.D., King Dharmapala founded a monastery at Vikramsila which

[1] Beal's translation of the Life of Hiuen-tsiang, 1888, (Trubner & Co), page 110 ff.

is said to have included 107 temples and six colleges. Among the subjects studied were grammar, metaphysics including logic, and ritualistic books. The king endowed his foundation with grants for the maintenance of monks and students. The kings of this period used to hold debates in their courts in order that students might show their talent, and thus obtain appointments in the practical government. This was also the period when the title of 'pandit' (learned) was conferred on distinguished scholars by the king himself.

Members of the archæological department of India by their explorations during the last twenty years have brought to light many valuable records giving some idea as to the extent the kings and corporate bodies in ancient India bequeathed properties for educational purposes. Most of the records brought to light in Southern India belong to the period, eleventh to thirteenth centuries A.D. Some of them have been published in the Madras Epigraphy Reports, and show that schools and colleges at Kancipuram, Tiruchattipuram, Sembaikkudi, Tiruvorraiyur, Bahugrama, Belgami and at several other ancient cities and villages were founded by the kings and corporate bodies.

The Madras Epigraphy Reports also show that in the eleventh century A.D., at the time of King Rajendra-Cola I, a college for Vedic studies was endowed and maintained by the assembly of the village named Rajaraja-caturvedi-mangalam.

Attached to it there was a hostel accommodating 340 students and 10 professors.

"It is interesting to note that the teachers in some of the subjects were paid for their instruction according to what economists know as the 'piece-work' system. Thus the professor of Vyakarana (Grammar) was paid one 'Kalañju' of gold per adhyaya (chapter) taught."[1]

These inscriptions show that even in ancient times the village assemblies, the then local authorities, maintained schools and colleges.

At Bijapur till this day some detached pillars of an ancient temple remain here and there, and the Agrahar or College attached to it is still wonderfully perfect, though necessarily out of repair. This building is the most venerable in Bijapur, and is a remnant of the Hindoo sovereignty which existed in Southern India before the invasion of the Muhammadans at the end of the thirteenth century.

A huge pillar inscription at Malkapuram in the Guntur taluk of the Guntur district records gifts by the Kakatiya kings for the establishment of a school, a hospital and a feeding house. It should also be mentioned here that in a few areas the village communities levied a special tax for the maintenance of public institutions. One archæological record registers "an agreement by which the residents of Pularkoltan submit

---

[1] R. K. Mookerji—'Local Government in Ancient India', page 280.

to a special tax levied in the northern and southern divisions of Tirruvorraiyur for maintaining the Mandapa (school-building) and other similar buildings of the temple."[1]

The *Pathsalas* were the real elementary schools in ancient India, imparting instructions in reading, writing and arithmetic. These schools are still very numerous throughout the country. One can possibly trace the history of village education in India to the beginnings of the village community. The schoolmaster was an officer of the community. Either rent-free lands were assigned to him or he was given some grains out of the village harvest. The early schoolmaster was of course a Brahmin. His chief function was to offer worship to the idol—the village deity—on behalf of all classes of people who lived in the village. His subsidiary function was to impart instruction to the children of the higher castes in the three R's in the vernacular together with precepts of morality as embodied in compilations and enforced by Puranic legends. Vyakaran (Grammar), Abhidhan (wordbook or dictionary), and Kavya (poetry) in Sanskrit, were also taught to the most advanced students of the superior castes. The pathsala teacher, however, could charge fees for his tuition or could receive offerings in kind from the scholars and parents. "The outstanding characteristics of the schools of

[1] Mookerji—'Local Government in Ancient India', page 274.

the Hindu village community were that they were democratic, and that they were more secular than spiritual in their instruction and their general character."[1]

The Aryans when they penetrated into the east and south, gradually absorbed many non-Aryan populations and moulded and assimilated them into Hinduism. The non-Aryan deities were given places in the Hindu pantheon; and new castes were created in the Hindu community for the absorption of the better class non-Aryans. They were given places in the four superior castes. The pathsalas, or the village schools, were open to all the superior castes alike, and in this sense they were democratic. But it must be admitted that even these pathsalas were closed to those who lay outside the regular caste system, to those who were considered untouchables and to the innumerable aboriginal inhabitants of the country. "Throughout the long history of indigenous education in India, it is impossible to find any indications that these classes ever came within the range of the vast system of public schools which existed in the country from ancient times."[2]

The second characteristic of the village elementary schools, namely that they were more secular than spiritual in their instruction, seems

---

[1] John Matthai—'Village Government in British India', page 40.
[2] *Ibid.*, page 40.

rather surprising to many. But the fact is that although the village priest was the schoolmaster, he was not allowed to teach the Sastras (scriptures) to children not belonging to the priestly class. The pathsalas, we have noticed, were started for the instruction of all the higher castes without distinction. Hence though religion had entered so largely into the life of the people, the schools remained secular. As has been stated moral precepts were taken from the legends. In all likelihood prayers were offered at the beginning of the day's work, but no direct religious instruction was given in such schools.

The advent of Buddhism with its attack on the caste system further strengthened the secular character of the schools. Buddhism exercised immense influence on Hinduism and for a time being caused the position of the Brahmin priest to disintegrate. This necessarily reacted to a very great extent on the character of the schools in which he taught and altered considerably the personnel of the pathsala staff. "It is to the Buddhistic time, in all probability, that we must trace the beginnings of that change under which the village school master is not found to be invariably the village priest and Brahmin, as he certainly was in early Hindu times. Thus was taken the second step in secularising the elementary schools of the country a step which was not retraced (as such steps never are retraced) when Buddhism, after living side by side with Hinduism for some centuries, finally gave place to its rival."[1]

SECTION III—MUHAMMADAN EDUCATION

The Muhammadans began to come to India in the eighth century A.D., but the first real invasion for aggressive purpose took place under the leadership of Mahmud of Ghazni in the early part of the eleventh century. He is credited as a great patron of learning. Briggs' Ferishta says that in the neighbourhood of a magnificent mosque at Ghazni was founded "a university supplied with a vast collection of curious books in various languages. It contained also a museum of natural curiosities. For the maintenance of this establishment, he appropriated a large sum of money besides a sufficient fund for the maintenance of the students and proper persons to instruct youths in arts and sciences." He spent the money he had obtained by plunder and bloodshed for the encouragement of learning as an expiation for his sins. His successors, too, founded several schools and colleges. The Ghazni kings did not however settle down in India. A new power sprang up at Ghor, west of Ghazni. This power over-threw the Ghazni dynasty, invaded India and really laid the foundations of Muhammadan dominion in India. In 1192 Muhammad Ghori established his

[1] Indian Education Commission (1882-83)—Bengal Report, para 6.

rule at Delhi. He destroyed many temples in different parts of Northern India and built in their places mosques with which were attached *Maktabs* and *Madrasahs.* The 'maktabs' were the primary schools and 'madrasahs' the secondary schools and colleges of higher learning. It is related that Muhammad Ghori while he was at Ajmere "destroyed the pillars and foundations of the idol temples and built in their stead mosques and colleges, and the precepts of Islam and the customs of the Law were divulged."[1]

Muhammad Ghori had no children except one daughter; he was very fond of his talented young slaves, and adopted some of them as his sons and gave them a good education. Kutb-ud-din was one of the slaves whom Ghori thus educated. He became the general of Ghori's army and the successes gained were largely due to his ability. When Ghori was murdered on the road to Ghazni, Kutb-ud-din succeeded his master at Delhi in 1206 A.D. Kutb also built mosques and maktabs. His lieutenant, Bakhtiar Khilji, raided the Buddhistic monasteries at Vikramsila in Bihar which were all places of learning. The Muhammadan onslaught extinguished the life of Buddhism in its old home and last refuge. The Muhammadan invaders also started a number of maktabs and madrashahs at different places in Bengal. Kutb's successors King Altamash,

[1] N N. Law—'Promotion of Learning in India by Muhammadans', page 18.

Sultanâh Raziyah, Sultans Nasiruddin and Balban all encouraged the starting of schools attached to mosques and gave grants for their maintenance.

Then came a period during which the Muhammadan kings gave no encouragement to learning.. When the dynasty of the Turkish Slave Sultans of Delhi ended in 1290, Jalaluddin one of the Turkish chiefs of the Khilji tribe, occupied the throne. Ala-ud-din one of the kings of the Khilji dynasty intoxicated by the success of his arms confiscated all endowments for educational purposes and "ordered that wherever there was a village held by a proprietary right, in free gift (inam) or as a religious endowment (waqf), it should by one stroke of pen be brought under the exchequer. So rigorous wás the confiscation that beyond a few thousand *tankas*, all the pensions, grants of lands (in'am-wa-mafruz), and endowments in the country were appropriated."[1] The endowments were however restored by his successor Mubarak Khan.

Some of the Muhammadan rulers of the Tughlak dynasty (1325-1413) helped a good deal in the starting of a number of schools. The third king of the line, Firuz Tughlak, spent large sums of money for the encouragement of education. "He spent 136 lacs of tankas (13,600,000 rupees) in pensions and gifts, of which 36 lacs were given to the learned and religious."[2] He also took great

[1] N N. Law—'Promotion of Learning', page 35.

[2] *Ibid.*, page 51.

care in the preservation of the archæological remains in the country and showed a respect for Hindu monuments, which was rare in those days. "Like some of the Muhammadan sovereigns of India before him he had a special interest in educating young slaves though he carried it to a further extent than any of his predecessors. It is said that he maintained no fewer than eighteen thousand of these lads, and large sums must have been spent by him for their support and education. He had some of them apprenticed to craftsmen, while others were set to learn the Koran, or the art of copying manuscripts. In the inscription which Firuz placed upon a mosque in his capital of Firuzabad, he mentions amongst his other good works the repair of schools and the alienation of revenue for their support. The Muhammadan historian Ferishta says that Firuz built no less than thirty colleges with mosques attached. In the college which he founded at his capital students and professors all lived together in the institution, and stipends and scholarships were given for their support. It is evident that under this sovereign considerable advance must have been made in the education of Muhammadans."[1]

Firuz's three immediate successors Ghiyasud-din II, Abu Bakr, and Nasiruddin practically did nothing for the promotion of learning. They were all puppet sultans, all equally wanting in

---

[1] Rev. F. E. Keay—'Ancient Indian Education', page 117.

personal merit and as such passed rapidly across the stage. The kingdom, in fact, ceased to exist and the governor of every province assumed practical independence. Two rival sultans had to find rooms within the precincts of the Delhi group of cities. Sultan Mahmud a boy grandson of Firuz, was acknowledged king in old Delhi, while another member of the family claimed similar rank in Firuzabad, a city few miles distant from old Delhi, where Firuz Tughlak removed his capital when he ascended the throne. In 1398, during the reign of Mahmud Tughlak, Timur invaded India, occupied Delhi and proclaimed himself king. He had no intention of staying in India and so destroyed many institutions. He quitted India leaving anarchy, famine and pestilence behind him. The progress of education received a great set back after the devastation that he caused.

The kings of the Sayyid and Lodi dynasties (1414-1526) did not do much for the spread of education. During Sikandar Lodi's reign, however, Agra became a centre of learning. It was insisted that those who were sultan's favourites should take up a course in literature.

Before the time of Sikandar Lodi, the Hindus as a body did not like the idea of learning Persian. There were of course a few cases of Hindus prosecuting the pursuit of the language and literature of the invaders but the majority of the Hindus preferred learning Sanskrit and Pali.

Sikandar's reign is noted for the fact that the Hindus for the first time began to learn Persian. The new language of this period, Urdu, is the outcome of the intercourse between the Muhammadans and the Hindus. "The name Urdu, by which this language is usually known, is said to be of Turkish origin, and means literally 'camp'. The Moghuls of India first introduced it within the precincts of the Imperial camp; so that Urdu-i-Muali (high or supreme camp) came to be a synonym for new Delhi after Shah Jahán had made it his permanent capital, so Urdu-ki-zabán meant the lingua franca spoken at Delhi........ The classical languages of Arabia and Persia were exclusively devoted to uses of law, learning and religion; the Hindus cherished their Sanskrit and Hindi for their own purposes of business or worship; while the Emperor and his Moghul courtiers kept up their Turkish speech as a means of free intercourse in private life....... Out of such elements was the rich and still growing language of Hindustan formed, and it is yearly becoming more widely spread over the remote parts of the country, being largely taught in government schools."[1] Though in the sixteenth century only a few Hindus learnt Persian, before the expiry of another century a large number of them became very proficient in that language and

---

[1] H. C. Keene—'The Fall of the Moghul Empire' (W. H. Allen & Co, 1887) page 5 f.

many of them came up to the Muhammadans in point of literary acquirements.

While the Pathan sovereigns at Delhi and Agra were trying in their own way to spread education among their own moslem subjects the kings of smaller states in other parts of India helped considerably in the starting of schools in their own territories. We find the records of the founding of a number of village schools in the Bahmani Kingdom of the Deccan, and a splendid library at Bidar containing about three thousand volumes. Some of the kings made special provisions for the education of the orphans in village schools, allocating special funds for their support. In the states of Bijapur, Ahmadnagar, Golkonda, Malwa, Khandesh, Jaunpur, Multan, Sindh, Guzrat, Kashmir and Bengal the ruling chiefs in their own way helped the spread of education.

As to education in the Bahmani Kingdom the following interesting account is given in Capt. M. Taylor and J. Fergusson's 'Architecture at Beejapur':—

"If we cannot compare the Bahmani kings with their European contemporaries from Edward III to Henry VIII, yet there can be no doubt that high civilization according to the standard of Muhammadanism existed. While all previously existing elements of social union and local government were not only preserved, but strengthened by the Mahomedans who so far from interfering with or remodelling local institutions and hereditary offices turned them to their own use, and employed them. Education in Persian and Arabic literature was extended as much as possible by village schools, which were attached to mosques and endowed with lands sufficient for their maintenance. There were few villages without mosques of one kind or other, however humble; but the system was the same, everywhere, and tended as well to the spread of literature as of the faith of the ruling power, and its effects are still distinctly traceable throughout the wide extent of their dominions."[1]

Babar, the first of the Moghul Emperors (1526-30) hardly did anything for education as he died suddenly after four years' rule. His son Humayun, too, could not do much for education as for a number of years he was banished from India by Sher Khan, who occupied the throne of Delhi assuming the title of Sher Shah (Shah means king or sultan). Blochmann however narrates in his translation of Ain-i-Akbari that Humayun built a madrasah at Delhi of which Sheik Hussain was a teacher. Mr. Stephen in his Archæology of Delhi also testifies that a madrasah was housed in the tomb of Humayun:—"The college which is on the roof of the tomb, was at one time an institution of some importance and men of learning and influence used to be appointed to the charge of the place." Sher Shah during

[1] Taylor and Fergusson—'Architecture at Beejapur', page 12. (John Murray, 1866).

the short period of his reign, while Humayun was in exile, built a madrasah at Narnaul.

Akbar is regarded as the greatest of all the Moghul Emperors of India. He came to the throne in 1556 and reigned till 1605 A.D. He was a great patron of learning although as a boy he had steadily refused to learn his lessons, and because of this was supposed by many to have been unable to read or write. He however used to take an active part in the discussion of literary and abstruse subjects and showed a keen interest in endless debates on the merits of rival religions which he examined from a strangely detached point of view. He was very tolerant in religious matters. Jains, Parsees, Hindus of various denominations and even Christians took their share in modifying the opinions of the Emperor and determining the lines of his policy. He encouraged art and literature. The architecture of Akbar's reign is noted for a happy blending of Hindu and Muhammadan styles which is no doubt an expression in stone of his personal feelings and convictions. As an emperor with tolerant views he not only encouraged Muhammadan learning but helped the spread of Hindu learning a great deal. He gave grants for translating a number of Sanskrit books into Persian. He appointed a number of prominent Hindus as his ministers. One of them, Todar Mal, issued a circular insisting that official accounts should be kept in Persian. This compelled many

Hindus to study that language. We have noticed that during Sikandar Lodi's reign the Hindus for the first time began to learn Persian but this circular helped a good deal in the growth and development of Urdu which soon became the lingua franca of the northern India. Sir George Grierson says—"His influence in making Hindus learn Persian is especially noteworthy as it accounts for the formation and acceptance of Urdu."[1] Akbar, with the assistance of ministers like Abul Fazl, framed schemes of instruction and regulations for the guidance of schools.

Jahangir (1605-1627), the successor of Akbar, also helped in the matter of building schools and repaired a number of old institutions. "He made a law that when any wealthy man died without leaving an heir his property was to escheat to the crown and be used for the repair of schools, monasteries and other religious buildings."[2]

Shah Jahan (1627-1658), who lavishly spent money on the erection of many fine buildings, of which the Taj Mahal at Agra is the finest, did not spend any large amount on educational purposes. He, however, founded a college north of the Jumna Musjid, the buildings of which fell

---

[1] Sir George Grierson—'Modern Vernacular Literature of Hindustan', published by the Asiatic Society of Bengal, 1889, page 35 (printed as a special number of the Journal of the Society).

[2] F. E. Keay—'Ancient Indian Education', page 128.

into ruin before the rebellion of 1857 and were pulled to the ground soon after that event.

Shah Jahan's son, Prince Dara, was well versed in Arabic, Sanskrit and Persian and translated a number of best Sanskrit works into Persian. Aurangzib, who came to the throne in 1650 and reigned till 1707 A.D., was a very bigoted Muhammadan. He would not have anything to do with Hindu culture and Hindu teaching. He abolished a large number of schools attached to temples He showed, however, a great desire for the spread of Muhammadan education. Keay quotes from the Mirat-i-Alam that, "All the mosques in the empire are repaired at the public expense. *Imams,* criers to the daily prayers, and readers of the *Khutba,* have been appointed to each of them, so that a large sum of money has been and is still laid out in these disbursements. In all the cities and towns of this extensive country, pensions and allowances and lands have been fixed for scholars according to their abilities and qualifications."[1] He helped in the starting of a large number of colleges and schools for Muhammadans. He also issued orders that in backward provinces like Gujarat, Oudh, etc., all Muhammadan students should be given special monetary help. The Bohras of Gujarat were very backward in education, and for their instruction he appointed special teachers and asked that their

---

[1] F. E. Keay—'Ancient Indian Education', page 131.

progress, as shown by the results of the monthly examinations, should be communicated to him.

SECTION IV—SPECIAL EDUCATION

Technical education flourished in two ways. The first is that in ancient times the arts and crafts received encouragement at the hands of the kings and landholders. As a matter of fact many of them maintained their own craftsmen who were organised on a feudal basis. The second is by the domestic training due to the caste system. Moreover, in villages the craftsmen formed guilds regulating their duties and remunerations. The payment of craftsmen was either a payment in kind or a grant of land besides perquisites on special occasions. The princes, great nobles and wealthy gentry, were the chief patrons of works of art. They collected together in their own palaces and houses all who gained reputation for special skill in the production of beautiful articles. These men received a fixed salary, besides food and clothing, and were so little hurried in their work that they had plenty of time to execute private orders also. Their salaries were continued even when through age or accident they were past work; and on their death such appointments passed to their sons, if they became skilled in their father's art. Upon the completion of any extraordinary work it was submitted to the patron, and some honour was at once conferred on the artist, and his salary increased. It was under such conditions that the best art work of the East had been produced.

Asoka passed stringent laws for the protection of craftsmen. Capital punishment was inflicted on any person who impaired the efficiency of a craftsman by causing the loss of a hand or an eye. Shipbuilders and armour-makers were considered salaried public servants, and were not permitted to work for any private person. Special state regulations were also issued for the supervision of the work of woodcutters, carpenters, blacksmiths and miners. Many of the Muhammadan rulers, especially Akbar and Shah Jahan, were great patrons of craftsmen.

Due to the caste system any particular boy had to follow the profession of his father. He had practically no choice in the matter. Hence the system of education was a domestic one. The young craftsman was brought up and educated in the actual workshop, and was the disciple of his father. If the father had no time or was not in good health, the boy's master might be an elder brother or even an unrelated person of the same caste. A few master craftsmen received a number of apprentices also belonging to the same caste. Thus the education of the young craftsman in India was entirely vocational, and the method of teaching followed was observance and handling of real things. The teacher, moreover, took a great delight in passing on to his pupils the skill which he himself possessed. Hereditary craftsmanship can be traced to the Code of Manu (according to Vincent Smith the date of its composition may lie between 200 B.C. and A.D. 200: others put it to about 500 B.C.). This code "has secured in the village system of India a permanent endowment of the class of hereditary artisans and art workmen, who of themselves constitute a vast population; and the mere touch of their fingers, trained for 3,000 years to the same manipulations, is sufficient to transform whatever foreign work is placed for imitation in their hands 'into something rich and strange' and characteristically Indian."[1]

Such is the history of indigenous education in India, in its different branches, elementary, secondary, collegiate, and vocational.

SECTION V—GENERAL REMARKS.

Aurangzib was the last great Moghul Emperor who reigned in Delhi. Even during his life time, towards the end of the seventeenth century, a number of states in Southern India declared themselves independent; the mightiest power that arose in the south was the Marhatta under the leadership of Sivaji. The powers both in the north and south began to fight with each other for the supremacy in India. While the country was in such a state it was impossible to expect anything

[1] Sir George Birdwood—'Industrial Arts of India', Vol. I, page 130; (South Kensinghton Museum Art Hand Books Series, 1880).

from the rulers towards the spread of education. More or less secular village schools for both Muhammadans and Hindus continued to exist, but the schools and colleges attached to the temples and mosques which were then receiving any help from the states had to be closed down dispersing the teachers and the students. In an unsettled country there could be no progress in education. A few of the successors of Aurangzib tried in a feeble way to keep the torch of education lighted but could hardly make their influence felt in the eighteenth century.

It has been shown that the Hindu and Muhammadan kings did something for the spread of education out of the state revenue. But too glowing a picture cannot be drawn. It must be admitted that the education which they provided was not for the masses but for special classes who were willing to avail themselves of it. There was no such thing as an education department of the state. No comprehensive scheme of education was ever drawn up. The schools which the kings founded, or which came under their personal notice, flourished for some time owing to their beneficence. The very fact that a number of kings had to spend large sums of money on the thorough repair of school buildings proved that within a few years of the establishment of these institutions they had fallen into disuse. Whether they were attached to mosques or temples or not, whenever any pious founder died or his interest in the cause of education failed the tutors and pupils used to desert the buildings. Moreover, the country could hardly be then called settled. Wars and strife, especially during the seven hundred years of Muhammadan rule, continued at frequent intervals. These conflicts hardly gave the kings any time for thought for the development of education. They were all more or less busy owing to their desire for territorial acquisitions and aggrandisement of powers. Their grants for education were of the nature of private benefactions. As a matter of fact individuals with their private benefactions helped the cause of education more than it was helped by the sporadic grants of kings. Individuals made endowments for education and therefore the schools started with such foundations continued to flourish. Whereas the schools started by the kings ceased to exist as soon as they lost the patronage of royalty. Hence we find a rather gloomy picture of the state of education in the eighteenth century, when the strife for supremacy in India was long and in it were involved not only the Hindus (Marhattas, Sikhs, etc.) and Muhammadans, but also the French and the English. While the country was in such a state, profound and universal ignorance was the natural consequence. Occupations and offices of trust and dignity were not many and were not open to all classes. There was nothing to excite the ambition and the hopes of the young students. That was not the age of science, the mastery of which requires ability and skill. The English, when they settled down in the country after the battle of Plassy (1757), found two parallel sets of institutions, viz., the 'pathsalas' and 'tols' for the Hindus, and the 'muktabs' and 'madrasahs' for the Muhammadans. These schools used to be run by the village communities in which the school-master had a definite place assigned to them. It has been clearly shown how the village schools for the Hindus were secularised and even the personnel of the pathsala staff changed with the advent of Buddhism.

There is even now a striking similarity as between the different provinces in the constitution and methods of management and instruction in these indigenous elementary schools which have survived in India. The diverse characteristics and variety of customs prevailing in different parts of the country had had very little effect on the system of education in the indigenous schools. A 'pathsala' in Bengal is almost identical in character with a 'pial' school in Madras. And one could hardly find any difference between a 'Mullah' school in Sindh and a 'Muktab' in the United Provinces of Agra and Oudh. If we leave aside Burma we notice that the indigenous schools were started in different parts of India by one or other of the three communities—the Hindu, the Muhammadan and the Sikh. While the Hindu pathsalas have steadily aimed at a secular education, the Sikh 'Gurumukhi' schools and the Muhammadan 'Muktab' and 'Mulla' schools have always tried to keep spiritual instruction in the forefront The Muhammadans have all along insisted on teaching the 'Koran' in their elementary schools and the Sikhs have tried to teach the precepts of the *Granth* (the precepts as recorded by Nanak, the first Guru of the Sikhs). Except this emphasis on spiritual instruction in the Muhammadans and Sikh schools the differences between the Hindu, Muhammadan and Sikh schools are almost inappreciable. Burma in many respects lies outside of India, and its 'Pongyi-kyaungs', the Buddhistic monastic schools, are peculiar to Burma.

CHAPTER II.

EDUCATIONAL ENTERPRISES BY THE EARLY MISSIONARIES AND THE EAST INDIA COMPANY PRIOR TO 1814.

Early enterprises in the field of education commenced both by the missionaries and the East India Company were mostly confined to the presidencies of Madras and Bengal. A little work was also done in the Bombay Presidency.

SDCTION I—THE MADRAS PRESIDENCY.

The English when they arrived in India started their most important colony in Madras. The earliest record that one could trace regarding the educational work of the English settlers, chronicles the fact that in 1677 Ralph Ord came out to India as a schoolmaster for a salary of £50 per annum.[1] This salary was then almost equal to that of a junior member of the Council. He was a Protestant and besides teaching his own religion he taught the elements of English.

In 1687 the Court of Directors asked the Governor of Madras to form a Municipality for the town of Madras. In their letter of the 28th September of the same year they made the following suggestions regarding the administration of

---

[1] Arthur Howell—'Education in British India Prior to 1854 and in 1870-71' (published by the Superintendent of Government Printing, Calcutta, 1872), page 3.

education by the municiual authorities:—"The Court of Aldermen may, by virtue of the powers granted by our intended charter assess and *levy a rate upon the inhabitants for the building of one or more free school or schools* for teaching the English tongue to Gentoos or Moors. or other Indian children and for salaries to the school-masters, and by degrees for many other good works. Their constitution being so framed that our President and Council shall always influence their debates and resolutions."

On receipt of that letter Governor Yale formed a Municipal Corporation and asked them to levy a rate for educational purposes. *They levied a rate but did nothing in the way of providing schools or in drawing up any scheme of education.* The Governor waited for a few years but as he found that no school was started from the money raised by the rate he asked the municipal authorities to pay the amount thus collected to the Government Treasury. This they did; but the Government too did nothing to start or aid any school.

Till the end of the seventeenth century more than one company had been carrying on trade in India with charters from the British Government. In the early years of the eighteenth century they amalgamated and formed the 'United Company of Merchants trading to the East Indies.' For the purpose of this amalgamation the authorities in England had to give them a new charter. For the instruction of the children of the Company's servants the Court of Directors asked the Company to provide schoolmasters in all their garrisons and factories. But even then the Company did nothing to help in that direction. In the meantime, the Danish missionaries under the leadership of Ziegenbalg wanted to open a mission centre at Tranquebar. They desired to work hand in hand with the Society for Promoting Christian Knowledge founded in 1698. The authorities of the S. P. C. K. in 1711 approached the Court of Directors in England for permission to provide and maintain charity schools at Madras through the agency of the Danish Missionaries. The Court of Directors sent their application to the Governor of Madras and in 1713 the Madras Government gave the S. P. C. K. and the Danish missionaries permission to open schools in the Presidency of Madras. The Government also promised to give them financial aid. With the increase in the number of Company's servants the local authorities also realized their responsibility in the making of provision for educating the children. They therefore founded the St. Mary's Charity School for Protestant children. The Danish missionaries came to Madras in 1717 and with the permission of the government opened two charity schools in the city of Madras, one for the Portuguese and the other for the Tamil children. In the same year the Company also started a school for Indian children at Cuddalore. This was the beginning of the Anglo-Vernacular system of schools maintained by Government in the Presidency of Madras. The people of Madras at first did not like to join the mission schools in large numbers; they preferred joining the government school. But slowly they realized the benefits of education, and owing to the great personal influence of the missionary Schultze a number of students joined the mission school opened for the Tamils in 1726. This was the origin of the present Anglo-Vernacular school at Vepery (a part of the city of Madras). Encouraged by the success they gained in filling up their schools with students, the Society for Promoting Christian Knowledge started a few more schools. It has been mentioned that the Madras Government promised to help them with grants but so far it had done nothing in that direction. Consequently these schools at different places had to be supported for many years entirely from funds raised by the S. P. C. K.

Another sister society had been started in 1701, called the Society for the Propagation of the Gospel. The older society, the S. P. C. K. engaged itself in semi-missionary operations, namely education, while the S. P. G. provided the missionaries. The two societies always worked hand in hand. Ziegenbalg, who had been the leader of the Danish missionaries and who had prepared the ground for the spread of the mission education in the early part of the eighteenth century, returned to Europe, in 1714, on leave for two years. He was presented to the King of Denmark and on visiting England was admitted to the presence of George I. While in Europe he tried to promote the cause he was engaged in and was warmly encouraged by both kings. Ziegenbalg went back to Madras in 1716. On his return there he found in Rev. William Stevenson a ready helper in his cause. Stevenson at first helped him in organising the school for Portuguese children mentioned before. Later on, leaving the Portuguese school to the Danish missionaries, he himself founded a school for the children of the English soldiers. Ziegenbalg died suddenly in February, 1917, at the early age of 36. Rev. Stevenson returned to England. The number of students in his school fell off and it was finally closed. But the enthusiasm of Mr. Schultze, who by his personal influence made the mission schools popular, enlisted the sympathy of the Governor. With the sanction of the authorities of the S. P. C. K. he focussed all his attention on educational work in the town of Madras. In 1736 he erected a church and established two more schools.

The French under the command of La Bourdonnais besieged Madras in 1746; the fort St. George surrendered; and for the purpose of improving the defences in case of any future insurrection the French authorities levelled to the ground a great part of the city mostly inhabited by the South Indians. The Germans had a Mission-House in this part of the city; with other houses this was also razed to the ground and the mission abolished. The French leader, Dupleix, became the Governor of Madras for a short time; he gave the Armenian Roman Catholics permission to erect Mission buildings at Vepery, and they actually erected a few. When the English regained Madras, the Vepery premises were confiscated by the Government and presented to the Protestant Mission. In November, 1760, the French under the command of Count Lally again besieged Madras, but the town did not surrender; the missionaries at Vepery were allowed to leave the city. They returned to Madras in February 1761, when it was relieved and came completely under the control of the English. That was a death blow to French ascendancy in India. In the same year the English captured the French town, Pondichery, and found a printing press there. The Government presented it to the Protestant Mission which thereupon removed it to Madras and set it up at Vepery. Although a printing press had been sent out from England to Tranquebar in 1710, the first press established in the city of Madras was the one, confiscated from the French Government at Pondichery, set up at Vepery.

In 1784, the S. P. C. K. engaged a special teacher at £50 a year to give instruction to the children of Indian mothers by English fathers.

In 1786 the Female Orphan Asylum was started with money raised for the purpose by Lady Campbell, the wife of the Governor of Madras. Arrangements were made for the teaching of orphan girls. The buildings were presented to the Asylum Committee by the Nawab of Arcot who purchased them for the purpose at a cost of 8,000 pagodas or £2,800 (a pagoda was a coin at one time current in Southern India of about the value of seven shillings). The local people also contributed a good deal towards the upkeep of the institution. The missionary Gericke was appointed the first superintendent of the asylum. The Government agreed to pay a grant of five rupees (ten shillings) per head per month. In the first year of the opening of the asylum there were 60 girls; hence the Government contribution was Rs. 300 (£30) per month. In 1790 the number of girls rose to 150 and the government grant was increased to Rs. 750 a month. Within ten years the girls in residence increased to 200, but the government were unable to give any grant higher than Rs. 750 per month. The success of the Female Asylum from the very first year of its existence encouraged the same committee to start a similar institution for the boys. On the 1st June, 1787, the Male Orphan Asylum was established.

It must be mentioned here that these two asylums were intended for those children of military officers and soldiers in the service of the company who had been left destitute by the sudden death of their fathers. The Vepery Mission for many years, even before the starting of military asylums for boys and girls, had been conducting an orphan asylum for children of the civil population. This orphanage was probably the origin of the present Civil Orphan Asylums. The missionary Gericke first came to Madras as the superintendent of the Vepery Civil Asylum. Later on, as has been mentioned, his services were placed at the disposal of the Female Orphan Asylum Committee.

The Military Male Orphan Asylum was opened with 21 children in June 1787, and in the next month 36 more were admitted. The opening of this institution marked an era in the history of elementary education not only in Madras but throughout the world. Its first superintendent was the famous Dr. Andrew Bell. From the very starting of the institution he had to face many difficulties; firstly, for want of means he had to reject a large number of applicants for admission; secondly, there were no competent teachers who could be engaged to assist him. The latter difficulty led Dr. Bell to invent what since became known as the *Monitorial System* of education. Known at first as Bell's or the Madras system, it at once revealed how education could be both efficient and inexpensive and thus became the basis of much modern progress in elementary education. Even the pupil teacher system, in vogue in England and India till lately, was a modification of Bell's Madras System. We can best judge of the success of this new movement by references to it by Dr. Bell himself in his frequent letters to friends in England and Scotland:

"The orphans educated here are bound out to an art or trade by which they may be useful to themselves and society. We have already saved from perdition, and given to the world, a number of apprentices, clerks, apothecaries, sailors and mechanics. In the course of two years I have had boys taught to speak, and write, and spell English, and to advance in arithemetic. Many of them wrote beautifully. But the great lesson is, in opposition to the making and breeding of the country, to speak truth and to leave off deceit.'

'Every boy is either a master or a scholar, and generally both. He teaches one boy, while another teaches him. The success has been rapid.'

'The school promises fair to present to us the sole reward I have sought of all my labours with my young pupils, by giving to society an annual crop of good and useful subjects, many of them rescued from the lowest state of depravity and wretchedness.'

'I think I have made great progress and almost wrought a complete change in the morals and character of a generation of boys."[1]

---

[1] Quoted by A J. Saunders from letters of Dr. Bell to various friends, *vide* 'The Problem of Religious Education in the Public

The Madras Government sanctioned a monthly grant of Rs. 500 towards the upkeep of the institution.

In 1805 the London Missionary Society commenced its work in Madras by opening a school there. This society gradually started a number of schools in different parts of the Madras Presidency. Its schools were efficient and popular but did not aim at academical distinctions

The Military Chaplain of the cantonment at St. Thomas' Mount, with the help of money raised by contributions from a number of Europeans of the Presidency, opened a Sunday School in January, 1812. His intention was to impart elementary education, following the Lancastrian method, to the children of the residents of the cantonment. "The object, as well as the plan of tuition being highly approved by the Government, an endowment of 300 pagodas (£105) per annum was granted from the 1st January, 1812."[1]

The work of the early missionaries, occasionally aided by government grants, was particularly interesting as the beginning of a now widely-prevalent system of education, especially in South India. Mr. F. W. Thomas writes:—"Its chief importance lay, however, in the fact

---

School as seen in the Bell-Lancaster Controversy (published by the Christian Literature Society), page 21.

[1] Arthur Howell—'Education in British India prior to 1854 and 1870-71', page 68.

that it was the means of attracting the attention of the Government both in India and at home to what soon became a plain duty. The first project for native education which can in any way be ascribed to the Government was that of Mr. Sullivan, resident at Tanjore, who in 1784 propounded a scheme for setting up English schools for the higher classes of every province. With the assistance of the missionary Schwartz a few schools were started. They maintained a flickering vitality until the year 1787 when the Court of Directors took them in hand. £100 sterling was assigned as the yearly endowment of each of the schools, and a course of reading was drawn up which included English, accounts, writing, Tamil, Hindustani, and some Christian instruction. But it was not the intention of the Government to patronize Christianity and the last item was subsequently very much curtailed. The schools, in spite of some opposition, for a time succeeded. The pupils, mainly Brahmins, made no objection to a little Christianity through the medium of the English language, and those in authority went so far as to contribute to the maintenance of the schools."[1]

SECTION II—THE BENGAL PRESIDENCY.

After the battle of Plassey (1757) the East India Company which assumed wider administra-

---

[1] F. W. Thomas—'The History & Prospects of British Education in India' (published by George Bell & Sons, 1891), page 20 f.

tive powers, did not specially interest themselves in the education of the people of Bengal. There were of course the indigenous schools in different parts of the country. At that time there was no state system of education in England and no one thought of introducing any in India as everybody believed that education could be spread without state organization.

Warren Hastings, the first Governor-General, founded the Calcutta Madrasa in 1781 at the special request of distinguished Muhammadan gentlemen. "The main and special object of the institution was to qualify the sons of Muhammadan gentlemen for responsible and lucrative offices in the State, even at that date largely monopolised by the Hindus, and to produce competent officers for the Courts of Justice to which students from the Madrasa on the production of certificates of qualification were to be drafted as vacancies occurred."[1] Until the end of 1782 the monthly cost of Rs. 625 for the upkeep of the institution was privately defrayed by the Governor-General, but in that year the Government took over the charge of the institution and even paid Warren Hastings the money he had so far spent on it.

Mr. Jonathan Duncan, the President at Benares, founded in 1792, the Benares Sanskrit College. This institution was maintained from the very beginning by the Government. Lord

[1] Arthur Howell—'Education in British India', page 1.

Cornwallis, who was then the Governor-General, sanctioned Rs. 20,000 per annum for its maintenance. "This College was designed to cultivate the laws, literature, and religion of the Hindus, to accomplish the same purpose for the Hindus as the Madrasa for the Muhammadans, and specially to supply qualified Hindu Assistants to European Judges."[1]

In 1789 the Calcutta Free School Society was established for the education of the children of the European residents in the city. The Governor-General became the patron of the society. The Civil Servants of the Company agreed to pay a rateable contribution for the maintenance of the schools started by the society.

The East India Company, after they had assumed control of the administration of Bengal, were not very willing to help the Christian Missionaries in their work of proselytisation through educational institutions. Towards the end of the eighteenth century Carey, Marshman and Ward of the Baptist Mission Society reached India. As they were afraid they might be sent back to England they settled down in the small Danish colony of Serampur, twelve miles north of Calcutta. From Serampur in 1807, they published certain addresses to the Hindus and Muhammadans. There was consternation among the Indian public The Government issued orders to confiscate the mission press; but, the

[1] Arthur Howell—'Education in British India', page 2.

missionaries having expressed their regret and promising to issue no more addresses of a similar character, the orders for the confiscation of the press were withdrawn. The Government was afraid of the religious susceptibilities of the people who had come under their sway. They dared not give active support to or even countenance a movement directed against the religious faiths of the people, lest there might be rebellion shaking their position as rulers of the country. The Court of Directors in England approved of the proceedings of the Government. They, in their despatch of the 7th September, 1808, made their first declaration of strict religious neutrality. The Despatch also contains the following passage: "They (missionaries) must be aware that it is quite consistent with doing all justice to the excellency of the motives on which they act, to apprehend that their zeal may sometimes require a check, and that it may be useful and necessary to introduce the control and superintendence of Government, whose responsibility for the public tranquillity will force it to direct its views to those political considerations which the zeal of the Missionaries might overlook."[1]

It will be interesting to narrate here what the British Parliament did, at this period, for the spread of education in India.

In 1792 Charles Grant, a former servant of

[1] H Sharp—'Selections from Educational Records' (Government publication), page 6.

the East India Company, wrote a treatise entitled 'Observation on the state of Society among the Asiatic Subjects of Great Britain, particularly with respect to Morals, and on the means of Improving it.' He became a Director of the Company, and a member of Parliament. He and Wilberforce, the philanthropist, urged before the authorities in England that education in India should not be left entirely in the hands of voluntary organisations like the missions, and that some responsibility for the spread of education lay upon the Government. They at any rate could give pecuniary aid to the missionaries to carry on the educational work. At the time of the renewal of the Company's Charter in 1793, Wilberforce and Grant carried a resolution in the House of Commons to the effect "that it is the peculiar and bounden duty of the British Legislature to promote by all just and prudent means the interest and happiness of the inhabitants of the British dominions in India; and that for these ends such measures ought to be adopted as may gradually tend to their advancement in useful knowledge and to their religious and moral improvement."[1]

The resolution, as carried in the House of Commons, would have enabled the Government to give grants to the mission bodies for the spread of western education. But the labours of the missionaries, as has been already stated, excited

[1] Arthur Howell—'Education in British India', page 3.

profound alarm in India and England, and the clause was interpreted to be positively 'dangerous', 'absurd', and 'impracticable', and in the House of Lords it was negatived.

On the 6th March, 1811, the Governor-General, Lord Minto, wrote a minute recording the decay of learning in India and proposing additional expenditure for starting two more Sanskrit Colleges, one at Nuddea (now known as Nabadwip in the District of Nadia in Bengal) and the other at Bhour[1] (in the District of Tirhoot in Behar), and two Muhammadan Colleges at Bhagalpur and Jaunpur[2] (where Persian and Arabic literature formerly flourished). The people of Bengal, especially in cities came in contact daily with Englishmen in office or in trade, and were anxious to receive western education for the purpose of earning a livelihood. They thought that orental learning would not help them in their pursuit of trade and commerce and in earning a decent living. But the Court of Directors sanctioned Lord Minto's proposals. The reason being that "orthodox English education was then dominated, almost as completely as Indian, by reverence for classics, and by dogmatic theology. To substitute one set of classics for another might well seem futile; to attempt to substitute one system of dogma for another appeared to all but those who were touched by mis-

---

[1] Sharp—'Slections from Educational Records', page 20.

[2] *Ibid.*, page 21.

sionary zeal for the Christian faith, at once dangerous and hopeless."[1]

The question of the further renewal of the Charter of the East India Company came up again before the House of Commons in 1813. In order to ascertain the views of all parties the House resolved itself into a Committee for the purpose. One of the important items referred to this Committee, for opinion, was the nature and need of education in India. The Committee of the House examined many witnesses including Warren Hasings, Lord Teignmouth, Sir John Malcolm, Sir Thomas Munro, and a number of other persons who were once officially connected with India. A large number of witnesses in their evidence stated that the State should not interfere in educational matters and that no encouragement should be given to western missionaries to undertake educational work in India. The party for giving state recognition to education in India was also a strong one. This party was again led by Mr. Wilberforce.

The following resolution (being item No. 13 concerning the affairs of the East India Company) was discussed by the Committee of the House:—

"Resolved, that it is the opinion of this Committee, that it is the duty of this country to promote the interest and happiness of the native inhabitants of the British dominions

[1] Calcutta University Commission (1917-19) Report, Vol. I, Chapter III, para 1.

in India, and that such measures ought to be adopted, as may tend to the introduction among them of useful knowledge, and of religious and moral improvement. That, in the furtherance of the above objects, sufficient facilities shall be afforded by law, to persons desirous of going to and remain in India for the purpose of accomplishing those benevolent designs."

"Provided always,, that the authority of the Local Governments respecting the intercourse of Europeans with the interior of the country, be preserved, and that the principles of the British Government, on which the natives of India have hitherto relied for free exercise of their religion be inviolably maintained."[1]

Animated by a true spirit of friendship for the Indians, Mr. Wilberforce made a lengthy speech, on the 22nd of June, in support of the resolution. He emphasized that the course he was recommending, viz., the propagation of useful knowledge through mission agencies supported by the State, would tend no less to promote their temporal well-being, than their eternal welfare. He wanted Parliament to endeavour to communicate to the Indians the benefits of Christian instruction. He hesitated not to affirm that a regard for their temporal well-being would alone furnish abundant motives for the government's attempt to diffuse among them the blessings of Christian

---

[1] Hansard—'Parliamentary Debates', Vol. XXVI (May to July, 1813), page 562.

light and moral instruction. After prolonged discussion when the House divided, 89 members voted for the resolution and 36 against it.[1]

On the 1st July it was again brought forward before the House. An amendment was moved by Sir T. Sutton to the effect that the Christian Missions should not be entrusted with the work of the spread of education. He said that if too open and avowed efforts were made to propagate Christianity, the Indians might say: "You have taken from us our territories, you have seized upon our revenues; and not content with taking our country from us you wish to deprive us of our religion. But our religion you shall not take from us."[2] With a view to removing these objections he moved, that after having declared the necessity of spreading useful knowledge, that it be put down that it was expedient to send persons to India "for various lawful purposes,"[3] instead of the words "for the purpose of accomplishing those benevolent designs."

Mr. Charles Marsh, who had amassed a fortune at the Madras Bar and was a prominent member of the anti-educational party, supported the amendment in a lengthy speech, in the course of which he said: "I ask you, then, whether it is worth while to make an attempt which must

---

[1] Hansard—'Parliamentary Debates, (May to July 1813, Vol. XXVI, page 873.

[2] *Ibid*, page 1017.

[3] *Ibid.*, page 1018.

be subversive of our existence in India? The moral obligation to diffuse Christianity, binding and authoritative as it is, vanishes, when it is placed against the ills and mischiefs of the experiment. There never was a moral obligation to produce woe and bloodshed and civil disorder. Such an obligation would not exist, were the wildest barbarians the subjects of experiment. But when in addition to these considerations, which are sanctioned by justice, and policy, and virtue, it is remembered that the people we are so anxious to convert, are, in the main, a moral and virtuous people; not undisciplined to civil arts, nor uninfluenced by those principles of religion which give security to life, and impart consolation in death; the obligation assumes a contrary character; and common sense, reason, and even religion itself, cry out aloud against our interference. I shall therefore vote for the amendment."[1] Wilberforce again rose to give reply to the remarks made by Mr. Marsh. When the House divided there were for the original clause 54 members and for the amendment only 32. So the amendment was lost.[2]

A final effort was made by Mr. A. Robinson, to suppress the clause on the 12th July, 1813: he moved that "the preamble be omitted."[3] When

---

[1] Hansard—'Parliamentary Debates, (May to July 1813), Vol. XXVI, page 1051.

[2] *Ibid*, page 1082

[3] *Ibid*, page 1192

the House divided 24 members voted for the amendment and 48 against it.[1]

In accordance with the resolution of the Committee of the House of Commons, which subsequently received the assent of both the House of Parliament, the following clause was inserted in the East India Company Act of 1813. It was moved by Mr. Robert Percy Smith, a member of Parliament and late Advocate-General of Calcutta. The Earl of Buckinghamshire, then President of the Court of Directors, was also entirely in favour of the clause.

"It shall be lawful for the Governor-General in Council to direct that out of any surplus which may remain of the rents, revenues, and profits arising from the said territorial acquisitions, after defraying the expenses of the military, civil interest of the debt, in manner hereinafter provided, a sum of not less than one lac of rupees in each year shall be set apart and applied to the revival and improvement of literature and the encouragement of the learned natives of India, and for the introduction and promotion of a knowledge of the sciences among the inhabitants of the British territories in India; and that any schools, public lectures, or other institutions, for the purposes aforesaid, which shall be founded at the presidencies of Fort William, and Fort St. George, or Bombay, or in any other part of the British territories in India, in virtue of this Act shall be

[1] Hansard—Vol. XXVI, page 1196.

governed by such regulations as may from time to time be made by the said Governor-General in Council; subject nevertheless to such powers as are herein vested in the said Board of Commissioners for the Affairs of India, respecting colleges and seminaries: Provided always, that all appointments to offices in such schools, lectureships and other institutions, shall be made by or under the authority of the Governments within which the same shall be situated."[1]

This clause is justly regarded as the foundation stone of the present system of education in India. The meaning of the clause, however, was not quite clear. The members of the Government in India were divided into two parties, one of which maintained that the money was asked to be spent exclusively for the purpose of spreading oriental learning; the other party was distinctly in favour of introducing the knowledge of western literature and science. The nature of the controversy and the ultimate decisions will be noticed in the next Chapter. It needs to be recorded here that the Act was meant to be applied to the whole of India then under British control, viz. the presidencies of Fort William (Bengal), Fort St. George (Madras) and Bombay.

SECTION III—THE BOMBAY PRESIDENCY AND RAJPUTANA

Because the presidencies of Bengal and Madras first came into the possession of the

[1] H. Sharp—'Selections from Educational Records', page 22.

English, all the educational activities of the East India Company, prior to 1814, were carried on in those two presidencies. There were however several schools and colleges in the Bombay Presidency during the sixteenth and seventeenth centuries. These were mostly started by the Portuguese. The earliest of these was the Jesuits' College established in Chaul, in 1580. It is said that more than 300 students used to attend the college. During the time of the early Portuguese settlement Jesuit colleges were also established at Margav and at Rachol. Thomas Stevens was the Rector of one of these. In 1620 a college called the 'College of St. Anne' was founded at Bandora in Salsette. "Another college was at Monpacer, over the door of which is an inscription in Portuguese with the arms of Portugal above it, purporting that the erection was made in 1623, by order of Infant Don John II of Portugal."[1] In 1674, Dr. John Fryer when he visited the presidency of Bombay, saw two colleges, one started by the Jesuits and the other by the Franciscans.

The Marhattas expelled the Portuguese in 1739, and with the suppression of the Catholic Orders the orphanages and colleges broke up. But the work of the parish schools were carried on by the Indian Christians with the aid of private liberality. These parochial elementary schools were started during the seventeenth century and

[1] N. N. Law—'Promotion of Learning in India by Early European Settlers', page 81.

maintained by the members of the Franciscan and Jesuit Orders, in Bombay and smaller adjacent islands.

In 1719, the Rev. Richard Cobbe opened in Bombay a school for the education of the Protestant children. The school was located within the fort and was supported by voluntary contributions until 1807, when it began to receive a grant from the Court of Directors. It continued within the fort till 1825 when the government ordered the removal of the school from the fort to the present buildings at Byculla. Originally it was called the 'Charity School' but later on it came to be known as the Bombay Education Society School. A 'Portuguese Eurasian School' also existed in Bombay in 1790.

In 1808 the Court of Directors of the East India Company issued a despatch declaring strict religious neutrality and refusing to lend authority to any attempt to propagate the Christian religion in any part of India. In some missionary schools the order of the Court of Directors was not rigidly followed. Mr. Carey, son of Rev. Dr. Carey of Serampur, was reprimanded by Government for not adhering strictly to the policy of neutrality in a missionary school in Rajputana. A letter dated the 15th July, 1822 (addressed to Sir D. Ochterlony)[1] records—"His Excellency the Governor General in Council has perceived with much regret the highly injudicious and objectionable course

[1] H. Sharp—'Selection from Educational Records', page 6.

pursued by Mr. Carey in introducing the sacred books of scripture as school books in institutions of so recent a date and in such a state of society as that of Rajputana. Mr. Carey will receive injunctions through his father, the Reverend Doctor Carey, to discontinue the use in schools under his charge of the Christian Scriptures and all religious tracts calculated to excite alarm as to our motives in the minds of the Natives." In the old days the missionaries used to regard the Indians as heathens; and in the first half of the nineteenth century the British administrators looked upon the Christian missionary as a bigoted busybody arousing unnecessary animosity. The British officials excluded the Bible even from the libraries of government schools and forbade their teachers to explain any references to religion in English literature or history. Bentinck, Macaulay, Trevelyan and other high officials thought that Indians would slowly get converted to Christianity as a result of a purely secular western education.

CHAPTER III

THE PERIOD 1814—1859

SECTION I—THE BENGAL PRESIDENCY

The East India Act of 1813 contained a clause which empowered the Governor-General to spend one lakh of rupees (£10,000) each year for the purpose of education. This was the first legislative admission of the right of education to participate in the public revenues of India. The Court of Directors in Bengal while they communicated the clause to the Governor-General had no definite scheme in mind. They, however, sent a Despatch, dated the 3rd June, 1814, to the Governor-General asking him to formulate definite schemes; but at the same time gave him certain ideas as to the way in which the money should be spent. They emphasized the need of spending more money on higher Oriental studies, including Indian systems of Philosophy and Ethics, Codes of Laws, Astronomy, Geometry and Algebra, than on elementary education. Their Despatch, however, did not definitely exclude the vernacular instruction imparted in the village schools: "We refer with particular satisfaction upon this occasion to that distinguished feature of internal policy which prevails in some parts of India, and by which the instruction of the people is provided for by a certain charge upon the produce of the soil, and by other endowments in favour of the village teachers, who are thereby rendered public servants of the community."[1] They also urged that the protection of the Government should be afforded to the village teachers in all their just rights and immunities.

Lord Moira, the Governor-General of India, wrote on the 2nd October, 1815, a minute on the Judicial administration of Bengal. In this minute, though he agreed to spend a large sum of money on higher Oriental studies, he yet emphasized the foremost claims of the village school-masters in the reorganisation of education in India. He wrote "the humble but valuable class of village school-masters, claims the first place in this discussion. These men teach the first rudiments of reading, writing and arithmetic for a trifling stipend which is within reach of any man's means, and the instruction which they are capable of imparting, suffices for the village zamindar, the village accountant and the village shop-keeper. As the public money will be ill-appropriated in merely providing gratuitous access to that quantum of education which is already attainable, any intervention of government either by superintendence, or by contribution should be directed to the improvement of existing tuition, and to the diffusion of it to places and persons now out of its reach. Improvement and diffusion may go hand in hand; yet the latter is to be considered matter

[1] Sharp—'Selections from Educational Records', page 23.

of calculation while the former should be deemed positively incumbent....... I must think that the sum set apart by the Honourable Court (of Directors) for the advancement of science among the natives would be much more expediently applied in the improvement of schools, than in gifts to seminaries of higher degree."[1]

At the present moment when every one is clamouring for universal elementary education in India it is interesting to note the concluding paragraph of Lord Moira's minute, a paragraph which has all along been overlooked by the administrators of India:—"The lapse of half a century and the operation of that principle (confinement of legislation to the primary principle of justice) have produced a new state of society, which calls for a more enlarged and liberal policy. The moral duties require encouragement and experiment. The arts which adorn and embellish life will follow in ordinary course. It is for the credit of the British name that this beneficial revolution should arise under British sway. To be the source of blessings to the immense population of India is an ambition worthy of our country. In proportion as we have found intellect neglected and sterile here, the obligation is the stronger on us to cultivate it. The field is noble: may we till it worthily!"

---

[1] Sharp—'Selections from Educational Records', pages 24 and 28.

For the next eight years the government could hardly do anything for the spread of education and the despatch of 1814 remained a dead letter. The government, during those years, were engaged in wars with the Gurkhas in Nepal, the Pindaris in Central India, and the Marhattas in different parts of India. During these years the missionaries started several schools in Bengal. In 1814, the Rev. Robert May opened sixteen schools in and near Chinsurah (a place 25 miles north of Calcutta). These schools were highly successful and attracted a large number of pupils, Hindus and Muhammadans. The government sanctioned for them a monthly grant of Rs. 600, which was later on increased to Rs. 1,800 when the number of schools also rose to 36. Mr. May died in 1818. Messrs. Pearson and Harley took charge of these and also started several more at Khulna, Shamnagar and Patna. The Serampur missionaries also established 20 schools in the vicinity of Calcutta. They had a printing press at Serampur and published a series of vernacular school books. The Church Missionary Society opened ten vernacular schools with about one thousand children, in and around Burdwan. David Hare established one Vernacular school and one English school, in close proximity, in Calcutta. "The two schools held classes at different hours—the Vernacular from sunrise to 9 o'clock and the English from 10-30 to 2-30, and the Vernacular again from 3-30 to sunset. By this arrangement boys in the vernacular schools were enabled to attend the English school if they so desired."[1] It was found out that almost all students desired to learn English. Private English schools were set up by Indians and Eurasians. The schools started by the mission-aries flourished because they taught English. The dearth of suitable school books was felt and the Calcutta School Book Society was established in 1817. In 1821 the government gave it a donation of Rs. 7,000, and sanctioned a monthly grant of Rs. 500. In 1819 the Calcutta School Society was founded under the patronage of the Governor-General. It established a number of schools, both English and vernacular all over Bengal, commencing with Calcutta as the centre. The satisfactory work of the Calcutta School Society drew the attention of the government which in 1823 sanctioned a monthly grant of Rs. 500 for the maintenance of the schools under its care. In 1825 the Court of Directors approved of this sanction by the government. *It was the first recognition on the part of the Court of Directors in England of the claims of education for the masses of India.* Before this grant the money from the state revenue was mostly spent for higher studies. The Calcutta School Society also made arrangements for educating teachers for the indigenous schools. Thus it combined the

---

[1] Stark—'Vernacular Education in Bengal, 1813 to 1912' (published by the Calcutta General Publishing Company), page 9.

double function of giving elementary instruction and educating teachers for the vernacular schools.

The East India Company Act of 1813, as interpreted by the despatch of 1814, made it almost impossible for the elementary schools to receive direct grants from the state revenue. But the despatch requested the Governor-General to make a survey of the condition of education in the country and to report the results of such inquiries, at regular intervals, to the Court of Directors. In 1823 Mr Adam, the acting Governor-General, appointed a General Committee of Public Instruction "for the purpose of ascertaining the state of public education, and of the public institutions designed for its promotion, and of considering and from time to time submitting to Government the suggestion of such measures, as it may appear expedient to adopt with a view to the better instruction of the people, to the introduction among them of useful knowledge and to the improvement of their moral character."[1]

The General Committee consisted of ten members, all Europeans. They were assisted by local committees at various centres. On the local committees were appointed a few Indians, the others being the principal officers of the local government. Two great principles guided the

[1] Para I of the Resolution constituting the Committee of Public Instruction dated the 17th July 1823 Quoted from Selections from Educational Records, page 53.

policy of the General Committee. The first was the avoidance of any suspicion of proselytisation. Therefore the committee encouraged the learning and literatures which the Hindus and the Muhammadans respected. The second principle was that the encouragement should be given to higher education as the funds at the disposal of the Committee were inadequate for any purpose of general education. The local committees were not much of a success as they were apathetic to their duties of the promotion of education in their respective districts.

From the very beginning of the constitution of the General Committee the members were divided in their opinion whether oriental or occidental learning should be fostered by the government. Half the members were for giving encouragement to oriental learning, the other half were in favour of the introduction of western learning. Amongst the Indians also there grew up a small, but strong, party headed by Raja Ram Mohan Roy, which advocated the introduction of the sciences and arts of Europe. On behalf of this party Raja Ram Mohan Roy wrote a letter in December, 1823, to the Governor-General, Lord Amherst, requesting the government to spend money for the instruction of the Indians "in Mathematics, Natural Philosophy, Chemistry, Anatomy and other useful sciences, which the Nations of Europe have carried to a degree of perfection that has raised them above the inhabitants of other parts of the world."[1]

The Court of Directors were in favour of familiarising the Indians with European Literature and Science, but asked the Government of India to decide the question. The controversy raged for 12 years. So evenly were the two parties balanced that nothing could be carried by vote. Lord Macaulay arrived in India in 1834 as the Legal Member of the Supreme Council. Lord William Bentinck, the then Governor-General, appointed him as the President of the General Committee of Public Instruction. From the very outset he urged that nothing should be done till the decision of the Supreme Government on the main question at issue was pronounced. Both parties addressed the government. Lord Macaulay himself had to decide the question when the letters came before him in his capacity as Law Member. In the latter capacity he wrote a long minute (dated the 2nd February, 1835) replying fully to the arguments advanced by the orientalists. He declared that English was better worth learning than Sanskrit or Arabic.

Moreover Macaulay wrote that "we must at present do our best to form a class who may be interpreters between us and the millions whom we govern—*a class of persons Indian in blood and*

---

[1] Address, dated 11th December 1823 from Raja Ram Mohan Roy to Lord Amherst; 'Selections from Educational Records', page 99.

colour, but English in tastes, in opinions, in morals and in intellect. To that class we may leave it to refine the vernacular dialects of the country, to enrich those dialects with terms of science borrowed from the Western nomenclature, and to render them by degrees fit vehicles for conveying knowledge to the great mass of the population." Everybody now admits that Macaulay made a great mistake in imagining that Western education would assimilate Indians to Englishmen in everything but their complexions. It may however be mentioned that he visualised the larger implications of the new departure he was advocating. Macaulay declared—"It may be that the public mind of India may expand under our system until it has outgrown that system; that by good government we may educate our subjects into a capacity for better government; *that having become instructed in European knowledge they may in some future age demand European institutions.* Whether such a day will ever come, I know not. But never will I attempt to avert or retard it. Whenever it comes *it will be the proudest day in English history.*"[2] Never on this earth was a more momentous question discussed. Nearly seventy years after Macaulay's declaration, even Lord Curzon admitted that *"ever since the cold breath of Macaulay's rhetoric passed over the field of Indian languages and Indian text-*

[1] Sharp—'Selections from Educational Records', page 116.

[2] Quoted by Valentine Chirol in "India Old and New", page 79.

books, the elementary education of the people in their own tongue has shrivelled and pined." In 1835, however, Lord William Bentinck wholly endorsed Macaulay's views. Mr. H. T. Prinsep again pressed the orientalist's point of view before the government by writing a strong note in reply to Macaulay's minute. But the Government put a stop to the controversy by issuing the following resolution on the 7th March, 1835:—

"The Governor-General of India in Council has attentively considered the two letters from the Secretary to the Committee of Public Instruction, and the papers referred to in them.

1st—His Lordship in Council is of opinion that the great object of the British Government ought to be the promotion of European literature and science among the natives of India; and that all the funds appropriated for the purpose of education would be best employed on English education alone.

2nd—But it is not the intention of His Lordship in Council to abolish any College or School of native learning, while the native population shall appear to be inclined to avail themselves of the advantages which it affords, and His Lordship in Council directs that all the existing professors, and students at all the institutions under the superintendence of the Committee shall continue to receive their stipends;......he directs that no stipend shall be given to any student that may hereafter enter at any of these institutions; and that when any professor of Oriental learning shall vacate his situation, the Committee shall report to the Government the number and state of the class in order that the Government may be able to decide upon the expediency of appointing a successor.

3rd—It has come to the knowledge of the Governor-General in Council that a large sum has been expended by the Committee on the printing of Oriental works; his Lordship in Council directs that no portion of the funds shall hereafter be so employed.

4th—His Lordship in Council directs that all the funds which these reforms will leave at the disposal of the Committee be henceforth employed in imparting to the native population a knowledge of English literature and science through the medium of the English language; and His Lordship in Council requests the Committee to submit to Government, with all expedition, a plan for the accomplishment of this purpose."[1]

When this resolution was communicated to the General Committee, they decided that as funds became available schools should be established in the principal towns (district headquarters) of the presidencies. These schools were to be called Zillah Schools (the vernacular word 'Zillah' means district) and were to be started for the teaching of English literature and science through the

[1] Sharp—'Selections from Educational Records', pages 130 and 131.

medium of the English language. The Government Resolution practically barred any new expenditure on vernacular teaching. In some provinces, e.g. in Madras, the immediate result was the prohibition of the use of the vernacular languages as media of instruction in all government schools, and the employment of Government fund exclusively for English education.

The Calcutta Committee, however, interpreted that the resolution merely intended to secure the preference to European learning taught through the medium of the English language, over Oriental learning taught through the medium of the Sanskrit and Arabic languages. These expressions of opinion, however, referred not at all to the question through what ultimate medium was to be conveyed such instruction as the mass of the people was capable of receiving. The teaching of the language of the province was therefore encouraged by attaching a vernacular teacher to all government schools. Moreover, in the lower forms of the zillah schools the vernacular language was taught exclusively. The zillah school had ten or eleven forms, the last four or five of which might easily be classified as the Elementary Department of the Secondary School. Hence the first public elementary schools in Bengal started by the State were merely the lower forms of the secondary schools.

But Bentinck's government did not stop here. They were anxious to improve the lot of the masses. They wanted to find out how education among the masses of the people could be widely diffused. In 1835 Lord William Bentinck appointed Mr. W. Adam, who first came to India as a missionary in 1818, as Special Commissioner for the Survey of the state of Education in Bengal. Mr. Adam spent three years (1835-38) in the inquiry and submitted three very elaborate reports. Mr. Adam in his reports mentioned that there existed in the first half of the nineteenth century three types of institutions in the country viz. (a) Indigenous Elementary Schools (b) Elementary Schools not Indigenous and (c) Indigenous Schools of Learning (mostly for advanced work). He also made inquiries regarding the courses of studies in elementary schools, the stages of instruction, the qualifications and remuneration of the teachers of elementary schools, the school buildings, quality of instruction given in the domestic schools, and the state of instruction amongst females. *Mr. Adam estimated that in Bengal there were about 100,000 schools for the education of the people.*

Mr. Adam in his report said that "there is probably no district in Bengal and Behar in which the amount and proportion of juvenile and adult instruction are so high as in Burdwan or so low as in Tirhoot, and we may thus assume without much danger of error that we have ascertained both the highest and lowest existing standard of instruction in those two provinces. Actually the state of instruction of nearly eight millions of its subject is before Government with a degree of minuteness, which, even if it should fatigue, may give some assurance of an approach to accuracy, and exhibiting an amount of ignorance which demands the adoption of practical measures for its diminution. Virtually, the state of instruction of more than thirty-five millions of its subjects is before Government, that portion of the Indian population which has lived longest under British rule, and which should be prepared or appreciate and enjoy its highest privileges."[1]

He calculated that in the District of Burdwan the proportion of the population above fourteen and below five to the population between 14 and 5 (the school-going age) was as 100 to 18.4; and in the District of Tirhoot the same was as 100 to 25.5. He also showed that though in the cultured districts about 16 per cent of the school-going population were receiving some kind of instruction, in the backward districts the percentage was only 2.5; the aggregate for all the districts was about 7 per cent. Thus at that time about 93 per cent of the children of school-going age were not receiving the benefit of any kind of instruction.

Mr. Adam not only described the state of education that he had found but also made certain

---

[1] Adam's Reports on Vernacular Education in Bengal and Behar, submitted to Government in 1835, 1836, and 1838, (printed with a note by the Rev. J. Long and published by the Home Secretariat Press, Calcutta, 1868), page 250 f.

recommendations to improve it. His proposals might be summarised as follows:—

(1) that to improve the indigenous schools, the teaching staff must be improved and that inspectors should be appointed to supervise the work of the schoolmasters; that such inspectors of village schools should co-operate with the local committees,

(2) that on the results of the examinations held periodically by the inspectors if the *gurus* (masters) could show that their students had made fair progress, then they themselves should be encouraged by rewards and grants,

(3) that a normal school for the training of teachers should be established in each district,

(4) that small *jagirs* of land should be assigned in each village for the support of these improved teachers,

(5) that a few districts should first be selected for the trial of the scheme,

(6) that an educational survey, giving exact details of the population, the existing means of instruction, and the state of its schools and attendance, should be made in each district so selected,

(7) that the Government should take the responsibility of preparation and distribution of text books suited to the needs of the vernacular schools.

Mr. Adam urged that the scheme as outlined by him would form the basis of a truly national system of education for Bengal and that the Government ought to spend the greater part of the amount sanctioned annually for education under the Act of Parliament to give effect to his scheme. In 1836 the amount at the disposal of the government for educational purposes was nearly Rs. 400,000 (£40,000).

It might be mentioned in this connection that throughout the nineteenth century the government had followed the policy that knowledge should descend from the higher strata of the society to the lower. Mr. Adam as early as 1838 was the first person in India to point out the unsoundness of this policy. Because of financial difficulties the Government was not moved by Mr. Adam's arguments. But it is worth while quoting Mr. Adam's views on this policy:—

"Instead of beginning with schools for the lower grades of native society, a system of Government institutions may be advocated that shall provide, in the first place, for the higher classes, on the principle that the tendency of knowledge is to descend, not to ascend; and that, with this view, we should at present seek to establish a school at the head station of every *zillah,* afterwards *pergunnah* schools, and last of all village schools, gradually acquiring in the process more numerous and better qualified instruments for the diffusion of education. The primary objection to this plan is that it overlooks entire systems of native educational institutions,

Hindu and Muhammadan, which existed long before our rule, and which continue to exist under our rule, independent of us and of our projects, forming and moulding the native character in successive generations. In the face of this palpable fact, the plan assumes that the country is to be indebted to us for schools, teachers, books—everything necessary to its moral and intellectual improvement, and that in the prosecution of our views we are to reject all the aids which the ancient institutions of the country and the actual attainments of the people afford towards their advancement. We have to deal in this country principally with Hindus and Muhammadans, the former one of the earliest civilized nations of the earth, the latter in some of the brightest periods of their history distinguished promoters of science; and both, even in their present retrograde stages of civilization, still preserving a profound love and veneration for learning nourished by those very institutions of which I have spoken, and which it would be equally improvident on our part and offensive to them to neglect........ The efficiency of every successive higher grade of institution cannot be secured except by drawing instructed pupils from the next lower grade which, consequently by the necessity of the case, demands prior attention. Children should not go to college to learn the alphabet. To make the superstructure lofty and firm, the foundations should be broad and deep;

and, thus building from the foundation, all classes of institutions and every grade of instruction may be combined with harmonious and salutary effect."[1]

As soon as Lord William Bentinck left the shores of India (April, 1835) the orientalists again raised their voice of protest against the decision of the government. Lord Auckland came to India as successor to Bentinck. He waited for nearly four years before he could pronounce any definite opinion on the controversy raised again. In the meantime Mr. Adam's reports on elementary education were placed in the hands of the government. Lord Auckland carefully examined the whole position and expressed his views in a minute dated the 24th November, 1839. He maintained that the funds assigned for the purpose of education were small and consequently disputes had arisen in the General Committee. He realized that on account of the transfer of funds for the support of English classes the Oriental schools and colleges had suffered, and that as more and more attention was being paid to the teaching of English the vernaculars were relegated to a very subordinate position. He therefore ordered that the money originally used to be spent for oriental schools and colleges prior to the

[1] Adam's Reports on Vernacular Education in Bengal and Behar, submitted to Government in 1835, 1836 and 1838, (printed with a note by the Rev. J. Long and published by the Home Secretariat Press, Calcutta, 1868), page 257 f.

resolution of Lord William Bentinck should be supplied again for the said purpose, and that the instructions in English should proceed from the additional grants, from the public treasury, which the Government might sanction annually. In 1840 Lord Auckland increased the allotment by Rs. 150,000. As regards the medium of instruction experiments were being carried on in two presidencies. *In Bengal instruction through the medium of English was in vogue whereas in Bombay it was through the vernacular languages.* Lord Auckland was in favour of both methods being given a fair chance. The General Committee, under the presidency of Lord Macaulay, gave their attention only to the spread of education through the medium of English among the upper and middle classes of Bengal. They had no intention of giving education to the masses. They firmly delieved that education would spread from the higher ranks of society to the lower orders. This principle they called the "Filtration Theory," i.e. education would filter down from the upper classes to the masses. The committee's intention was to raise up an educated class in Bengal who would hereafter be the means of diffusing among their countrymen some portion of the knowledge they had received. Holding this view *the committee rejected Mr. Adam's recommendations regarding the starting of elementary schools throughout Bengal.* But the majority of the members of the committee were willing to give a trial on a small scale to Mr. Adam's scheme in a group of schools in a selected area in the neighbourhood of Calcutta. The proposal of the committee, however, was not accepted by the Government. The Court of Directors in England also agreed with the Government that Mr. Adam's proposals might be carried out with success when the educational needs of the upper classes had been provided for.

The support of the Court of Directors encouraged the General Committee to concentrate their attention on the education of the upper and middle classes of the society. They directed their efforts to the establishment of Anglo-Vernacular schools in the important towns. They, however, recognised the importance of the vernacular studies by providing a set of teachers for vernacular subjects in addition to the set of teachers for English subjects. In spite of all these precautions it must be admitted that the study of English tended to eclipse the study of the vernaculars. So far all the money at the disposal of the Government for educational purposes had been disbursed through the General Committee of Public Instruction. In 1840, the educational funds were increased to nearly 550,000 rupees.

The Government realized that the business of the committee had attained very great dimensions and the time had arrived when education should come directly under their own supervision.

Hence, in 1842, the General Committee was dissolved and a Council of Education was installed in its place. This Council assumed control of all the schools and colleges, except the purely indigenous schools, and practically became a department of the state.

Lord Hardinge, as Governor-General, issued a resolution in 1844 which gave a new impetus to the study of English. The resolution stated that, in the selection of candidates for public employment, preference should be given to those who had been educated in the institutions established or recognized by the Council of Education, and 'especially to those who had distinguished themselves therein by a more than ordinary degree of merit and attainment.' Lord Hardinge's resolution further ruled that, in selecting for employment in the lowest offices under Government, preference should be given to one who could read and write to one who could not. The last part of the resolution clearly paved the way for the recognition by the state of the indigenous schools. The Government went further and resolved to take direct measures for the diffusion of elementary education in the villages, independently of the Council of Education.

"The Right Hon'ble the Governor of Bengal has determined to sanction the formation of village schools in the several districts of Bengal, Behar and Cuttack, in which sound and useful elementary instruction may be imparted in the vernacular language.

"The number of schools which the funds at the disposal of the Government will admit of being formed, is 101, to each of which a master will be appointed capable of giving instruction in vernacular reading, writing, arithmetic, geography and the histories of India and Bengal."[1]

The Government decided that these schools should only be located in those areas where the inhabitants would be willing to provide suitable buildings for the purpose, and keep them in proper repair. A fee of one anna a month per pupil was fixed. To encourage diligent work on the part of the teachers some part of the income from fees was to be given to the teachers in addition to their fixed pay. The Government remained liable for fixed salaries of the teachers; all other expenses were to be met from the fee fund. School books were not to be supplied free but should be purchased by the scholars. A variety of causes contributed to the failure of these schools. Every year a number closed down and by 1852 only 26 survived. "The Reports of the Council of Education—for the schools were eventually put under its management—contain such observations as the following:—Elementary education is to be had in numerous private schools. There are few large villages in which

[1] Lord Hardinge's Resolution of the 11th October 1844 Vide H. A. Stark, Vernacular Education in Bengal, page 66.

elementary vernacular instruction cannot be obtained at little or no expense."[1] The cry for instruction in English, even in the village schools, was also one of the causes of failure of the Hardinge schools. For effective supervision of the schools under the Council of Education an Inspector of Schools was appointed in 1844.

After the failure of the Hardinge schools, Lord Dalhousie, who was now the Governor-General, called upon the Council of Education in October, 1853, to frame a scheme 'best calculated to provide the most efficacious means of founding and maintaining a sound and well adapted system of Vernacular Education to all the provinces of this government.'

In 1854 the charter of the East India Company was once more renewed, and in the same year was issued by the Court of Directors a very comprehensive Education Despatch which came to be regarded as the Charter of Education, the most important proposals therein being the institution of universities at the presidency towns in India and the appointment of a Director of Public Instruction in each of the provinces of British India. The Directors assumed the functions of the Council of Education, which from that date ceased to exist. The Sepoy Mutiny broke out in 1857 and the Government could not give effect to the majority of the proposals contained in the Des-

[1] H. A. Stark—'Vernacular Education in Bengal', page 70.

patch of 1854. After the Mutiny had been suppressed the Crown in England assumed charge of the administration of India. The East India Company was dissolved. On the 1st November, 1858, Queen Victoria was proclaimed the Empress of India. Lord Stanley on behalf of the Queen's Government sent a Despatch in 1859 supplementing the Despatch of 1854.

"The Despatch of 1854 commends to the special attention of the Government of India, the improvement and far wider extension of education, both English and Vernacular, and prescribes as the means for the attainment of these objects:—

(1) the constitution of a separate Department of the administration for education,

(2) the institution of Universities at the Presidency towns,

(3) the establishment of institutions for training teachers for all classes of schools,

(4) the maintenance of the existing Government colleges and high schools and the increase of their number when necessary,

(5) the establishment of new middle schools,

(6) increased attention to vernacular schools, indigenous or other, for elementary education; and

(7) the introduction of a system of grants-in-aid.

"The attention of the Government is specially directed to the importance of placing the means of acquiring useful and practical knowledge within reach of the great mass of the people.

"English is to be taught wherever there is a demand for it, but it is not to be substituted for the vernacular languages of the country.

"The system of grants-in-aid is to be based on the principles of perfect religious neutrality. Aid is to be given (so far as the requirements of each particular District as compared with other Districts and the funds at the disposal of Government may render it possible) to all schools imparting a good secular education, provided they are under adequate local management, and are subject to Government inspection, and provided that fees, however small, are charged in them. Grants are to be for specific objects, and their amount and continuance are to depend on the periodical reports of Government Inspectors. No Government colleges or schools are to be founded where a sufficient number of institutions exist capable with the aid of Government, of meeting the local demand for education; but new schools and colleges are to be established and temporarily maintained where there is little or no prospect of adequate local effort being made to meet local requirements. The discontinuance of any general system of education entirely provided by Government is anticipated with the gradual advance of the system of grants-in-aid; but the progress of education is not to be checked in the slightest degree by the abandonment of a single school to probable decay.

"A comprehensive system of scholarships is to be instituted so as to connect lower schools with higher, and higher schools with colleges.

"Female education is to receive the frank and cordial support of Government.

"The principal officials in every district are required to aid in the extension of education.

"In making appointments to posts in the service of Government, a person who has received a good education is to be preferred to one who was not. Even in lower situations ,a man who can read and write is, if equally eligible in other respects, to be preferred to one who cannot.

"The Second great Despatch on education, that of 1859, reviews the progress made under the earlier Despatch, which *it reiterates and confirms with a single exception as to the course to be adopted for promoting elementary education.*" The Despatch of 1859 recorded that no general scheme of popular education could be framed suitable for all parts of India; but it was most important that the greatest possible use should be made

[1] Summary given in the Indian Education Commission Report (1882), page 22.

of the existing schools and of the masters to whom, however inefficient as teachers, the people had been accustomed to look up with respect. It noticed that the grant-in-aid system had been freely accepted by private schools both English and Anglo-Vernacular, missionary and secular. But it was not so with respect to vernacular schools, the requisite local co-operation of the Indian community being wanting. The grant-in-aid system could not therefore be made the basis of any extended system of popular education. In this view the Lieutenant Governor of Bengal, Mr. Halliday, concurred. The Despatch emphasized that care should be taken that a prejudice against education was not created, and the Government itself rendered unpopular, by the efforts of educational officers to obtain the necessary local support for the establishment of vernacular schools under the grant-in-aid system. By such proceedings the dignity of the Government might also be compromised. The soliciting of contributions from the people was prohibited. The grant-in-aid system, as hitherto in force, was pronounced unsuited to the supply of vernacular education for the masses of the population. The despatch, therefore, strongly recommended that means of elementary education should be provided by the direct instrumentality of the officers of Government. As it asked to relinquish the existing grant-in-aid system as a means of providing popular vernacular schools throughout the country, *it commended to the careful consideration of the Government the levying of a special rate on land to defray the expense of schools for the rural population.*

During the time of the East India Company the Governor-General of India had been the head of the administration of the Presidency of Bengal with headquarters in Calcutta. All the despatches of the Court of Directors had been addressed to the Governor-General of India in Council. Though some of these principally concerned the Presidency of Bengal, they to a large extent shaped the educational policy of the governments of Bombay and Madras. Before 1842 the Presidency of Bengal had practically comprised the whole of Northern India except the Punjab. In 1842, the North-western Provinces, at present known as the United Provinces of Agra and Oudh, were separated from the presidency and placed under a new government with a Lieutenant-Governor as the head of the administration. The progress of education in this province from 1842 to 1859 will be noticed in Section IV of this Chapter. When Queen Victoria was proclaimed Empress of India in 1858, the Governor-General became the Viceroy of India, and the administration of the Presidency of Bengal was placed under a Lieutenant-Governor.

The Despatch of 1854 is the first code on which Indian Education rests. For the first time it clearly laid down in the following paragraph that measures should be devised for the education of the mass of the people.

"Our attention should now be directed to a consideration, if possible, still more important, and one which has been hitherto, we are bound to admit too much neglected, namely, how useful and practical knowledge, suited to every station in life, may be best conveyed to the great mass of people, who are utterly incapable of obtaining any education worthy of the name by their own unaided efforts, and we desire to see the active measures of Government more especially directed, for the future, to this object, for the attainment of which we are ready to sanction a considerable increase of expenditure" (para. 41 of the Despatch of 1854).

This policy was reaffirmed by Lord Stanley, the first Secretary of State for India, in his Despatch of 1859.

"There can be no doubt of the great advantage of promoting in the native community a spirit of self-reliance, in opposition to the habit of depending on Government and its officers for the supply of local wants; and if Government shall have undertaken the responsibility of placing within reach of the general population the means of a simple elementary education, those individuals or classes who require more than this, may, as a rule, be left to exert themselves to procure it with or without the assistance of Government" (para. 55 of the Despatch of 1859).

SECTION II—THE MADRAS PRESIDENCY.

We have seen in the previous Chapter that, under the patronage of the Society for Promoting Christian Knowledge, the Protestant Mission had had a number of schools at different parts of the Madras Presidency. Some of them especially those at Madras, Cuddalore, Tanjore and Trichinopoly, became very famous because eminent persons like Ziegenbalg, Gericke, Kierander, Swartz, had been connected with those schools. They taught a large number of South Indians in those schools. The Court of Directors gave them permission to receive from the Society's office in England various supplies free of freight. Besides these they also got occasional aid from the local governments. The Court of Directors authorised a permanent annual grant of 250 pagodas each towards the support of three schools which had been established with the sanction of the respective Rajahs (Indian chiefs) at Tanjore, Ramnadapuram and Shivaganga. These schools were under the direction of Mr. Swartz. The Court further directed that a similar allowance should be granted to any other school which might be opened for the same purpose. "Later on there appears to have been a school at each of (the towns of) Tanjore and Kumbakonam costing Rs. 4,200 per annum. In 1820 a request was received by Government for titles to certain plots of ground connected with the schools and chapels in Tanjore."[1]

In 1814 Mr. Ross, the Collector of Cuddapah, suggested to the Government that it would be advisable to provide education for the higher classes first, and subsequently an arrangement might be made for other classes. He offered to the consideration of the Government a scheme for establishing a school in every district for imparting mental and moral instruction to young men of the upper classes of the Indian society. The Government however had great doubts whether the proposed scheme would succeed. They, however, authorized an experiment to be made at Cuddapah under the superintendence of Mr. Ross, whose superintendence they observed afforded the best prospect of success. But he died not long afterwards and the experiment was given up.

On the 2nd July, 1822, Sir Thomas Munro, the Governor of the Presidency, directed the Board of Revenue to make a survey of the actual state of education in its various branches among the inhabitants of the provinces under the Madras Government. A circular letter was accordingly sent by the Board to the several Collectors of the districts. Sir Thomas wrote:—"It is not my intention to recommend any interference whatever in the native schools.... The people should

[1] 'Fisher's Memoir', given in the Appendix to the Selections from Educational Records,' page 194.

be left to manage their schools in their own way. All we ought to do is to facilitate the operations of these schools, by restoring any funds that may have been diverted from them, and perhaps granting additional ones."[1] The collectors took over three years to make this educational survey; in the early part of 1826 the returns came to the hands of the Government ,and they in their turn forwarded them to the Court of Directors in England. Sir Thomas Munro wrote another Minute, on the 10th March, 1826, reviewing the returns. This was also forwarded to the Court of Directors. The Government found from the returns that the schools then existing in the country were for the most part supported by the payments of the people who sent their children to them for instruction. The rate of payment for each student varied in different districts and according to the pecuniary circumstances of the parents of the pupils "from one anna to four rupees for mensem; ordinarily about four annas and seldom exceeding half a rupee."[2] There were endowments for the support of schools only in the following seven districts:—Rajamundry, Nellore, Arcot, Salem, Tanjore, Trichinopoly, and Malabar. But it was also reported that public endowments for the purpose of education had been diverted in a number of other districts from their original purpose.

[1] 'Fisher's Memoir', given in the Appendix to the 'Selections from Educational Records', page 194.

[2] *Ibid.*, page 195.

Sir Thomas Munro's Minute records "It is remarked by the Board of Revenue, that of a population of 12½ millions there are only 188,000 or 1 in 67 receiving education. That is true of the whole population, but not as regards the male part of it, of which the proportion educated is much greater than is here estimated; for if we take the whole population as stated in the report at 12,850,000 and deduct one half for females, the remaining male population will be 6,425,000; and if we reckon the male population between the ages of five and ten years, which is the period which boys in general remain at school, at one-ninth, it will give 713,000 which is the number of boys that would be at school if all the males above five years were educated; but the number actually attending the school is only 184,110, or little more than one-fourth of that number. I have taken the interval between five and ten years of age as the term of education, because, though many boys continue at school till twelve or fourteen, many leave it under ten. I am, however, inclined to estimate the proportion of the male population who receive school education to be nearer to one-third than one-fourth of the whole, because we have no returns from the provinces of the number taught at home. In Madras the number taught at home is 26,903 or above five times greater than that taught in the schools. There is probably some error in this number, and though the number privately taught in the provinces does certainly not approach this rate, it is no doubt considerable, because the practice of boys being taught at home by their relations or private teachers is not unfrequent in any part of the country. The proportion educated is very different in different classes; in some it is nearly the whole; in others it is hardly one-tenth."[1]

He further observed that though the state of education in India was low compared with that of England it could favourably be compared with most other European countries, at no very distant period. It had no doubt been better in earlier times but, during the eighteenth century, war and other causes made the population migrate from place to place and they disorganised the ancient educational system of the country. The ignorance of the professed teachers and the poverty of parents were considered as the causes which combined to keep education in a low state. Owing to the comparatively large number of professed teachers, the number of scholars attached to each was small, and the monthly rate paid by each scholar was only from four to six or eight annas. So that teachers did not earn more than six or seven rupees per month, which was not considered an allowance sufficient to induce men properly qualified to follow the profession.

To remedy these defects Sir Thomas Munro suggested "the endowment of schools throughout the country by Government." As a first step

[1] 'Selections from Educational Records', Part I, page 73

towards removing the defects he proposed that a school for educating teachers should be started by Government at Madras, and that the Treasury should give a grant of Rs. 700 per month. His second proposal was that two principal schools—one for the Hindus and the other for the Muhammadans—should be established in each collectorate. And as more and more trained teachers could be found the number of schools for the Hindus should be increased, so that ultimately each *Tahsildaree* might possess one such school. The number would then be about 15 to each collectorate. The Muhammadan population not amounting to more than one-twentieth of the Hindu, it was considered sufficient to establish one Muhammadan school in each collectorate, except Arcot and a few other collectorates, where the proportion of the Muhammadan population was greater. Sir Thomas Munro added "whatever expense the Government may incur in the education of the people, will be amply repaid by the improvement of the country, for the general diffusion of knowledge is inseparably followed by more orderly habits, by increasing industry, by a taste for the comforts of life, by exertion to acquire them, and by the growing prosperity of the people."[1] The Minute of March 1826, by Sir Thomas Munro concluded by recommending the appointment of a Committee of Public Instruction, and by an expression of his entire confidence in the

[1] 'Selections from Educational Records', Part I, page 75.

7

final success of the measure, but he declared that success must be progressive and would be slow.

The members of the Governor's Council entirely agreed with Sir Thomas Munro's suggestions, which were accordingly sent to the Court of Directors for sanction. The Court approved the scheme and a Committee of Public Instruction at Madras was appointed in 1826. A sum of Rs. 48,000 per year was sanctioned for the scheme.

The Committee of Public Instruction first established a Normal School for the training of teachers. An English Head Master was appointed at a salary of Rs. 300 per month. Arrangements were also made so that headmasters in the Oriental and Vernacular Departments of the Colleges could give part-time services to the Normal School at a small cost. The next step taken by the Committee was to procure forty students to be trained as teachers in Madras for the projected collectorate school. The Committee thought that if it could get candidates for these situations from the districts in which they were intended to serve, they would undoubtedly be able to exercise great local influence. It accordingly asked the district magistrates to select two youths from each district—one Hindu and one Muhammadan—to be trained for the situation of teachers of collectorate schools. Each of these students was given a stipend of Rs. 15 per month. This sum was the minimum they were eventually to receive as teachers. In the case of Hindu candidates preference was to be given to the Brahmins. The Committee had not made any plan for training teachers for the *tahsildary* schools. It expected that a batch of trained collectorate teachers would gradually help in introducing the necessary improvements into inferior schools in the *tahsils*. "The Committee also proposed that in three of the principal towns of each collectorate a tahsildary teacher should be appointed on Rs. 9 per mensem. The schools should be open to Brahmins and Sudras alike."[1]

The Committee insisted upon the necessity of securing the sympathy and co-operation of the people. With this view the selection of the masters was left to the principal inhabitants of the towns. This resulted in the appointment of a number of very incompetent persons even inferior in calibre to the village schoolmasters. They got themselves appointed because of their influence with those to whom the selection was entrusted. Eventually 61 tahsildary schools were established in the province. In addition to these, nine schools of a similar character were set up in the town and suburbs of Madras under teachers trained in the Normal School. The headmasters of the collectorate schools were asked to inspect them periodically. For the time they appeared to have tolerable success. In them, as in the tahsil-

[1] 'Fisher's Memoir' in the 'Selections from Educational Records', Part I, page 196.

dary schools in the provinces, the instruction imparted was entirely vernacular, the study of English being reserved for the central collectorate schools.

It was, however, soon found that except for the Madras Schools, the scheme did not work well. The people were anxious to gain a good English education; they did not care much for the prolonged vernacular instruction. The Normal School became very successful, not because the pupils wanted to become teachers, but because there they obtained an opportunity to learn English. The tahsildary schools in the town of Madras were more or less successful because of the inspection introduced there; but in the mofussil such schools were failures as there was no provision for due inspection.

In 1834 the Committee of Public Instruction proposed that the Normal School should be enlarged and a few more tahsildary schools should be established in the town of Madras. The Committee also decided in 1835 to abolish the collectorate and tahsildary schools in the mofussil, because they were not much of a success. The decision was due to a large extent to the suggestions of the Government of India. Macaulay issued his famous Minute about this time in Bengal. Though his Minute had direct reference to education in Bengal still it affected educational policy in Madras. The Madras Government was advised by the Government of India to spend the earmarked public money almost exclusively on English education, and chiefly on higher English education.

On the receipt of the Bengal Despatch in 1835 the old Committee of Public Instruction was abolished and a new committee under the designation of "the Committee for Native Education" was appointed by the Government of Madras. This Committee consisted of five members, with a member of the Governor's Council as President. The new committee made several proposals: first, the immediate establishment of four English Schools in the town and suburbs of Madras; second, the organising of a normal class for training teachers of English in connection with the best high school in the Presidency; third, the establishment of a college as soon as the materials for such an institution could be procured; fourth, the engagement of a small number of well qualified persons to lecture at the college and teach the normal class, as well as to exercise a general superintendence over all town schools; fifth, the award of premiums to the teachers of the best conducted schools.

The Committee also decided to open immediately four good elementary schools, from which pupils were eventually to be qualified for instruction in the normal class attached to the High English School. At these four elementary schools English was also to be taught which, therefore, should be so located, as not to interfere with the

English schools already in existence. They proposed that these schools should be placed under European headmasters, and should provide instruction for about 100 scholars each.

All these proposals were not, however, accepted by the Government; only the Central Normal School was remodelled; the old method of gratuitous instruction to selected candidates from the districts was given up, and a fee of half a rupee per month was levied. The students were also required to provide themselves with school books. Affairs remained in this state until 1839.

Lord Elphinstone became Governor of Madras shortly after the plans of the Committee for Native Education were submitted to the Government. In 1839 he wrote a Minute, dated the 12th December, in which he stated "that the endeavours made in the Presidency to introduce a general system of education had produced nothing but disappointment and that their discontinuance had been ordered. A new direction was to be given to our efforts, and the plan which had been found to succeed in Bengal and Bombay was to be introduced, with such modifications as local circumstances might require at Madras. Among the principal points urged upon the attention of the Madras authorities by the Supreme Government and the General Committee was the discontinuance of the system of frittering away the sums allowed for educational purposes upon more elementary schools and upon eleemosynary scholars."[1]

As a result of Lord Elphinstone's Minute the Committee for Native Education was dissolved; it was succeeded by a Board called the 'University Board.' Its duties were to establish one central collegiate institution—called in the scheme 'university,'—at Madras, and a number of provincial colleges and high schools in connection with the central institution. This Board strongly felt that at first the instruction in the Government schools should be restricted to the upper classes of the Indian community, and that no scheme for the education of the masses should be formulated until an educated class should have been formed among those who had means and leisure to continue their studies after finishing their high school course. This Board was strongly of opinion that the light must touch the mountain tops before it could pierce to the levels and depths. Lord Elphinstone also held similar views, but at the same time agreed with the Governor-General that the elementary education of the mass of the people was not necessarily to be neglected or postponed to an indefinite period. He, therefore, proposed that in some of the principal towns in the interior a number of higher secondary schools should be started. Their status would be something like that of Intermediate College and would become the centre of a circle of zillah schools. In

[1] 'Selections from Educational Records', Part I, page 52.

the provincial schools the medium of instruction was to be English; and an acquaintance with it was made a necessary condition for admission to these schools; but at the outset this condition was relaxed in a few cases.

When these proposals came before the Court of Directors they disapproved of the entire abandonment of vernacular instruction in the provincial schools. They also thought that the time was not ripe for the starting of the higher collegiate or University department, and so did not sanction this part of the proposed scheme. The University Board was, therefore, not a successful institution, and a Council of Education was created to supplement it. This in its turn was dissolved in 1847, and a Board of General Education was created to administer a total Treasury grant of Rs. 100,000. Half of this sum was earmarked for higher secondary or collegiate education, Rs. 30,000 was assigned to five provincial schools, and Rs. 20,000 was set aside for grants-in-aid to elementary schools. Out of this money two provincial schools were started, one at Cuddalore in 1853, and the other at Rajahmundy in 1854. Then came the Despatch of 1854, the provisions of which have been enumerated in Section 1 of this Chapter.

One of the most important steps taken to give effect to the Despatch of 1854 was the creation of a Department of Education in each province under a Director of Public Instruction.

Mr. Alexander Arbuthnot, formerly Secretary to the Board of General Education, was appointed Director of the Presidency of Madras in 1855; and in the course of the next year four Inspectors of Schools, twenty Assistant Inspectors afterwards styled Zillah Visitors, and sixty Sub-Assistant Inspectors called Taluk Visitors were appointed. A scheme was drawn up and money sanctioned for the establishment of a Normal School, four provincial and eight zillah schools, a hundred Taluk schools, a depot for school books, education presses, and a number of scholarships of different grades.

These measures could not be carried out in one year; and some changes were occasionally made in the details of the plan when the work was taken in hand. Thus the full number of Taluk schools was never established, and schools of a somewhat higher grade known as Anglo-Vernacular schools took the place of some of the Taluk schools. Besides the Madras Normal School several others of a more elementary type were started in the provinces. A special school for Muhammadans known as the Madrassa-i-Azam was remodelled in 1859.

The first government grants-in-aid rules, that is to say, rules for regulating State aid given to private schools, were published in 1855. Though they were not very definite and did not specify by what considerations the exact amount of the grant was to be determined still they embodied some important principles. It is interesting to note the conditions upon which the first systematized grants were made:—

"1st. It will be a condition of all Grants towards the erection, enlargement, or repair of School buildings, that such rules as shall be laid down in regard to the dimensions and arrangements of the School buildings, with reference to the number of Scholars they are designed to accommodate, shall be duly observed, and that the permanent assignment of the buildings for School purposes shall be adequately secured.

"2nd. Applications for Grants for the provision of School furniture must be accompanied by a declaration on the part of the applicants that they will be personally responsible for the due preservation of the furniture of the School, and for its being reserved for the purposes for which it is supplied.

"3rd. Applications for Grants in augmentation of the salaries of teachers or for providing additional teachers, like other applicants for aid, will be referred to a Government Inspector, for report, on the merits of the School and qualifications of the teachers, and their continuance will depend upon the periodical reports of the Inspector on the merits and proficiency of the teachers, as ascertained at his periodical examinations of the School.

"4th. Grants for the payment of stipends to pupil teachers will be made only to those Schools in regard to which the Inspector may report that the master is competent to instruct such pupil teachers; and the continuance of such stipends, as well as the amount of gratuities, to be assigned to the masters for the instruction of the pupil teachers, will depend upon the proficiency of the latter.

"5th. Grants for School books, maps, or apparatus at reduced prices will be accompanied by the condition that the books shall be appropriated bonafide to the use of the masters and scholars, and that due means shall be taken for their preservation."[1]

Besides fulfilling the above conditions the rules provided that the grants were not to exceed in amount the sum raised by the school authorities, from fees, endowments or other sources for the specific purposes for which the aid was sought. Except in the case of Normal and Female schools no free schols were to receive any aid; the grants were to be confined to schools in which a certain rate of fees was levied. Every aided school was to be periodically inspected by Government inspectors and a teacher would receive a grant only when his qualifications had been reported as satisfactory by them. Experience showed that more definite rules were needed, for it was soon found that the original rules did not mention what deficiencies should be deemed a bar to any grant

[1] S. Satthianadhan, History of Education in the Madras Presidency' (published in 1894), page 51 f.

at all. In 1858 a new Code appeared. It was to a large extent an adaptation of the old English Code. Its main feature was an elaborate system of teachers' certificates in connection with the salary grants. Nine standards of qualification were laid down for schoolmasters and five for school mistresses, and for each standard there was a departmental examination. To each class of certificate a specific grant was attached which represented one-third of the teacher's salary.

SECTION III—THE BOMBAY PRESIDENCY

The Bombay Education Society was established in 1815. Although it depended solely on voluntary contribution, it opened and maintained a number of schools in the Island of Bombay, Thana and Surat. In order to take steps to spread elementary education a special committee was appointed by the society. The first work they attempted was the preparation of text books suitable for vernacular schools. With the increase in the scope of the work the society broke up in 1822 into two distinct societies, one retaining the original name confined its efforts to the education of European and Indo European children, and the other which confined its work among the Indians was named the Bombay Native School Book and School Society, commonly known as the Native Education Society.

During the period 1814 to 1859 elementary education in the Bombay presidency was largely developed by the operations of the Native Education Society and of the missionaries from the several Christian Churches of Europe and America of which the following did very good work:—The American Missionary Society, the Scottish Missionary Society, the London Missionary Society, the Irish Presbyterian Missionary Society and the Church Missionary Society. Some of these societies gradually began to receive state aid but the larger part of their income was derived from voluntary contributions. During the early part of this century primary education in the Bombay presidency was extended by missionary enterprise and the state only helped the higher education.

In 1823 the Native Education Society submitted a report in which they pointed out that the chief defects in primary education were the want of books, proper methods, teachers and funds. The society applied to the Government for assistance. Mr. Elphinstone, then Governor of Bombay, held that primary education should be spread by the agency of the Government as well as by private societies, and that these societies might receive grants from the Government. A grant of Rs. 600 per month was accordingly made to the Native Education Society.

"Mr. Elphinstone suggested that all contributions from these local funds towards education should be taken from the gross income of the village before the Government share was separated, so as to avoid the semblance of a too close connection between schools and taxation; and he further proposed to supplement such local contributions with other specified funds, which had hitherto been drawn from the Government treasury for objects that were of no utility and that were equally lost to the State and to the people. All schools so aided, were to be placed under the general supervision of the district collectors, who would have power to resume the grants in cases of gross neglect."[1]

The Governor's Council were divided in opinion on these matters; so effect was given to only a part of his scheme. The survey that was made by the collectors showed that the number of primary schools was 1,500, and the number of children attending them 31,000. It also showed that the education imparted hardly touched the masses of the people. There was an immense number of entire *mahals* (villages), without any schools whatever, and the number of villages destitute of schools was far greater than the number which possessed them. The instruction imparted in the schools extended with very limited exceptions, to the rudiments of writing and ciphering necessary for the business of a shopkeeper; and only a small proportion of the people acquired even this knowledge.

The progress of the Native Education Society

---

[1] Bombay Report of the Indian Education Commission (1882-83), page 6.

with financial grants from the Government appeared to have been steady and uniform from the year 1824. In 1832, the Native Education Society gave up its executive connection with the District Schools in Guzrat, which were then placed under Revenue officers, and the head inspector was placed under the orders of the principal collector of Surat. "The effects of this measure appear to have been most pernicious. The collectors regarded the schools as of trivial importance, and neither took pains to remove the indifference of the people with regard to them nor gave any instructions for the guidance of the inspector. The latter persevered, indeed, in visiting the schools and applying to the collectors for books and necessaries; but his applications were disregarded, and the masters, finding that he had no power over them, obeyed or neglected his instructions according to their inclination."[1] A Board of Education was therefore created in 1840 to take charge of the administration of education in the presidency. It consisted of six members, three of whom were appointed by the Native Education Society as its final act, and the other three by the Government. This Board took over all the Education Society's vernacular schools in Bombay and the mofussil. It also assumed charge of the English Schools, the

[1] Report of the Educational Inspector Gujratha Division, 1855-56, quoted in the Bombay Report of the Indian Education Commission (1882-83), page 9.

Oriental Colleges, the Normal classes and the Elphinstone College. From this time till 1855 the Board carried on all the educational activities of the presidency. It divided the area into three divisions for educational purposes, each of which was placed under a European Inspector. It also established studentships and school committees in important centres and undertook to open a vernacular school in every village containing not less than 2,000 inhabitants provided the people of the locality agreed to give a school house, furnish it and keep it under repair.

The English schools were considered the secondary schools; an entrance examination test was prescribed and a number of free studentships for poor and deserving boys from the vernacular schools was provided. In the vernacular rural schools the pupils were taught to read, write and to keep accounts, so that they might not be cheated when they began to earn their own living. A school census was taken in 1842 and it was ascertained that there was in all 1,420 indigenous schools in the province attended by upwards of 30,000 pupils. This figure indicated that 13 per cent of the total number of male children between 10 and 5 years of age were then attending the elementary schools.

From 1843 to 1852 Sir Erskine Perry was the Chairman of the Board of Education. He firmly believed in the growth of English Schools and advocated the downward filtration policy. In

1842 the Court of Directors sanctioned a subsidy of Rs. 1,45,000 to the Board of Education by the Government of Bombay. Out of this sum Rs. 45,000 were set apart for collegiate education; and the remaining Rs. 1,00,000 per annum used to be spent on English as well as on vernacular schools. Due to the acceptance by the Government of Sir Erskine Perry's views not much attention was paid to the elementary schools. During the time he was the Chairman of the Board only 43 vernacular schools were added to the list of Board-schools, whilst the number of English schools and the attendances were doubled. His encouragement of higher education also acted as a stimulus to private enterprise and nine English schools were started by the citizens at important towns. Endowments were also created for the establishment of girls' schools in Ahmedabad. When Sir Erskine Perry left, the Government began to give more attention to primary education. In 1853 the Board offered small grants-in-aid to the masters of indigenous schools. The Government also increased the grants to the Board which now stood at Rs. 2,50,000. In 1854 the Board agreed to pay half of the master's salary for any new school opened by the inhabitants in any village. The school-room, class books and the other half of the master's salary were to be provided by the villagers. At this time the Despatch of 1854 came in and the Board was abolished in 1855. A Department of Public

Instruction was organised on the basis of the Despatch and Mr. C. Erskine of the Indian Civil Service was appointed as the first Director of Public Instruction, Bombay.

Mr. Erskine proposed to organise the following system of Vernacular and English institutions:—[1]

(1) The Indigenous Primary School, which should be encouraged to place itself under the control of the Department by the offer of a grant, equivalent to half the master's salary.

(2) The Village School to be established aided and controlled by the Department. One such school to be provided to every 2,000 inhabitants.

(3) The Town School to be similarly aided and controlled by the Department. It was to have two more advanced classes than the village school. The pupils of the town schools were to be given the option of learning the rudiments of English in the highest class.

These three types were to be elementary schools. Besides these he proposed to start the Pargana or Taluka School and the Zillah or High School. He also made proposals how the different types of schools should be linked up by examina-

[1] Bombay Report of the Indian Education Commission (1882-83), page 16.

tion tests and scholarships. But his health broke down in August, 1856, and he was compelled to resign his office. His proposals regarding aiding and controlling the indigenous, village and town schools were to a large extent carried out by his successor Mr. E. I. Howard. In 1858 the Government of India interpreted that the Despatch of 1854 only empowered the giving of grants to the indigenous schools, and that the Government of Bombay had no power to establish the village and town schools on the partially self-supporting system. "The Bombay Government replied that the partially self-supporting system was substantially the same as the grant-in-aid system, inasmuch as the Department paid only a moiety of the schoolmaster's salary, while the people paid not only the other half and school fees, but the whole expenditure on account of the school building, furniture and contingencies. The Supreme Government acquiesced in this view but desired that no new schools of this class should be opened without their sanction. The extension of primary education being thus virtually stopped,—for the grant-in-aid rules sanctioned by the Government of India were wholly unsuited to the indigenous schools—the work of the Educational Department was limited to consolidating and improving its existing schools."[1] It must also be stated here that more than 90 per cent of the villages in the

[1] Bombay Report of the Indian Education Commission (1882-83), page 25.

Presidency were at this time without any indigenous schools. The Government of India interpreted the Despatch in the manner mentioned above because they wanted to divert more money to higher education. The net result was the stoppage of the extension of primary education according to the plan of Mr. Erskine. If Mr. Erskine's plan had been fully acted upon the Bombay Presidency would have had by that time a network of primary schools. The whole question of State aid was soon after discussed in the Despatch of the 7th April, 1859, the effects of which on primary education in Bombay will be described in the next chapter.

Section IV—The United Provinces of Agra & Oudh

The area covered by the United Provinces of Agra and Oudh was a part of the Presidency of Bengal till 1842. In that year this portion was separated from the Bengal Presidency. It was then given the name of North-Western Provinces and was placed under the administration of a Lieutenant-Governor. The name N. W. Provinces was changed to the United Provinces of Agra and Oudh in 1902. The development of education in this area prior to 1842 was on the lines adopted for the Presidency of Bengal, an account of which has been given in Section I of this Chapter. Mr. Thomason was the first Lieutenant-Governor and was familiar with the recommendations which Mr. W. Adam had submitted during 1835 to 1838 for consideration of the General Committee of Education in Bengal. Although Mr. Adam's proposals were not carried into practice in Bengal, Mr. Thomason regarded them as worthy of acceptance in the N. W. Provinces.

In this province the rights in the land were of several kinds, and the properties were minutely subdivided. Complete registration was therefore required to protect the interests of the ryots. It was necessary that they should be able to understand that the figures were accurately put down in the books of the registration office. For this purpose it was necessary that they should be able to read and write, and should understand the elementary rules of arithmetic. In 1846 the government laid down the policy for the extension of primary education. There were four types of indigenous primary schools then in existence: first, those in which the teacher received no remuneration whatever; second, those in which the teacher was a domestic tutor, entertained by his patron; third, those supported entirely by the scholars; fourth, those supported by the patron with a certain contribution from boys allowed to read with his sons. In those days trustworthy statistics were not to be had easily, but it was roughly ascertained that out of a population which numbered in 1848, twenty-three million souls and in which there were more than 1,900,000 males of a school-going age only 68,000 were receiving any education whatever. Nearly half of them attended Hindi schools, and in these hardly anything deserving the name of education was given.

Mr. Thomason gave a permanent impulse to popular education. In 1850 the government issued a resolution whereby "there will be a Government village school at the headquarters of every tahsildari (subdivision) which will be conducted by a schoolmaster, who will receive from Rs. 10 to Rs. 20 per mensem, besides such fees as he may collect from his scholars." The curriculum in the tahsili school was comprehensive. It included besides the three R's, history, geography and geometry through the medium of the vernacular and accounts and land mensuration. In 1854 there were nearly five thousand students in the tahsili schools and the state expenditure was only ten thousand rupees.

The *halkabandi* or primary vernacular schools which during this period thronged the North-Western Provinces in thousands, originated about 1851 in an experiment made by Mr. Alexander, Collector of Muttra. The plan was this. "A *pargana* being chosen, it was ascertained how many children of school-going age it numbered, what revenue it paid, and what expense it could therefore bear. A cluster of villages, some four or five, was then marked out, and the most central of the villages fixed upon as the site of the school. The rate of aid originally varied a good deal in the different districts, but ultimately the *zamindars* (landlords) agreed to contribute towards education at the rate of one per cent on their land revenue. Mr. Alexander's idea was quickly caught up by other Collectors; in 1853, Agra, Bareily, Etah, Etwah, Mainpuri, Muttra, and Shahjahanpur all had a certain number of halkabandi schools, and at the close of 1854 there were about 17,000 boys receiving education in them. The teacher's pay varied from Rs. 3 to Rs. 7, the average being about Rs. 4-10-0. Reading and writing with a little arithmetic, mensuration, and geography, were the subjects taught, and though later on others more abstruse were added, it is doubtful whether such ambition served any useful end."[1]

As in other provinces a Director of Public Instruction was appointed in 1854. Mr. H. S. Reid, who had so long acted as the Visitor-General of the Vernacular Schools, was appointed as the first Director. Two Inspectors of Schools and a few Deputy Inspectors were also appointed. The first Normal School was established in 1855 to train teachers for the *tahsili* and *halkabandi* schools. There were 758 halkabandi or primary vernacular schools in 1854 with about 17,000 boys on the rolls. The system was then confined to a few districts only. Gradually it spread to almost all the districts in the provinces and at the beginning

---

[1] N. W. Provinces Report of the Indian Education Commission (1882-83), page 18.

of 1857 there were 1,491 schools with about 31,500 boys on the rolls. The Sepoy Mutiny broke out in that year and the work was more or less disorganised; Lucknow, Agra, Bareilly, and Delhi suffered a good deal. School buildings were deserted; some even were demolished by the mutineers. When the year closed there were left but 892 schools with 13,220 boys. The depression, however, did not last long after mutiny was suppressed, and by the end of 1860 there were 84,723 boys attending 3,086 schools.

Section V—The Punjab

The Punjab was annexed to British India only in 1849. Immediately after the annexation the Government declared their intention of educating the masses, but no serious steps were taken to carry the intention into practice till 1854: only when the Despatch from the Court of Directors came did the government of the Punjab realize their responsibility. In January, 1856, Mr. W. D. Arnold, a son of the distinguished headmaster of Rugby, was appointed as the first Director of Public Instruction in the Punjab. The Inspectors and Assistant Inspectors of Schools were also appointed in the same year.

The Punjab Education Department found three types of indigenous schools existing in the country—(a) the Hindu village schools, (b) the Sikh schools, a large proportion of which taught in the Gurmukhi character the language of the Sikh scripture or *Granth,* (c) the Muhammadan schools; the majority of the boys attending these schools were Muhammadans. It is also noteworthy that a large percentage of the Hindu students were then attending the Muhammadan schools. The Punjab was for centuries the stronghold of the Muhammadan kings. Hence to court the patronage of the rulers even the Hindus preferred to learn Persian.

After making a preliminary survey of the educational needs, Mr. Arnold tried to improve the indigenous schools by giving them state aid from the yield of the one per cent cess. It was distinctly given to understand that the people of the locality would have to maintain the indigenous schools though they would get some help from the government for their improvements. But the people tried to throw the entire burden of their support on the state. In some localities the teachers accepted state aid to improve their salaries but paid no attention to departmental rules regarding the method of instruction, class management etc. Thus all efforts to elevate the standard of indigenous schools failed. An attempt was then made to introduce the village school system of the North-Western Provinces described in the previous section of this chapter. These schools were supported entirely from the yield of the one per cent cess. A few simple rules were drawn up for the guidance of the teachers, and a plan of an elementary course of instruction was prescribed for adoption in the schools. The salaries of the teachers were fixed at Rs. 5 each per month. The subordinate officers of the department made very bad selections of teachers. To meet the wishes of the people they mostly selected the old teachers of the indigenous schools. They followed the old time-honoured but useless system. So the new schools became no better than the old indigenous schools. Hence we find that the *tahsili* and *halkabandi* systems which worked so well in the North-Western Provinces failed to produce any effect on education in the Punjab. The fanatic character of the teachers belonging to two of the communities rendered all progress impossible. Moreover, the language which was adopted in the Courts of law, and which later on became almost exclusively the medium of instruction in schools for boys was not the principle vernacular of the people. So the reforms in the Punjab had to be effected very slowly. Gradually all schools supported entirely by the state were removed from mosques and other buildings of a religious character. Old and inefficient teachers, who were originally appointed only for priestly qualifications, were removed. The Government had to throw out prospects of advancement in order to secure the services of efficient teachers in village schools. The village school teachers were divided into three grades on salaries of Rs. 5, 7 and 10.

SECTION VI—OTHER PROVINCES

The other administrative units which we find at present in India e.g. the Central Provinces, Assam, etc., were not constituted during the period under review. These territories were gradually acquired or annexed. The Central Provinces were placed under one administration in November, 1861, with a Chief Commissioner at the head. Before 1859 the northern part of the area known as the Saugor and Nerbudda territories formed part of the North-Western Provinces. The Eastern part e.g. Sambalpur and adjoining feudatory states were under Bengal. The Southern parts formed part of Berar.

Before 1854 in the Saugor and Nerbudda territories there were a few Hindi and Persian indigenous schools. A small number of English schools were started by Capt. James Paton and Mr. Rao Krishna Rao, and they received some grant from the Government of Lord William Bentinck. Later on in these parts attempts were made to start a few schools on the *halkabandi* system of the North-Western Provinces, but not much success was gained as the Government at first refused to select those territories as experimental districts. Moreover, there was a good deal of social prejudice against educating the masses of the people. As an example it may be cited that one of the English schools was broken up because nearly all the students left, when a few boys belonging to the lower castes were admitted.

On account of the unbridged rivers, mountains and forests the light of modern civilization could hardly pierce into the interior of the territories and there was a good deal of opposition from the higher caste Hindus to any State system of education.

In 1841 the German Agricultural Mission under Pastor Grossner of Berlin tried with the sanction of the Government to establish schools especially for the aborigines, the Gonds etc., but as four of the six missionaries died very shortly after their arrival the mission was given up.

After the receipt of the Despatch of 1854 the Lieutenant-Governor of the North-Western Provinces appointed two inspectors of schools for the country and started a few schools in the Nerbudda and Saugor territories. The Central Provinces report of the Indian Education Commission states that prior to 1861 "there was a system of State education in the Saugor and Nerbudda territories imperfectly adopted after the mode of the North-Western Provinces, and inferior to the system existing in the North-West. In the districts of the late Nagpur Provinces there had been no State education at all. In Sambalpur and its dependencies existed only one school for general education: in short more than half of the Central Provinces were without education at all, and the remainder possessed an incomplete system only. The people, as remarked by Sir Richard Temple, were thoroughly uneducated. In no part of

British India could there be found a population of less education. There were no places of Native learning and no learned classes. There was not one indigenous school to fifty villages."

CHAPTER IV.

THE PERIOD 1860—1881.

In Section I of the previous chapter the main features of the Secretary of State's Despatch of 1859 have been reviewed. The gradual development of the policy of the Government of India regarding elementary and secondary education has also been traced. We have seen why and how the Government tried to give more encouragement to secondary and collegiate education than to elementary education. From this chapter our attention shall primarily be devoted to the development of elementary education in India.

SECTION I—THE BENGAL PRESIDENCY

As regards the education of the masses of the people the Despatch of 1859 clearly stated that the grant-in-aid system alone would not be able to supply education to all children of school-going age; therefore it was necessary to start schools under the direct instrumentality of the State. It was also laid down that, if required, educational rates might be levied for the purpose of meeting the increased expenditure. From the beginning of this period, the controversy between the Governments of India and Bengal centred round the levying of an education rate in the presidency. An educational rate on land had been introduced in several provinces in British India but the Bengal Government urged that the Permanent Settlement of Lord Revenue in Bengal by Lord Cornwallis precluded its being levied in that presidency. Moreover, about a third of the children then attending the *pathsalas* (primary schools) belonged to the non-agriculturist classes. So it was argued, it would be unfair to have an educational rate on land only, and would be much better to levy a general tax for education. While the controversy was raging, Mr. James Wilson, was sent by the British Government to advise the Government of India regarding the adjustment of the finances of the country after the Sepoy Mutiny. He examined the problem of levying an education rate on land in Bengal; and was of opinion that the Permanent Settlement of Land Revenue in Bengal did not exempt the landholder from liability to share in the national expenditure. The Government of Bengal, however, was not moved by Mr. Wilson's opinion. But the Duke of Argyll's Despatch, dated the 12th May, 1870, ended the controversy. This Despatch declared "that rating for local expenditure is to be regarded, as it has hitherto been regarded, in all the provinces of the empire, as taxation separate and distinct from the ordinary land revenue; that the levying of such rates upon the holders of land, irrespective of the land assessment, involves no breach of faith on the part of Government, whether as regards holders of permanent or temporary tenures.... Her Majesty's Government can have no doubt that, as elsewhere so in Bengal, the expenditure required for the education of the people ought to be mainly defrayed out of local resources. This, however, is precisely the purpose of rates which the present condition of the people may render them least able to appreciate. I approve therefore of Your Excellency proceeding with great caution."[1]

Soon after a terrible famine swept over Bengal and a Commission was appointed to inquire into the causes of it. In 1875 the Famine Commission declared that the cultivators had already been taxed to the utmost extent and it was desirable that they should pay a smaller proportion of the national charges. The decentralization of finances also greatly improved the financial position of the local Governments. The question of levying an education rate on land in Bengal was therefore dropped. With it the idea of drawing up any comprehensive scheme of education for the masses fell through. The Government then thought of improving the existing indigenous schools by giving encouragement to the Circle School System already adopted in the N. W. Provinces and Punjab, and in a few districts in Bengal. A chief *guru* (teacher) was appointed to supervise the work of a small number of schools in close proximity to one another. His position was not like an

[1] Bengal Report of the Indian Education Commission (1882-83), page 29.

inspector of village schools but like that of a Visiting teacher. He was required to instruct the upper classes of the small group of schools placed under his charge as well as to help the local guru in his difficulties. This system was known as the Circle School System and it worked with a fair amount of success for some years. This system was introduced in Behar, which was then a part of the presidency of Bengal, in 1876. The Indian Education Commission of 1882-83 thus recorded their opinion of the system:—"This system supplies a close net-work of organization, which has been found very effective in bringing to light in Behar the smallest schools of the people, hid in the remotest corners of districts. In Orissa, the results of an almost identical scheme have been the same. Introduced lately into some of the Bengal districts, it has been found to be far more effective of its object than any system heretofore tried. It appears to be the best calculated to preserve and bring under organisation whatever indigenous schools exist in the country, which are or can be utilized as a part of the educational system."[1]

Another important feature of this period was the holding of a conference at Simla to discuss the constitution of a standing committee, in each of the presidencies and provinces, for the selection and recommendation of suitable text books in schools

[1] Bengal Report of the Indian Education Commission (1882-83), page 43.

of different grades. In 1877 the Bengal Text-Book Committee was appointed. This committee brought out a new and uniform series of text books which they thought would be suited for use in the vernacular schools. But the series was not very good as the books were mere translations of English originals, and as such were not quite suited to the primary schools in Bengal.

Mr. (afterwards Sir) H. L. Harrison, while he was the district Magistrate of Midnapur, encouraged the *gurus* (teachers) of the primary schools by the award of monetary grants on the results of examinations of the pupils held by the inspectors. This was possibly *the origin of the system of payments by results in India.* Mr. Harrison undoubtedly was guided by the Report of the Newcastle Commission (published in 1861) and the Revised Code of England of 1862. The scheme worked so well in the district of Midnapur that the attention of the Government was drawn to it; and Sir George Campbell, the Lieutenant-Governor of Bengal, asked the Director of Public Instruction in 1873 to introduce it in other districts of Bengal. Two examinations were held annually—first, a Sub-centre examination in Reading, Writing, Arithmetic, *Zamindari* (land) and *Mahajani* (cash) Accounts, Dictation and Explanation of Passages. The results of the successful candidates were classified into two divisions, higher and lower. "The reward paid to the teacher for each pupil who passed by the former was one rupee (2 shillings), and for each who passed by the latter, eight annas (1 shilling). One rupee was the reward for each pupil who passed in Accounts. For satisfying the examiners in Dictation and Explanation of Passages, the reward was Rs. 2 to pupil and teacher alike. In addition a special prize was given in every group of 50 candidates examined. For girls the rewards for the first three subjects were doubled. Then there were rewards in small sums of money for register-keeping and stability of schools, so that the earnings of the less fortunate *gurus* might in some slight measure be augmented."[1] The second, or Central Examination, was held for the award of scholarships and prizes to the deserving candidates. For this examination a more advanced knowledge of the subjects of the Sub-centre examination was required Besides these the candidates had to pass an examination in Mensuration. These examinations were held for the first time in 1876-77. "In 1876-77, the date of the first systematic examination, there were 11,462 candidates from 3,110 schools, and 5,246 passed the test. In 1880-81, after a lapse of four years, there were 26,293 candidates from 7,887 schools, and 13,951 passed. That is to say, more than half of the indigenous schools which in 1876-77 had been brought under control, had in 1880-81 advanced to the full primary scholarship

[1] Stark—'Vernacular Education in Bengal', page 96.

standard."[1] The main feature of the system of payment-by-results was the eagerness with which a great many of the indigenous schools entered into the departmental system. The Government also did their best to encourage the traditional methods of indigenous education. They wanted to improve the schools gradually by the central scholarship examination and by the removal of inefficient teachers. The scheme at first was such a success that every year more and more schools came within the departmental system. The Government, however, were unable to keep pace with meeting the increasing demands made upon their finances. The teachers began to earn less than half the amount they used to get when the scheme was launched. They, therefore, became discouraged. But the system held the field of elementary education for a long time even after this period; for, as we shall see in the next chapter, the Education Commission of 1882 recommended its retention.

SECTION II—THE MADRAS PRESIDENCY

In Rajamundry the ryots were anxious to have a few vernacular schools established in their villages. They agreed to contribute a fixed annual addition to the revenue demand on their villages for the maintenance of the schools. The Sub-collector assented to their proposals and started a

[1] Bengal Report of the Indian Education Commission (1882-83), page 46.

few schools. This system was confined only to Rajamundry. The Director of Public Instruction remarked that the system could not be introduced in other districts as the principle on which its introduction had been sanctioned in Rajamundry was that the rate should be raised voluntarily. Though the people of Rajamundry offered to pay the rate, the Director was extremely doubtful whether even in Rajamundry the rate could properly be called voluntary. An Act [1] was therefore passed in 1863 known as the Voluntary Education Act to give legal sanction and permanence to the Rajamundry schools. The operation of the Act could, however, be extended to other districts to enable the schools to be supported partly by grants-in-aid and partly by a quasi-voluntary rate. But the scheme did not work well in other districts because the people preferred to do without improved education rather than pay a cess. Its operations were limited to only nine districts. This Act, however, was cancelled by the passing of the Madras Acts III and IV of 1871.

The Madras Act III of 1871 is known as the Town Improvement Act. This Act, though mainly intended to deal with the administration of the municipalities in towns, gave the Municipal Commissioners certain powers to devote part of their funds for the diffusion of education by (1) construction and repair of school houses,

[1] The Madras Act VI of 1863.

(2) establishment and maintenance of schools, either wholly or by means of grants-in-aid, (3) inspection of schools, and (4) training of teachers. The Madras Act IV of 1871 known as the Madras Local Funds Act empowered all local authorities to spend a part of their money for educational purposes. The rules under the same Act laid down that "Villages or groups of villages in which Government might direct the imposition of a house tax for the support of a Local Fund school or schools situated therein, or for the reimbursement to Local Funds of grants-in-aid of a school or schools so situated, were to be denominated Unions. The proceeds of the house-tax levied within such unions, together with the school fees, donations, contributions, and other money accruing to the schools or for Union purposes, were to form subordinate branches of the Local Fund under the designation of Union Funds. They were to be applied in the first instance to meet the educational expenditure of the Union, but in the event of there being a surplus, it might be applied to other expenditure within the Union. Any elementary school in which 30 per cent of the pupils for two consecutive years qualified for results-grants was, as a general rule, to be permanently constituted a Union school, unless the inhabitants or other persons were willing to establish from their own resources an elementary school on the salary-grant system. Local Com-

mittees were to be appointed for the management of schools of sufficient importance to render such a measure desirable."[1]

We have seen in the previous chapter that the first grants-in-aid rules for the Presidency of Madras were published in August, 1855. A new Code was issued in 1858 modifying some of the rules. A revised set of grants-in-aid rules was brought into force from 1st January, 1865. A scheme for payments by results was also drawn up and came into operation on the 1st January, 1868 According to this scheme the examinations conducted by the inspectors were of four different standards. In the first (or the lowest) standard only the three R's were examined; in the second the examination was held in the same subjects but the course were slightly more advanced than in the first; in the third Vernacular Grammar, Geography and English (reading and writing only) were introduced, in addition to the courses prescribed for the second; in the fourth was included English Grammar besides advanced work in the subjects mentioned in the third. The scale of money grants to teachers and pupils was higher than that adopted in the presidency of Bengal. The authorities in Madras were better off financially because they were allowed by Acts III and IV of 1871 to levy an education rate.

---

[1] Rules under the Local Funds Act IV of 1871 have been given in Appendix F of Satthianadhan's History of Education in Madras Presidency, 1894).

The Government decided that all results-grants to lower forms of primary schools (often called lower class schools) should be paid out of the municipal and local funds. It became, therefore, necessary to demarcate between the upper primary (often called middle class) and lower class schools. It was finally decided that the third-results standard, which included reading and writing of English, should be the upper limit of instruction in a lower class school; and that the results-grants to the middle class schools should be paid out of the provincial revenues. The rate on houses levied to meet the cost of education in accordance with Acts III and IV of 1871 caused much discontent; the Government, therefore, discontinued it from the 1st April, 1873.

In the same year the Government thought that they were not spending as much as they ought on primary education. But as they had not sufficient money in the Treasury to sanction increased sums for primary education, they wanted to divert some money from the higher to elementary education. They asked the Director of Public Instruction, Mr. Powell, to devise means for the purpose. He pointed out that in a large number of higher class schools there remained a surplus from the fees and government grants after meeting the expenses. He, therefore, suggested to the Government that the salary-grants to the teachers in the higher class schools might be reduced and the amount thus saved could be devoted to primary education. The Government could not give immediate effect to the Director's suggestions, because they wanted to have the opinions of the representatives of the mission schools and the presidents of the local boards. But eventually an agreement was reached and the revised Salary-grant-rules were sanctioned early in 1880, but they were not enforced until the 1st April, 1883.

In May, 1877, revised rules regarding the payment of grants by results were sanctioned. These raised the standard in some respects, and reduced the scale by one third The inevitable result was a great fall in the number of scholars and schools in 1878. The famine that prevailed in that year might have been one of the causes of the decline in number but the stringency of the rules had a great effect on it. "The South Indian Missionary Conference forwarded a memorial to Government, in June 1879, suggesting some material alterations; and after further discussion, the rules now (1883) in force were issued. By these the standards were again lowered and the old rate of grants was restored."[1] The new code of rules was issued on the 16th February, 1880; this laid down among other things that in the interior or backward districts or in districts with exceptional climates the period of attendance of

[1] Madras Report of the Indian Education Commission (1882-83), page 29.

a pupil was to be reduced from 90 days to 75 days during the six working months preceding the examination.[1]

SECTION III—THE BOMBAY PRESIDENCY

When the despatch of 1859 came to the Government of India, Mr. Howard was the Director of Public Instruction in the Presidency of Bombay. He was not much in favour of giving large scale grants to missionary schools, as he held that the people would not like to be proselytized while receiving instruction in such schools; he was also against giving encouragement to the indigenous schools. He added that the people of his presidency much preferred the prestige, purity, and efficiency of government schools to those under private management. And to meet the expenses of state-maintained schools he suggested that the Government might levy with each rupee of land revenue the one-anna cess which had been reserved under the Revenue Survey Rules for education and local improvements. He also asked the Government to amend the Municipal Act to enable the authorities to spend a part of the Municipal funds on secular education.

The Bombay Government almost wholly agreed with Mr. Howard's proposals. Powers were given to the municipalities by Act II of 1862

---

[1] Clause 68 of the Educational Grant-in-Aid Code, Fort St. George, February 16th, 1880.

to spend money on the support of schools within their areas. As a result a number of municipalities began to spend money on primary education, but for a number of years the remaining ones did nothing for the purpose. In 1863 the Government sanctioned the imposition of the one-anna land-cess. It was laid down that one-third of the money realised in each district by this cess was to be spent on the support of primary education and the remainder on local public works. In the same year a provisional code offering grants-in-aid on the system of payment-by-results was issued. But the missionaries objected to the terms offered by Mr. Howard regarding religious instruction and refused to receive state-aid. In 1864 a conference was held with the prominent missionaries and managers of private schools and the code was revised. But so long as Mr. Howard was Director, that is till 1865, no missionary school received any state-aid.

The Government sanctioned the levying of the one-anna cess in 1863, but the first collection was not made until 1865. The cess was originally levied without the sanction of the legislature, but was imposed after receiving the sanction of the Secretary of State for India. In its first form the rate was an optional one which the local authorities might or might not impose. In 1869, however, an Act[1] was passed making the rate compulsory.

[1] Act III of 1869.

The Act also provided for the appointment of Local Committees to administer the funds thus raised, as well as any other funds that might be placed at their disposal. In this connection it must be noted that as the cess was levied on land the burden of taxation fell on the agriculturists. The non-agricultural community escaped from paying any cess; but in the schools their children numbered nearly half the total strength. Moreover three-fourths of the expenses of these schools were met from the income derived by the levying of the cess It was, therefore, urged by many, including government officials, that a school-rate in the form of a house-tax on the non-agricultural inhabitants of towns and villages should be levied. But no legislative action was taken to remove this defect.

The grants-in-aid rules on the system of payment-by-results were first introduced in the Presidency of Bombay in 1863; but unlike the rules in Bengal and Madras they embraced in this Presidency even secondary education. "The maximum grants offered under the several standards of instruction prescribed by the Code ranged from one rupee to four rupees a head, and in Anglo-Vernacular Schools from six rupees to thirty rupees a head, with a special grant of Rs. 100 for each pupil who passed the Matriculation Examination. A capitation grant of Rs. 2 in Anglo-Vernacular, and of eight annas in Vernacular schools was also given on the average attendance of the pupils during the year."[1] Although the education of the masses had the greatest claim on state-funds, yet the grants-in-aid rules were such that in practice they were found unsuited to primary schools.

These rules were in force till the end of 1870. To that time the Government of India had been contributing large sums to the provincial governments for the spread of education; but the Decentralisation-order of December 14th, 1870, compelled the Government of Bombay without any help from the Government of India to take the sole responsibility for the spread of primary education. So the Bombay Government had to formulate a provincial policy of education; they separated primary education from secondary. Up to 1871 whenever they had wanted to extend primary education the Bombay Government had invariably, applied to the Government of India for additional funds. But in conformity to the decentralisation order, the Bombay Government Resolution of December, 1872, made complete separation of the instruction, organisation, administrative control and finances of the primary and secondary schools. It was ruled that the cess-income should be entirely devoted to primary schools. This undoubtedly gave greater impetus to the linking up of the indigenous and the local board schools under one administrative control.

---

[1] Bombay Report of the Indian Education Commission (1882-83), page 34.

The Local Boards, District and Táluk Committees, also realized their increased responsibilities in the matter of primary education for the cess-income was placed entirely at their disposal for this purpose and for other local improvements.

Both types of schools, namely the local board and the indigenous schools, greatly influenced each other in improving the organization of primary education in the presidency. Where a cess-school, with better trained teachers, had been started by the local board, the indigenous school was unable to attract or keep their boys if it failed to supply the popular demand for improved education. As, however, not many cess-schools could be opened by the local boards on account of the limited amount of cess-funds, the indigenous schools, stimulated by the work of the neighbouring cess-schools, supplied in large measure the need caused by the shortage of primary schools. Regarding the work of the period the Education Commission of 1882 wrote as follows:—"It would appear that in Government and aided schools in the British districts of the Bombay Presidency there were 226,364 children in primary schools in 1881. Assuming the attendance in aided indigenous schools in the same area to be 61,000, there would have been 287,364 children under elementary instruction. According to the census of 1872 the population in the Presidency, excluding native states, was 16,228,774; and if 15 per cent represent the school-going age, there ought to be

2,434,316 boys and girls at school, of whom, as a matter of fact, not 12 per cent were under instruction. These figures suggest small reason for satisfaction with the results attained. But, on the other hand, if the popular prejudice to female education, the exceptionally backward condition of Sind, and the dead weight of a large aboriginal population are considered, it will be found that in some divisions of the Presidency the elementary education of male children has made remarkable progress; and in the city of Poona it has been stated that the whole population of school-going age, calculated as shown above, were attending primary schools at the close of 1881."[1]

Section IV—The United Provinces of Agra and Oudh

We have noticed that at the close of the last period three types of elementary schools existed in the United Provinces of Agra and Oudh (then known as the North-Western Provinces); they were the 'tahsili', 'halkabandi', and 'indigenous' schools. During the period 1859 to 1881 the *tahsili* schools were gradually raised to the status of lower secondary schools But as the majority of the boys in the *tahsili* schools only studied there for about four years, obviously they did not proceed beyond the elementary stage. In 1864 a

---

[1] Bombay Report of the Indian Education Commission (1882-83), page 45.

few schools of the type of *tahsili* schools were started by the Government in Oudh. They were called in that province Vernacular Town Schools.

The status of the *halkabandi* schools was not altered, as it was thought that it would involve the neglect of the lower classes for the sake of the higher. Moreover, the one per cent cess on land revenue was expressly levied for starting schools for the education of the masses. The number of such schools increased and the attendance of boys was satisfactory. Although during this period famine occurred on several occasions there was no considerable diminution in the number of attendance, which clearly proved the popularity of these schools among the general population. In 1863 the Government decided, with the approval of the Secretary of State for India, that the fund raised by the levying of the one-per-cent cess on land revenue in Oudh should be applied solely for the starting of the village schools and not for the maintenance of the *tahsili* schools in that area. These were permitted to be conducted on the lines of the *halkabandi* system or on any other plan which might be thought more suitable for the locality.

As the indigenous schools were not the outcome of any scheme of education formulated by the Education Department, they did not receive much encouragement at the hands of the state officials. But a few sympathetic inspectors tried to improve them by friendly inspection and distribution of approved text books as prizes to successful scholars.

"Among local Acts applicable to the North-Western Provinces and Oudh, the following make reference to the subject of education:—In Act XVIII of 1871, which was passed to provide, in the N. W. Provinces, 'for the levy on land of rates to be applied to local purposes,' Part IV lays down rules for the manner in which the rates are to be expended; and section 9 of the Act provides that 'the proceeds of all rates levied under this Act shall be carried to the credit of a general provincial fund.' Section 10 of the Act provides that the Local Government 'shall from time to time allot from such fund an amount to be applied in each district for expenditure on all or any of' certain purposes specified in various clauses of that section. Among such purposes clause (c) of the section includes 'the construction and repair of school houses, the maintenance and inspection of schools, the training of teachers, and the establishment of scholarships.' The Act was amended by Act VII of 1877, and was finally repealed by Act III of 1878, in which, however, the provisions above referred to were maintained. Similarly in the Oudh Local Rates Act VI of 1878, provision was made for the expenditure of a portion of the Local Fund on the purpose above mentioned".[1]

---

[1] N W Provinces Report of the Indian Education Commission (1882-83), page 79.

The first Grant-in-aid rule of these provinces laid down that no state aid should be given to schools which would not charge fees, however small, from the boys. The rule, however, was not rigidly enforced because in some schools run by the missionary bodies there were boys who mere anxious to receive education but who could not afford to pay even a small fee. The above mentioned condition regarding the grant-in-aid had, therefore, to be altered and a Revised Code was issued which laid down that schooling fees should be paid by at least two-thirds of the pupils. Exemption from payment might be granted to the limit of one-third of the total number of students if they could prove their inability to pay anything.

The elementary schools, maintained or aided by the state, were divided into two classes, viz., upper and lower primary. Boys were promoted to the former by their passing of an examination, which was conducted for the first time in 1879-80. A scholarship scheme was also instituted linking up primary, secondary and collegiate education.

Before the passing of Act XVIII of 1871 the cesses, including the education rate of one per cent, paid by landholders for local purposes, were credited separately to district funds. But by the passing of this Act all the cesses were consolidated into a single tax payable to the provincial fund. No doubt there were provisions that each district should get the full benefit of the amount raised within its area, and so far as education was concerned no district suffered any financial loss from this change, still it curtailed the freedom of the local authorities. The inevitable result was that the local authorities ceased to take any initiative in formulating any scheme for the further spread of education.

SECTION V—THE PUNJAB.

In May, 1860, the primary schools in the Punjab were transferred from the control of the officers of the Education Department to that of the Deputy Commissioners in charge of districts. The Department ceased to inspect the schools; the district officers asked the *tahsildars* to supervise the work of the schools as visitors and superintendents. The *tahsildars* had no professional qualification for doing this kind of work, and so they could not properly manage the work which the inspectors of the Department used to supervise before. This led to a large reduction in the number of schools; and the attendance of the pupils became very irregular. So the new system failed to work satisfactorily. Hence a compromise was made between the old and new systems by which the primary schools, though they remained under the control of the district officers for the purpose of administration, were supervised by the inspectors of the Education Department who gave professional advice when necessary, and who sent their reports both to the Department and to the district officers.

We have seen in Section V of the previous chapter that at the close of the last period (1859) the village schoolmasters were drawing pay on grades of Rs. 5, 7 and 10 per month. This scale was lower than the wages of a menial servant or a coolie. In 1868 Mr. Holroyd, the Director, submitted a proposal to the Government that no village school teacher should be paid less than Rs. 10 per month. This the Lieutenant-Governor sanctioned. So far the village schools had been maintained by money raised from the levying of the education cess and any other contributions from the local funds. The amount sanctioned for Education in the budgets of the Imperial and Provincial Governments had always been earmarked in the Punjab for expenses in connection with higher education, secondary and collegiate. Hence as the Director wanted to increase the pay of the village teachers he requested the Government to sanction an addition to the educational cess. The Government, however, did not sanction the increase in cess, but decided that the quality of instruction should be improved even at the risk of diminishing a large number of schools. The pay of the teachers was therefore increased by abolishing 300 primary schools and striking off the rolls 10,000 pupils.

In 1871-72 about 3.5 per cent of the children of school-going age were to be found in the departmental schools in the Punjab. In 1872 Dr. G. W. Leitner made a survey of the indigenous schools in the province and recommended the Government to improve these schools by extending the grant-in-aid system to them. The Government, however, could not do anything in that direction on account of financial and other practical difficulties, but declared that whenever possible every encouragement should be given to improving the indigenous schools.

In the Punjab the Local Rates Act of 1871 gave power to the district committees to provide a fund for the service of the people living in non-municipal areas This fund was similar to the municipal funds in towns. This Act gave an impetus to the spread of education. There was an eager desire for education at this time; and a number of schools was started by the local authorities, which were all filled up quickly. The guardians of the boys thought that by undergoing a course of instruction, even in an elementary school, their wards would obtain better appointments than they used to before; they therefore, sent them in large numbers to the schools and did not even grudge paying fees. Evidently a reaction set in before long, for the number of appointments in all departments was limited. It was, however, found in 1878 that more than half the number of those who received instruction occupied themselves with their fathers' business. Mr. Coldstream, who was asked by the Government to report on the future career of a number of boys of a group of selected primary schools, remarked in 1878 "The influx of intelligence and education into these pursuits (agriculture, trade, and manufactures) will doubtless, apply that stimulus to the development of the country which is so much needed".[1]

The enthusiasm for private effort in education was sadly lacking in the Punjab. Only the Mission organisations availed themselves of the benefits of the grants-in-aid system. In 1881-82, besides the cess-schools in the villages, there were only 278 aided primary schools with 14,616 pupils. Primary education in that province did not receive from the Government that support which had been urged by the Despatch of 1859. We have seen that the other provinces in India gave considerable support to the spread of mass education by grants from the provincial revenues. Some of them even tried to improve the indigenous schools. But no such attempt was made in the Punjab. For the spread of mass education hardly any money was sanctioned in the Provincial Budget, and very little thought was given to the improvement of the indigenous schools.

SECTION VI—THE CENTRAL PROVINCES.

In 1861, the Saugor and Nerbudda Territories, Sambalpur, Nagpur and adjoining districts, and Chattisgarh were grouped together under one administration, with a Chief Commissioner as

[1] The Punjab Report of the Indian Education Commission (1882-83), page 25.

its head. This part of India them came to be known as the Central Provinces. The Education Department of the administration was formed in 1862, with a Director of Public Instruction as its head. From the very beginning of his administration, the first Chief Commissioner sanctioned levying a one-per-cent cess on land which was subsequently raised to two per cent. The Government appointed school committees in a few districts. The members of these committees tried to make the educational scheme a success, but the agricultural community did not want any education. A few state schools were started, but private enterprises in education were spasmodic. Some of the energetic districts officers tried to create an enthusiasm among the higher class people in order to have private schools started; state aid was also promised for such schools. As a result a number of schools spread over a few districts but the enthusiasm of the people seemed to be merely temporary and the expenditure was felt to be burdensome. So the number of aided and unaided schools in the Central Provinces during this period fluctuated considerably.

In 1871 there were 658 state primary and vernacular schools for boys and 137 for girls; in 1881 the number of the former rose to 793 and the latter fell to 62. But in 1871 there were 422 aided and 666 unaided private primary and vernacular schools for boys, while in 1881 the number of the former dropped to 339 and the latter dwindled down to only 91. The Director reported that the fall in number was entirely in private schools which the people had opened because of the persuasion of district officers, but would not maintain except under compulsion. He pointed out in his report to the Government that the number of state primary and vernacular schools for boys had increased by nearly 20 per cent during this period. It must, however, be noted that though the number of aided schools diminished considerably, their quality improved a good deal as was evidenced by the increased, average, daily attendance. A thorough system of inspection was instituted which, however, increased the expenditure on primary schools.

We have seen that in the presidencies of Madras and Bombay, and in the N. W. Provinces and the Punjab some legislative measures were passed with reference to the provision of schools etc. But in the Central Provinces no such legislation was passed to help the private schools. Here only the grants-in-aid system was allowed to work. Two types of grants were instituted. The first was called 'the fixed grant' system by which half the cost of maintaining a school was paid by the Government, the other half being met by the managers of the school. Originally the proportion of the grants was fixed, but later on the amount given as aid was allowed to vary within certain limits, according to the receipts and expenditure in any school. The Inspectors had a fair control over such aided schools. The second was called the 'payment-by-results' system; the principles on which it was based were much like those in vogue in other provinces, but here the system was applicable only to middle vernacular and indigenous primary schools.

As regards the admission and the attendance of pupils of different castes in schools, the Central Provinces Report says:—"All sections of the Native community attend schools in the Central Provinces, except the very poor and low caste Dhers and Mahars, Mehtars, Gandas, etc. For Mahars, especial schools have sometimes been opened, but they rarely last long. The teacher generally is a Muhammadan, as Brahmins and others of the better castes amongst the Hindus object to be appointed to teach Mahar boys. After a time the low caste boys disappear and their place is taken by Muhammadans. We still have some special schools for Mahars, as at Hinganghat and Umrer. There is one aided Mahar school in Bhandara. It is a very good primary school and is supported by the Free Church Mission. Dhers and other low caste boys also attend village and other schools. These boys often read in the school-house verandah. Masters receive nothing from their hands. Slates, for instance, which have to be examined for the working of arithmetical questions or for composition or dictation are pushed along the ground to and from the master. If the master accidentally touches a boy, the master has to bathe before he is pure. Of course the low caste boys cannot be punished with a cane. Perhaps this is an advantage........ Chamars, too, are seldom seen in schools, except in Chattisgarh........ To Government schools boys of all castes are admitted, no questions are asked, but social prejudices do undoubtedly tend to keep the lower castes from school. Most of the Dhers are weavers, and their children are employed from their earliest years, that is from six years and upward, in their father's calling".[1]

SECTION VII—OTHER PROVINCES.

Assam formed a part of the Presidency of Bengal till 1874. In that year it was separated from Bengal and placed under the administration of a Chief Commissioner. The country is one of wide rivers, valleys, and hills. The people inhabiting the hill tracts are particularly backward. The Christian missions have done a good deal in spreading education among them. During the period ending 1881 the educational condition of the country was very much like that of the Central Provinces. But unlike the latter the bright feature in the former was that the indigenous schools were desirous of receiving state assistance and the children attending them numbered nearly ten thousand. Hence the Assam Government gave great encouragement to private enter-

[1] The Central Provinces Report of the Indian Education Commission (1882-83), page 18 f.

prise in education by the provision of liberal grants-in-aid rules. As a matter of fact the rates of aid to primary schools in Assam were far better than those sanctioned for schools in Bengal.

The indigenous schools in Coorg (in South India) did not receive any assistance from the Government.

In Berar there was no educational machinery such as School Committees and Local Boards. The Government, however, tried to develop the few indigenous schools existing there by giving them grants-in-aid. No attempt was made to educate the aborigines of this tract of land.

CHAPTER V

THE PERIOD 1882 TO 1917

SECTION I—THE EDUCATION COMMISSION 1882-83

Two of the most important recommendations of the Despatch of 1854 were the extension of primary education through the direct instrumentality of the state, and the system of grants-in-aid. But we have been in the previous chapter that the progress actually made in the spread of elementary education was very slow. The Government still believed in the 'Filtrartion Theory.' Moreover, the grants-in-aid rules were not quite fair to the institutions started by the religious bodies. Discontent among the Christian missionaries was particularly noticeable. Many of them, when they had retired from work in India and came back to England, started an organisation in London called the General Council on Education in India. From its very beginning in 1878 several prominent persons like the Earl of Shaftesbury, Lord Lawrence, Lord Halifax (once Sir Charles Wood, the author of the great despatch of 1854) became members of this Council. The Rev. James Johnston was appointed Secretary to the Council. A deputation of the members waited upon Lord Hartington, Secretary of State for India, and the Marquess of Ripon, before he went out to India as Viceroy and Governor-General, and urged that increasing efforts should be made to banish illiteracy from India. Lord Ripon promised that he would make a thorough and searching inquiry as to how far effect had been given to the principles laid down in the Educational Despatches of 1854 and 1859. Lord Ripon fulfilled his promise soon after his arrival in India. On the 3rd February, 1882, an Education Commission, with Sir W. W. Hunter as president, and twenty other members representing the officials, non-official Indians and Christian missionaries, was appointed by the Government of India, 'with a view to enquiring into the working of the existing system of Public Instruction, and to the further extension of that system on a popular basis.'

The terms of reference were too wide and therefore they had to review the whole field of education in India, primary, secondary and university. The representative members for each part of India were constituted a Provincial Committee. Each of these Committees submitted a separate report regarding the history and needs of their particular province. Ultimately one consolidated report was drawn up by the whole Commission.

The Commission defined an indigenous school as one established or conducted by natives of India on native methods. For the improvement of such schools they recommended[1] that—

(*a*) all such schools should receive encouragement from the State if they imparted any secular education whatsoever.

(*b*) the Hindu Pandits and the Muhammadan Maulavis should be consulted to find out the method which could be adopted to improve the indigenous schools of a high order.

(*c*) the 'payment-by-results' system would serve as a great stimulus in improving the elementary indigenous schools.

(*d*) the schoolmasters of such schools should be encouraged to undergo training, and if in any part of India the teaching profession was hereditary, the sons and relatives of indigenous schoolmasters should also be encouraged to receive a training in the profession, for it was desirable that there should be the least interference as regards personnel and curriculum of such schools.

(*e*) the standard of examination, the nature of inspection, the rules regarding the grants-in-aid on the results of the examination, should be so arranged as to suit the local conditions of each province.

(*f*) the aided indigenous schools should be open to all classes and castes of the community,

---

[1] The recommendations regarding the indigenous schools are given on pages 78 and 79 of the Report of the Indian Education Commission (1882-83). But as they are lengthy I have summarized them.

encouragement being given to the education of the backward and low-caste pupils by assigning special aid to them.

(*g*) where Municipal and Local Boards existed, the indigenous schools, whether receiving aid or not, should be placed under their supervision; but no supervision should be exercised over the unaided schools if they did not like it.

(*h*) such Boards should find the money to be given as aid to the elementary indigenous schools.

(*i*) every encouragement should be given by such Boards to developing the existing indigenous school system, and only in localities, where the system of aiding suitable schools of this type could not be adopted, were the Boards to start schools of their own.

(*j*) the inspecting officers of the Municipal or District Boards should be ex-officio members of such boards, and they were to receive assistance from the officers of the Education Department in securing a proportionate provision of education for all classes of the community and in selecting schools to be registered for aid.

The Commission found that, although every encouragement was given to the existing indigenous schools to improve themselves, they could never be expected to satisfy the growing desire for education among the masses. Moreover, to banish illiteracy the Government must make adequate provisions for the education of all. The Commission, therefore, made thirty-six recommendations regarding primary education. They were so important and far reaching, and modified the future policy of education of all the provinces in India to such an extent, that they deserve to be quoted in full.

The Commission recommended that:—

(1) "primary education be regarded as the instruction of the masses through the vernacular in such subjects as will best fit them for their position in life, and be not necessarily regarded as a portion of instruction leading up to the University:

(2) "the upper primary and lower primary examinations be not made compulsory in any province:

(3) "while every branch of education can justly claim the fostering care of the State, it is desirable, in the present circumstances of the country, to declare the elementary education of the masses, its provision, extension, and improvement, to be that part of the educational system to which the strenuous efforts of the State should now be directed in a still larger measure than heretobefore:

(4) "an attempt be made to secure the fullest possible provision for an extension of primary education by legislation suited to the circumstances of each Province:

(5) "where indigenous schools exist, the principle of aiding and improving them be recognised as an important means of extending elementary education:

(6) "examinations by inspecting officers be conducted as far as possible *in situ,* and all primary schools receiving aid be invariably inspected *in situ*:

(7) "as a general rule, aid to primary schools be regulated to a large extent according to the results of examination; but an exception may be made in the case of schools established in backward districts or under peculiar circumstances, which may be aided under special rules:

(8) "school houses and furniture be of the simplest and most economical kind:

(9) "the standards of primary examination in each province be revised with a view to simplification, and to the larger introduction of practical subjects, such as native methods of arithmetic, accounts and mensuration, the elements of natural and physical science, and their application to agriculture, health, and the industrial arts; but no attempt be made to secure general uniformity throughout India:

(10) "care be taken not to interfere with the freedom of managers of aided schools in the choice of text books:

(11) "promotion from class to class be not necessarily made to depend on the results of one fixed standard of examinations uniform throughout the Province:

(12) "physical development be promoted by the encouragement of native games, gymnastics,

school-drill and other exercises suited to the circumstances of each class of school:

(13) "all inspecting officers and teachers be directed to see that the teaching and discipline of every school are such as to exert a right influence on the manners, the conduct, and the character of the children, and that for the guidance of the masters a special manual be prepared:

(14) "the existing rules, as to religious teaching in Government schools be applied to all primary schools wholly maintained by municipal or local-fund boards:

(15) "the supply of Normal schools, whether Government or aided, be so localised as to provide for the local requirements of all primary schools, whether Government or aided, within the Division under each Inspector:

(16) "the first charges on provincial funds assigned for primary education be the cost of its direction and inspection, and the provision of adequate Normal schools:

(17) "pupils in municipal or local board-schools be not entirely exempted from payment of fees, merely on the ground that they are the children of ratepayers:

(18) "in all board-schools a certain proportion of pupils be admitted as free students on the ground of poverty: and in the case of special schools, established for the benefit of poorer classes, a general or larger exemption from pay-

ment of fees be allowed under proper authority for special reasons:

(19) "subject to the exemption of a certain proportion of free students on account of poverty, fees, whether in money or kind be levied in all aided schools; but the proceeds be left entirely at the disposal of the school-managers:'

(20) "the principle laid down in Lord Hardinge's Resolution, dated 11th October 1844, be re-affirmed, i.e. that in selecting persons to fill the lowest offices under Government, preference be always given to candidates who can read and write:

(21) "the Local Governments, especially those of Bombay and North-Western Provinces be invited to consider the advisability of carrying out the suggestion in paragraph 96 of the Despatch of 1854, namely, of making some educational qualification necessary to the confirmation of hereditary village officers, such as *patels* and *lambardars*:

(22) "night schools be encouraged wherever practicable:

(23) "as much elasticity as possible be permitted both as regards the hours of the day and the seasons of the year during which attendance of scholars is required, especially in agricultural villages and backward districts:

(24) "primary education be extended in backward districts, especially in those inhabited mainly by aboriginal races, by the instrumentality

of the Department, pending the creation of school-boards, or by specially liberal grants-in-aid to those who are willing to set up and maintain schools:

(25) "all primary schools wholly maintained at the cost of the school-boards, and all primary schools that are aided from the same fund and are not registered as special schools, be understood to be open to all classes of the community:

(26) "such a proportion between special and other primary schools be maintained in each school-district as would ensure a proportionate provision for the education of all classes:

(27) "assistance be given to schools and orphanages in which poor children are taught reading, writing, and counting, with or without manual work:

(28) "primary education be declared to be that part of the whole system of public instruction which possesses an almost exclusive claim on local funds set apart for education, and a large claim on provincial revenues:

(29) "both Municipal and Local Self-government Boards keep a separate school fund:

(30) "the Municipal school-fund consist of—

(*a*) a fair proportion of municipal revenues, to be fixed in each case by the Local Government;

(*b*) the fees levied in schools wholly maintained at the cost of the municipal school-fund;

(*c*) any assignment that may be made to the municipal school-fund from the local fund;

(*d*) any assignment from provincial funds;

(*e*) any other funds that may be entrusted to the municipalities for the promotion of education;

(*f*) any unexpected balance of the school fund from previous years:

(31) "the Local Board's school-fund consist of—

(*a*) a distinct share of the general local fund which share shall not be less than a minimum proportion to be prescribed for each Province;

(*b*) the fees levied in schools wholly maintained at the cost of the school-fund;

(*c*) any contribution that may be assigned by municipal boards;

(*d*) any assignment made from provincial funds;

(*e*) any other funds that may be entrusted to the local boards for the promotion of education;

(*f*) any unexpended balance of the school-fund from previous years:

(32) "the general control over primary school expenditure be vested in the school-boards, whether municipal or rural, which may now exist

or may hereafter be created for self-government in each Province:

(33) "the first appointment of schoolmasters in municipal or board-schools be left to the town or district boards with the proviso that the masters be certificated or approved by the Department, and their subsequent promotion or removal be regulated by the boards, subject to the approval of the Department:

(34) "the cost of maintaining or aiding primary schools in each school district, and the construction and repair of board-school-houses, be charges against the municipal or local board-school-fund so created:

(35) "the vernacular, in which instruction shall be imparted in any primary school, maintained by any municipal or local board, be determined by the school committee of management, subject to revision by the municipal or local board: provided that if there be any dissenting minority in the community, who represent a number of pupils sufficient to form one or more separate classes or schools, it shall be incumbent on the Department to provide for the establishment of such classes or schools, and it shall be incumbent on such Municipal or Local Board to assign to such classes or schools a fair proportion of the whole assignable funds:

(36) "Municipal and Local Boards administering funds in aid of primary schools adopt the rules prescribed by the Department for aiding

such schools, and introduce no change therein without the sanction of the Department."[1]

SECTION II—TRANSFER OF CONTROL OF PRIMARY EDUCATION TO LOCAL AUTHORITIES.

During the period 1882-5 several important measures were passed in the legislative councils introducing local self-government on the lines of the English system of County Councils and Rural District Boards; two of these, the Municipal Act and the Local Self-Government Act, later on played a very important part in developing the primary education of the country. Lord Ripon's administration is particularly remembered by the Indian people for the passing of these measures. In India from the earliest times there had been a system of Self-Government in small local areas known as the *Panchayat* (folknote) System. The two Acts mentioned above created a machinery of representative government responsible to the people upon the old *Panchayat* system. As a matter of fact the measures were an elaboration of the ancient system on modern western lines. Naturally, the Education Commission recommended the transfer of the primary and indigenous schools from official District Committees to the local authorities created by those two enactments.

We have noticed that *the Commission did*

[1] Report of the Indian Education Commission (1882-83), page 174 f.

not recommend making elementary education compulsory, nor did they recommend making it free. But they asked the local authorities to admit a certain proportion of pupils as free students on the ground of poverty in all schools managed by the local boards or municipalities.

The public primary schools were defined as those which, being maintained or aided by the state, would receive pupils of all classes and castes without distinction. Special primary schools were those which would take in pupils of particular castes or creeds. According to the recommendations of the Commission these were also eligible for aids from the local authorities. Prior to 1883 there had been two divisions of primary schools, English and Vernacular. In that year on the recommendation of the Commission the Government issued orders that the English Primary Schools (namely the primary departments of high and middle schools) were no longer to be considered primary schools. The primary schools were thenceforth regarded as being in the main vernacular. Even now they consist in the different provinces either of four or five classes, the two highest forming the upper primary section, and the classes below these the lower primary.

By 1886 the grants-in-aid rules were revised in almost all the provinces. The courses of instruction in both upper and lower primary schools were made more useful to the classes for whom they were designed, and as such were different in different provinces. The use of printed books was made obligatory in aided schools. Every aided school was asked to keep attendance and inspection registers. It was also announced that no school could seek a reward unless it had been in existence for six months and could show that it had on its rolls at least ten boys regularly attending the approved course of instruction. Srom this time onward till 1904 the payment-by-results system reigned supreme in the realm of primary education. Undoubtedly the system at first helped to bring about a steady, and often a rapid, increase of efficiency in all classes of primary schools: the standard of examination was also raised slowly. The results-grant system was gradually abolished in different provinces and was completely given up towards the end of 1906.

Besides the primary schools maintained or aided by the local authorities, a number of primary schools was established by the Department of Education of each of the provinces, in accordance with recommendation No. 24 of the Commission, in those areas which were mainly inhabited by the aborigines or backward races

From 1886 the Provincial Governments tried to carry out the important recommendations of the Commission of 1882-83. In some provinces no change of policy was required regarding district and municipal grants for education, for we have seen in the previous chapter that they had already levied an education cess in the areas under their control. In Bombay a part of both the district and municipal funds was already being devoted, either directly or indirectly, to the extension and improvement of primary schools. The Bombay Government also agreed, as a result of the recommendations of the Commission, to pay from the provincial revenues half as much as the local authorities would assign for education. In Madras and the Central Provinces the district funds had been applied to the same purpose for a number of years previous to the recommendations of the Commission. The rules framed under the Madras Local Boards Act of 1884 gave a further impetus to the extension of primary education, for they expressly laid down that the chief duty of the district board was to make a provision for improved elementary education. The Madras Government also announced that an amount equal to five per cent of its total revenues should in future be devoted to education. A part of it undoubtedly was allotted to primary education. In Bengal the local funds did not exist, for no education cess had been previously levied, and the municipal funds for educational purposes were as yet quite inadequate. The Government of Bengal took upon themselves the responsibility of financing primary education. In 1884 they increased the annual grant for primary education to eight lakhs[1] of rupees and by successive annual increments promised in nine years time to devote eighteen lakhs; but they could not carry out their promise because of the urgent necessity for retrenchment. Much the same thing took place in the United Provinces of Agra and Oudh (then known as the N. W. Provinces). In the Punjab the local bodies used to bear the expenses of inspection and training of teachers, but they were relieved of these charges which were henceforth paid by the provincial government. So the local authorities were able to devote the money thus relieved to the extension of primary education. In the Central Provinces the Government devoted five per cent of the provincial income to education. In Assam primary education received its full share of any increase in the general educational allotment.

At the close of the year 1891-92, in every province, there were a few primary schools entirely maintained by the Education Department As a matter of fact, the number was negligible, compared to the total number of such schools. But in nearly every case, where they existed, there was good reason for the retention of the control of these schools, for they served those areas where there was no definite machinery to take up this work.

The number of schools managed by the

---

[1] One lakh of rupees was then equivalent to £10,000

District Boards had increased from 13,318 on the 31st March, 1887, to 14,531 on the same date in 1892, and the number of pupils in them from 564,802 to 639,883. The Municipal Board Schools increased during the same period from 813 to 1,041 and the students in them from 79,763 to 101,291. The District Board schools were not so strong as the Municipal schools, because the former were all situated in the villages and the latter in the towns.

The aided schools formed a most important part of the primary school system. In March, 1892, they contained 53 5 per cent of the total number of pupils in primary schools. In a few cases they received aid direct from the Education Department; in the vast majority of schools aid was given from the District or Municipal funds. In accordance with the recommendations of the Commission of 1882-83, those of the indigenous schools which had adopted the departmental standards and methods of instruction began to receive aid from the local authorities.

The grants varied in different parts of India; even within the same province different kinds of grants were given. Some received fixed monthly grants for the salary of the teachers; while a large number had to depend on the amounts earned by their pupils at periodical examinations. Some again received aid under a mixture of both systems; while a number received merely a small annual sum for submitting returns.

During the period 1st April, 1892, to 31st March, 1897, the number of aided schools in the Madras Presidency increased rapidly, though a large percentage of them had to be placed on the list of temporarily recognised institutions for the purposes of the grant, for they could not fulfil all the conditions of full recognition regarding staff or accommodation. The Government asked the local authorities that one half of the land cess should be devoted to construction and repairs of roads and canals. As these authorities did not see their way to increase the cess, the educational expenditure of the Boards had to be cut down. The result was that the number of schools under Local and Municipal Boards showed a tendency to decline.

In Bombay during those years the local boards were not fully developed, hence the local-board schools, often known as 'cess schools' were really managed by the Education Department but maintained out of the money raised by the levying of the cess. On the other hand the Municipal Board schools in towns were managed and maintained by such boards.

The Government and Board schools in Assam during the same quinquennium increased by a small number; a few more schools were opened for the education of the children of the tribes occupying the Garo hills. In Bengal the number of aided schools decreased from 39,436 to 36,709 but the pupils attending them increased from

963,709 to 1,012,757; this caused an increase in the average strength of each school of from 24 to 28. The decline in the number of aided schools was due to the failure of the weak ones to earn even the minimum amount of Rs. 5 on the results of the periodical examinations.

In 1896-97 the Government of the N. W. Provinces and Oudh gave an additional recurring grant of Rs. 75,000 to district boards. The Lieutenant Governor, Sir Anthony MacDonell, asked the boards to devote this sum to the extension of primary education in those Provinces as they were then very backward compared with other parts of India. The number of aided schools there had steadily declined in number during the four previous years from 106 to 54, but this additional grant at once enabled the number to be increased to 1,490 and the pupils in them from 3,149 to 36,089.

In the Punjab a large number of indigenous schools came under the category of public elementary schools as they began to receive aid from the local authorities.

A rapid advance in Primary education was made in the Central Provinces where the number of schools increased by 38 per cent. Like the N. W. P. Government, the C. P. Government also made an additional grant of Rs. 50,000 to the district boards for the extension of Primary education.

In Assam most of the schools run by the

missionaries in the various hill tracts, inhabited by the aborigines, were helped out of the Provincial Revenues. In Coorg and Berar board schools were set up on the models of Madras and the Central Provinces respectively.

No further progress was made in the next few years. When the Education Department first directed their attention to the spread of primary education, they selected those areas for opening schools where they were sure that the population would value the benefits of education and would be eager to receive them. The more or less widespread indigenous schools also slowly came under the control of the Department. The progress so far made was comparatively easy under such circumstances. Then came a period of complete arrest of progress. In the interior and often times not easily accessible villages, the people were indifferent to the advantages of education. The boards in those areas were not very powerful; they were not willing to levy an increased rate for education. In some provinces they were not allowed to do so because the rules governing the boards were inelastic. Hence the further extension of primary education depended entirely on the additional sums which the Governments could sanction from the Provincial Revenues. Famine, plague and earthquake caused havoc in the country, and the financial conditions were such that it was not possible to make largely increasing grants from the Provincial Revenues. Though the progress of education was arrested, its quality was improved by raising the standard of instruction, inspection, and examination. The inefficient character of many of the village schools became a glaring defect in the light of the improvement of neighbouring ones; and in many parts of India the schools which could not improve themselves within specified periods were abolished. Thus closed the nineteenth century.

SECTION III—THE EDUCATIONAL POLICY OF 1904

Lord Curzon became Governor-General of India in January, 1899. At the request of the Government of India, Mr. Cotton made a review of the educational problems in the same year. The review covered the methods of organization, tendencies and results of Indian education as a whole, from the primary schools to the universities. Lord Curzon himself presided at a conference of the officials of the Department held at Simla in September, 1901. The resolutions of the conference were mostly unanimous. These were forwarded to the heads of provincial governments and local administrations. They also concurred with the general policy of education discussed in the conference and embodied in the resolutions. On receiving the opinions of the provincial heads, the Governor-General in Council issued a Resolution on the Indian Educational Policy on the 11th March, 1904.

The Resolution covered all branches of education. As regards primary education the policy enunciated therein was as follows:—

"The Government of India fully accept the proposition that *the active extension of primary education is one of the most important duties of the State.* They undertake this responsibility, not merely on general grounds, but because, as Lord Lawrence observed in 1868, 'among all the sources of difficulty in our administration and of possible danger to the stability of our Government there are few so serious as the ignorance of the people.' To the people themselves, moreover, the lack of education is now a more serious disadvantage than it was in more primitive days. By the extension of railways the economic side of agriculture in India has been greatly developed, and the cultivator has been brought into contact with the commercial world, and has been involved in transactions in which an illiterate man is at a great disadvantage. The material benefits attaching to education have at the same time increased with the development of scheme for introducing improved agricultural methods, for opening agricultural banks, for strengthening the legal position of the cultivator, and for generally improving the conditions of rural life. Such schemes depend largely for their success upon the influence of education permeating the masses and rendering them accessible to ideas other than those sanctioned by tradition." (para 14 of the Resolution).

"In so far as District or Municipal Boards are required to devote their funds to education, primary education should have a predominant claim upon their expenditure. The administration of primary schools by local bodies is already everywhere subject to the general supervision of the Education Department as regards tuitional matters; but the degree of control differs in different provinces, and where it is most complete, primary education is most advanced. It is impossible to extend that control to financial matters, as there are other objects besides education which have legitimate claims upon local funds. But it is essential, in order to ensure that the claims of primary education receive due attention, that the educational authorities should be heard when resources are being allotted, and that they should have the opportunity of carrying their representations to higher authority in the event of their being disregarded. In future, therefore, so much of the budget estimates of District or Municipal Boards as relates to educational charges will be submitted through the Inspector to the Director of Public Instruction before sanction." (para 19 of the Resolution).

Here for the first time we find the Government of India declaring that the rapid spread of elementary education is one of the foremost duties of the State. Effect was given to the resolution by the provincial governments. Though, on the whole, the changes made were much the same in all the provinces, yet they were modified to a certain extent to suit the local needs, exhibiting a great variety in their application.

Except in the Bombay Presidency in all other presidencies and provinces there were primary departments attached to the secondary schools. In the secondary schools in Bombay no such department had existed. They took in pupils who had passed through the first four standards of the common vernacular schools. But as education in the primary schools was not compulsory the children of the well-to-do and the middle class people used to receive their instruction in the three R's and the rudiments of History and Geography at home under private teachers, till they were fit to join the lowest form in the secondary schools. In other provinces, though there were primary departments attached to the secondary schools, all the pupils did not seek admission into the lowest form. Their guardians preferred to give them some education at home before they were admitted to any school. Thus they could be admitted to any form they were considered fit for. The result was that in all the provinces and presidencies, only the masses resorted to the primary schools. Besides the lower primary and upper primary schools, there was another type of school in all provinces, other than Bombay and Madras, which ought truly to have been classed under primary but at first used to be considered by the Government of India as secondary for statistical purpose; this type was known as Middle Vernacular Schools. They had five or six standards above the infants' class. The vast majority of the pupils of the primary schools did not proceed to the secondary; but those who liked to go up were drafted on to the latter at the point at which the teaching of English was begun.

The Government of India computed that in 1907 there were over eighteen-million boys of school-going age in India; of these only little over 3·6 millions, i.e. about one-fifth of the whole (actually 19·1 per cent) were attending boys' primary schools. As compared with the year 1902, the figure for 1907 showed an increase of ·6 million. From the beginning of the twentieth century the Government of India became anxious to do something to accelerate the progress of education. In 1902 the Imperial grant for education to all provinces amounted to 40 lakhs of rupees. In 1905 the Imperial grant was raised by 35 lakhs annually, as a result of the Resolution on the Educational Policy of 1904. It was orginally intended that this amount should be exclusively devoted to primary education. But it was not actually followed in practice; a large part of it was spent annually for education other than primary. Hence in spite of the Resolution of 1904 the progress of primary education continued to be slow. Still with the increased grant new primary schools were opened and the existing ones were enlarged. The number of schools increased from 92,226 in 1902 to 102,947 in 1907. In the former year there were on an average 33 pupils per school, in the latter year the average was 36. That the average number of school attendances increased in spite of extra provision of schools showed the willingness of the population to send their children to school. The Government report says—"this means that the spread of primary education has taken effect not only by the provision of new schools, but also by the enlargements of existing schools, or by improved attendance at them; and it tends also to show that the demand for new schools is equal to the supply, for otherwise the opening of new schools which remained unfilled would tend to reduce the average number of pupils to a school".[1] It is interesting to note that in 1907 out of 102,947 schools mentioned previously, only 24,715, i.e. 24 per cent, were under public management and the rest, i.e. 76 per cent, under private management. All these schools under private management followed the departmental curriculum and rules, and so were styled 'public institutions.' But a number of them did not take any aid from the District or Municipal boards. Such schools were mostly 'venture' schools in

[1] Fifth Quinquennial Review of Progress of Education in India (1902-07) Vol I, page 99.

which the schoolmaster somehow eked out a living by the fees and presents in crops from the pupils.' By this time, except in Bengal, the vast majority of schools all over India, under private management but conforming to departmental rules, were receiving grants from the boards. In most of the provinces the Government preferred to follow the policy, enunciated in the Despatch of 1854, of aiding private enterprise rather than opening large numbers of board schools. With limited financial resources they thought it was the cheapest way of multiplying facilities for education.

Besides these aided schools under private management, there were large numbers of schools not receiving any grants from the Government. They were mostly indigenous schools of a religious character. They refused to follow the departmental curriculum and were not under State inspection; they always preferred to remain outside the departmental influence. These were therefore called 'private institutions.' In 1907 a little over 550,000 boys were in attendance at these private institutions of an elementary character. The inclusion of this number would slightly raise the percentage of school-attendance of the male population of school-going age in 1907 from 19·1 to 22·6.

It has already been stated that the Education Commission of 1882-83 recommended the universal adoption of the principle of 'payment by results' in awarding grants to primary schools in India. In conformity to the Educational Policy enunciated in March, 1904, this system was slowly given up and by the end of 1906 it was almost entirely abolished, Burma being the only country where it still lingered on. To replace the system of payment by results the methods which had been contrived to assess grants in primary schools were characterized by a healthy variety in different provinces.

The simplest method was adopted in Madras. There for each teacher in a primary school Rs. 36 per year was sanctioned; besides an annual capitation grant of 8 annas[1] per pupil in average daily attendance was allowed. The total amount earned could, however, be reduced by the inspectors after examining the general condition of the school.

In Bombay each primary school was paid a fixed grant, subject to a maximum limit not exceeding one half of the local assets or one-third of the total expenditure of the school during the previous year.

In Bengal the grant to each school consisted of two parts: (1) a stipend not exceeding Rs. 5 and Rs. 3 per month for each head teacher and assistant master respectively: (2) an annual grant depending for its amount upon the number of

---

[1] One anna was then equivalent to a penny; a rupee was 1s. 4*d*.

children in regular attendance, the quality of instruction imparted, and the general character of the school as observed by the members of the local board and inspecting officers. Though the scale of grants had to be submitted to the Director of Public Instruction for approval, the District Boards in Bengal enjoyed the right of fixing the rates at which aid was to be given to primary schools. This privilege was not enjoyed by the Boards in other parts in India.

In the United Provinces of Agra and Oudh each school with an average attendance of 15 pupils was paid a grant of Rs. 4 a month per teacher. This amount could be increased to Rs. 5 or Rs. 6 a month if the aided school possessed text books, maps and other appliances, and followed the curriculum prescribed for the board managed schools. If a single master could manage a class of more than 25 pupils an extra rupee was paid. For assistant masters a grant of Rs. 3 per month per head was sanctioned. The experience of the inspector showed that the lower strata of indigenous schools were unable to earn grants-in-aid on the monthly payment system. A special scale of grants was approved for such schools.

In the Punjab the system adopted was called the 'block grants system.' It was based on (a) the average attendance of the pupils of the past five years and (b) a staff grant (in the case of a certificated teacher) of one-fifth of the average salary paid to a teacher in neighbouring board schools. An indigenous school having an average attendance of at least 10 scholars could receive a grant, if it taught them to read a printed book and to write. Such indigenous schools could also receive some extra aid if they kept returns and were open to inspection.

In Assam, except the mission schools, all other lower primary aided schools which had been located in the plains were gradually converted into board schools. In the hills the aided schools were chiefly supported by the Christian Missions. The mission schools in Assam, whether located in the plains or in the hills received lump grants from the provincial revenues instead of monthly grants from local bodies. The Missions in Assam worked among very backward peoples mostly aborigines. Hence the Government decided to give them large lump grants to carry on their work. The system of aid adopted for the upper primary schools established a strong departmental control and practically put a stop to the opening of 'venture' schools. To receive aid the upper primary school was required to show that it had raised a substantial portion of the cost of the school by proceeds of endowments or by private subscriptions, excluding fees. If in any school the local authorities provided a larger sum than had been raised by endowments and subscriptions, the appointment of a teacher could not be made by the managers without the previous approval of the

Inspector of Schools, and a teacher who was unfit for his duties could be dismissed by the Director.

In the Central Provinces all village schools, except those under the management of missions or other recognised societies, were converted into Board schools. Those under missions and societies received aid from the local authorities. Nothing, however, was laid down as to the scale upon which grants were assessed in the case of aided schools. The schools which showed an average attendance of 20 boys, received fixed quarterly grants not exceeding the difference between the receipts and expenditure.

In all the provinces grants were also made for buildings and furniture. In 1907 each aided primary school for boys received on an average Rs. 45 3 from public funds; the average amount received per boy worked out at Rs. 1 5 per year. The average annual expenditure on a boy's primary school stood at Rs. 85 in 1887 and at Rs. 133 in 1907. In 1887 the average cost of education per pupil in a primary school for boys had been Rs. 3; it became Rs. 3·7 in 1902 and rose to Rs. 3·9 in 1907. The size of the schools varied in different provinces according to the density of the population in India. Certain areas peopled by the higher castes had more schools than the areas inhabited by the lower. Still, when we consider that in 1907 there existed on an average only one primary school to every 109 square miles of the country, the picture becomes a gloomy one. The question of the extension of primary education was discussed every year in the Imperial Legislative Council. In the State of Baroda (Bombay Presidency) its Indian ruler made elementary education compulsory in 1907. The system worked there with a fair amount of success.

SECTION IV—GOKHALE'S BILL FOR THE EXTENSION OF ELEMENTARY EDUCATION

On the 19th March, 1910, the following resolution was moved by Mr. G. K. Gokhale, a non-official member representing the Bombay Presidency, in the Imperial Legislative Council[1] for the introduction of free and compulsory elementary education in British India.

"That this Council recommends that a beginning should be made in the direction of making elementary education free and compulsory throughout the country, and that a mixed commission of officials and non-officials be appointed at an early date to frame definite proposals."

In moving the resolution Mr. Gokhale made an able speech in the course of which he urged that—

(1) an Act, on the lines of the English Education Act of 1870, should be

---

[1] Prior to 1921 the Legislative Council of the Government of India was called the Imperial Legislative Council. In accordance with the Government of India Act of 1919, the name was changed, in 1921, to Indian Legislative Assembly; a second chamber known as the Council of State was also created.

passed conferring powers upon local bodies in India to make elementary education compulsory in their areas;

(2) compulsion should only apply to boys and not to girls;

(3) the period of compulsion should be between 6 years and 10 years of age of pupils;

(4) the principle of compulsion should be applied only in those areas where 33 per cent of the male population of school-going age was already undergoing instruction at school;

(5) compulsory education should be free;

(6) the cost of education should be divided between the Government and local bodies in the proportion of 2 to 1;

(1) there should be a separate Department of Education, in the Government of India, in charge of a Member of the Executive Council;

(8) the Government of India should take some responsibility for the spread of education instead of throwing the whole of it on the provincial heads; there should be a definite programme before the Government of India, just as there was a programme for railways, which should be carried out steadily year after year.

At the end of the debate on the resolution the Home Member (the post of the Education Member of the Government of India had not then been created) gave an assurance that the whole question would be carefully examined by the Government. So Mr. Gokhale withdrew the resolution.

In the same year (1910) the Government of India created a separate Department of Education in charge of a Member of the Executive Council and asked it to devise schemes for the extension of primary education. No definite proposals were made by the Department. Mr. Gokhale again pressed the question of compulsory education before the same council on the 16th March, 1911, by introducing a private Bill. The Bill had been drafted more or less on the lines put forward by him in the preceding year, at the time of the debate on his Resolution. The salient points of his Bill 'to make better provision for the extension of elementary education' may be summarized as follows:

(1) Before the provisions of the Act could be applied to any area, the municipal or district board authorities must satisfy themselves that a certain percentage of boys and girls had already been receiving instructions at schools in areas under their jurisdiction: the percentage was to be fixed by the Departmental rules and must receive

the sanction of the Governor-General in Council.

(2) Any local authority might, when the above condition was satisfied, apply the Act to the whole or any specified area within its jurisdiction; whether the Act should be applied or not was left entirely to its discretion; even when the percentage fixed had been attained, the local authority might not enforce the Act.

(3) Moreover, another check was proposed by providing a clause that even when any local authority was desirous of applying the Act, the consent of the Provincial or the Presidency Government was to be had before this could be done.

If in any area the Act was enforced, the guardian of every boy of not less than six years and not more than ten years of age, residing within that area, should cause him to attend a primary school. The provision of new schools and the recognition of the existing ones were to be left in the hands of the local authorities. The periods and number of days of school attendance were to be fixed by the Department of Public Instruction.

Provisions were made in the Bill for the exemption of individuals, and particular classes or communities from the operations of the Act. Primary Education was not to be free but remission of fees was to be allowed on the ground of a guardian's inability to pay, due to poverty or otherwise. No fee was to be charged for a pupil whose parent's income was less than Rs. 10 a month.

It was not contemplated in the first instance that the provisions of the Bill should be applied to girls; but later on the intention was that they might as well be made applicable to them. School attendance committees were to be appointed and provisions were made for the punishment of guardians for any failure of their wards in complying with the attendance rules. The local authority, with the sanction of the provincial or presidency government, might levy a special education rate. The income from the rate was to be supplemented by grants from the local government in a proportion to be fixed by the Governor-General in Council.

The Imperial Legislative Council gave Mr. Gokhale permission to introduce the Bill, and invited the opinions of the local governments, universities and public bodies upon it. These were obtained by February, 1912, and Mr. Gokhale on the 18th March moved that the Bill be referred to a Select Committee of 15 members of the Council for detailed examination of the clauses. This time he also urged that where education was to be made compulsory, it should be free. He said on that occasion—

"The Government of India are committed to a policy of mass education, and the rate at which we have been going for the last 60 years is hopelessly slow. Even at the accelerated pace of the last ten years, it will take enormously long periods for every boy and every girl to be at school. Moreover, this does not take into account the natural and necessary increases of population in the country. What then is to be done? Are we going to content ourselves with experiments of our own only, experiments which can only prolong the reign of ignorance in the country? India must profit by the example and by the experience of other civilized countries. And other civilized countries have come to only one conclusion in this matter, and that is *that the State must resort to compulsion in order to secure universal education for the people........* Local bodies cannot take the initiative (in introducing compulsion) unless there is legislation to empower them, and that is the reason why this Bill has been introduced. Whether this object is gained by enacting a special law for the whole country or by an amendment of the old Local Self-Government Acts of the different provinces is a minor matter. The great thing is to make a beginning in introducing compulsion. Once a beginning is made, the public mind in the country will be rapidly familiarised with the idea of compulsion, and it will then not take more than 20 years at the outside to have a system of universal education in the country in full operation"[1]

The debate lasted for two days. The Bill was opposed by all official members, who then constituted the majority of the council. A number of non-official members, especially the landholders, sided with the official members in opposing the measure. The grounds for opposition, as expressed in the speeches of the official members, were that (1) no popular demand for compulsory education had been felt; (2) the Local Governments were not in favour of it; (3) a strong minority of the educated Indians were against it; (4) the local authorities were unwilling to levy additional rates or increase the existing ones; (5) the attendance committees would not work satisfactorily and the machinery would be disliked by the ratepayers; and (6) there was still room for the extension of primary education on voluntary lines based on the grants-in-aid system. The Bill was, therefore, considered premature and its further progress was stopped by its rejection at this stage by 38 votes to 13.

Though the Bill was rejected the Government of India gave an assurance that every attempt would be made to ensure a larger extension of primary education, gradually making it free, and promised enhanced grants from the

---

[1] Proceedings of the Imperial Legislative Council—the Speech of Mr G. K. Gokhale on the 18th March, 1912.

Treasury. It also urged the Local Governments to pay more attention to the educational needs of the provinces.

The total number of pupils in primary schools and in primary departments of secondary schools was nearly 4 millions in 1907 and in 1912 it rose to 5 millions i.e. there had been an increase of 25 per cent. The extent of area per school had also been reduced; in the latter year there existed on an average one school to every 10·2 square miles of the country. The percentage of boys in the entire primary stage to boys of school-going age was 23·8 in 1912. As the length of time during which children remain at school has considerable bearing upon the question as to how far the population of any province is touched by education (for the numbers actually at school are affected by the duration of the school life) it is interesting to note the proportion of pupils in the upper primary stage to those in the entire primary stage in 1907 and in 1912. In the former year it was 12·3 per cent; in the latter it was 12·5 per cent. The vast majority of the pupils used to leave their schools after studying for only one year and very few proceeded beyond the third year.

The total expenditure on primary schools for boys was nearly 18 millions of rupees in 1912. The percentage of the total expenditure borne by public funds, fees and private contributions were 65·6, 22·8 and 11·6 per cent respectively. The average fee annually paid by a boy was 14 annas and 6 pies i.e. about one shilling and three pence.[1] By the end of 1912 primary education in the North-West Frontier Province was made free; the payment of fees in lower primary schools in Assam was made voluntary; in the Punjab elementary education became largely free; the fee-rate in the United Provinces and Central Provinces was made very low.[2] Except in Bengal, Madras and Bombay primary education practically became free for those who are unable to pay for it.

It is necessary to record here that though in one or two states, like Baroda, the Indian Chiefs introduced a compulsory system of primary education the vast majority of them were strongly against it. The Maharana of Rajpipla made a remark[3]:—"Make primary education as free as you choose, add as many further inducements as you can; but do not make it compulsory. In the case of the most advanced classes it is absolutely unnecessary, and would serve only to create irritation. In the case of the poor backward classes it would inflict harm where good was meant, would subject them to great harassment,

---

[1] Sixth Quinquennial Review of Progress of Education in India (1907—12), page 110

[2] *Ibid.*, page 133.

[3] Quoted by the Under Secretary of State for India in the House of Commons, vide Official Report of the Parliamentary Debates Vol. XLI (July 15 to August 7, 1912), page 1895.

would be positively cruel and unjust, and would be deeply though silently resented as such."

SECTION V—THE EDUCATIONAL POLICY OF 1913

Though Mr. Gokhale's attempts on three consecutive years to force the Government to pass an Education Act had failed, yet primary education in India received a great impetus when His Majesty in King-Emperor, George V, while on a visit to India, said on the 6th January, 1912:—

"It is my wish that there may be spread over the land a net-work of schools and colleges, from which will go forth loyal and manly and useful citizens, able to hold their own in industries and agriculture and all the vocations in life. And it is my wish, too, that the homes of my Indian subjects may be brightened and their labour sweetened by the spread of knowledge with all that follows in its train, a higher level of thought, of comfort, and of health. *It is through education that my wish will be fulfilled,* and the cause of education in India will ever be very close to my heart".[1]

His Majesty's pronouncement, coupled with the attempts of Mr. Gokhale's party, practically forced the Government to pay more attention to primary education. Even in the House of Commons at the time of the discussion on the Indian Budget the Under-Secretary of State for India had to make reference to the educational

[1] Quoted in Para I of the Indian Educational Policy of 1913.

programme. He said on the 30th July, 1912:— "Of the total population, 15 per cent of which may be taken to be of school-going age, only 4 per cent of the boys and ·7 per cent of the girls are at school. The educational grant of £330,000 a year announced at the Delhi Durbar is to be spent mainly on primary education, and that is but a prelude to a much more extensive programme. The programme which we hope to work up to in time is as follows:—We desire to increase the total number of primary schools by 90,000 or 75 per cent, and to double the school going population. The schools will cost £25 each per year, and they will be placed in villages and other centres of population which are at present without schools. We are going to improve the existing schools, which now only cost about £10 each per year, and the cost of these will probably have to be doubled".[1]

All these utterances in 1912 forced the Government of India to revise the Educational Policy of 1904. The new policy emanated in the form of Resolution of the Government of India from the Department of Education dated Delhi, the 21st February, 1913. It dealt with all branches of education, primary, secondary, agricultural, veterinary, forestry, technical, medical, legal, commercial and university. Paragraph 11

---

[1] Official Report of the Parliamentary Debates, House of Commons Vol. XLI (July 15 to August 7, 1912), page 1896.

of the Resolution, quoted below, deals with the general principles concerning primary education.

"For guidance in the immediate future, with the necessary modifications due to local conditions, the Government of India desire to lay down the following principles in regard to primary education:

(I) "Subject to the principles stated in paragraph 8 (1) *supra*,[1] there should be a large expansion of lower primary schools teaching the three R's with drawing, knowledge of the village map, nature study and physical exercises.

(II) "Simultaneously upper primary schools should be established at suitable centres and lower primary schools should where necessary be developed into upper primary schools.

(III) "Expansion should be secured by means of board schools, except where this is financially impossible, when aided schools under recognised management should be encouraged. In certain tracts liberal subsidies may advantageously be given to *maktabs*, *patshalas* and the like which are ready to undertake simple vernacular teaching of general knowledge. Reliance should not be placed upon 'venture schools,' unless by subjecting themselves to suitable management and to inspection they earn recognition.

(IV) "It is not practicable at present in most parts in India to draw any great distinction

[1] The principle refers to the steady raising of the standard of existing institutions

between the curricula of rural and of urban primary schools. But in the latter class of schools there is special scope for practical teaching of geography, school excursions, etc., and the nature-study should vary with the environment, and some other form of simple knowledge of the locality might advantageously be substituted for the study of the village map. As competent teachers become available a greater differentiation in the courses will be possible.

(V) "Teachers should be drawn from the class of the boys whom they will teach; they should have passed the middle vernacular examination, or been through a corresponding course, and should have undergone a year's training. Where they have passed through only the upper primary course and have not already had sufficient experience in a school, a two years' course of training is generally desirable. This training may in the first instance be given in small local institutions, but preferably, as funds permit, in larger and more efficient central normal schools. In both kinds of institutions adequate practising schools are a necessary adjunct, and the size of the practising school will generally determine the size of the normal school. As teachers left to themselves in villages are liable to deteriorate there are great advantages in periodical repetition and improvement courses for primary school teachers during the school vacations.

(VI) "Trained teachers should receive not less than Rs. 12 per month (special rates being given in certain areas); they should be placed in a graded service; and they should either be eligible for a pension or admitted to a provident fund.

(VII) "No teacher should be called on to instruct more than 50 pupils; preferably the number should be 30 or 40; and it is desirable to have a separate teacher for each class or standard.

(VIII) "The continuation schools known as middle or secondary vernacular schools should be improved and multiplied.

(IX) "Schools should be housed in sanitary and commodious but inexpensive buildings."

In conformity to the above Resolution, by the end of 1917, almost all the privately managed primary schools were converted into board schools in Bombay, the United Provinces, the Punjab, the Central Provinces, Assam and the North-West Frontier Province. In Madras, Bengal, and Bihar and Orissa the board schools were few, as the Governments of those provinces had largely depended in the past on privately managed schools for extension of primary education. The Government of Bengal however launched a scheme of development of primary education known as the *Panchayati Union Scheme.* This scheme aimed at providing each union, generally of 14 square miles, with one model primary school entirely at Government cost. These schools had only three classes teaching up to the Lower Primary standard. Although the Government provided the entire recurring and non-recurring expenses of these schools they were placed under the management of the District Boards. The scheme was not very successful, except in having proper buildings for the schools started. The chief defects of these schools were that (*a*) they were not suitably located, (*b*) their teachers were not well paid, (*c*) they were not free schools and at the same time the fees levied in them did not bring in any income worth the name to the teachers concerned and (*d*) provisions were not made for the teaching of full primary course. The scheme, in spite of defects, which were remediable with increased funds, formed the stepping-stone to a general system of publicly-managed primary schools for Bengal and could be linked with any comprehensive system of advance that might be devised in future.

In 1917 on an average one boys' school served 8·3 square miles as compared to 10·2 in 1912. In the same year the percentage of boys undergoing elementary education was 4·5 of the total male population as against 4 in 1912. Hence it may be said that even four years after the promulgation of the Educational Policy of 1913 less than a third of the total number of boys of school-going age were receiving instruction in primary schools.

The ratios borne by public funds, fees and private funds (endowments and subscriptions) to the total expenditure on primary schools in 1917 were 71 3, 16·3 and 12·4 per cent respectively. The figure for the public funds, viz., 71·3, consisted of 23·5 from Provincial funds, 38·4 from Local funds, and 9·4 from the Municipal funds. The greater part of the sum spent from the Provincial funds was derived from Imperial grants.

In the same year (1917) the average cost of a boys' primary school was Rs. 202 as against Rs. 133 in 1907, and the annual cost of educating a pupil Rs. 5 as against Rs. 3 9 in the latter year. We have noticed that the average fee paid by a pupil was 14·5 annas in 1912; but, in spite of the increase in the number of school and pupils, and in the salary of teachers, the average amount of fee paid remained just at the same figure in 1917. As a matter of fact in 1912, 22 8 per cent of the total expenditure on primary education was met from fees; in 1917 only 16 3 per cent was derived from the same source. Hence the increased expenditure was largely met by enhanced recurring grants given for primary education to the Provincial Governments by the Governcent of India.

CHAPTER VI

THE PASSING OF EDUCATION ACTS IN DIFFERENT PROVINCES.

(The Period 1918-1937)

In August 1917, the Secretary of State for India on behalf of His Majesty's Government made an announcement in the House of Commons regarding the change to be introduced in the administrative policy of India. She was gradually to become a self-governing country within the British Commonwealth of Nations It was then realized by all the Provincial Governments that unless rapid progress was made in breaking down illiteracy the mass of the people of India could not be expected properly to exercise their rights of citizenship of a self-governing country. Undoubtedly, in India, many causes combined to make the progress of education slow. The slight demand for education in an agricultural country, the early employment of children on account of bad factory laws, the caste prejudices, the existence of large depressed communities, the inferior social position of women and finally the reluctance of the authorities (both municipal and government) to introduce compulsion, terribly affected the progress of education in India. It is now unquestionably a recognized fact all over the world that one of the first conditions of self-defence, self-reliance, self-help and self-advancement is the gradual emancipation of the masses from gross ignorance. The system of local self-government and the principle of popular election presuppose that the mass of the population will by degrees attain at least that elementary knowledge which enables them to exercise judiciously their rights and powers Hence after the announcement of August 1917, the official and non-official members of the Legislative Councils of all the provinces in India began to pay serious attention to devise measures for the rapid breaking down of illiteracy.

During the years 1918 to 1920 the Government of India were busy formulating schemes for the successful working of the new Government of India Act, passed in both Houses of Parliament in December, 1919. During those years the Provincial Governments in India felt the need for universal education and passed measures giving powers to the local authorities to introduce a compulsory system of primary education in their respective areas. The Acts are different in different provinces; and the powers given to the local authorities vary to a considerable extent. In some provinces the Acts can be applied to the whole area, in others to municipal areas only. Some make provision for the education of both boys and girls, others for boys only.

SECTION I

—THE BENGAL PRIMARY EDUCATION ACTS

The Bengal Primary Education Act[1] was passed in 1919. Its main provisions can be summarised as follows:—

(*a*) It extends in the first instance to all Municipalities; later on the Bengal Government may extend the provisions of this Act to any area in a Union constituted under the Bengal Local Self-Government Act of 1885.

(*b*) Within one year from the commencement of this Act or within such other period as may be prescribed by the Government, the Municipalities shall make a survey of the educational needs in their respective areas, and shall submit to the Government a detailed statement regarding (1) the number of children between the ages of six and ten: (2) the school accommodation, staff and attendance of pupils at existing primary schools: (3) the school accommodation, staff and equipment required if suitable provision were to be made for the primary education of all all boys between six and ten years of age: (5) the existing expenditure incurred by the Municipality and the increased cost to be incurred annually in order to provide such school accommodation, staff and equipment: (5) receipts already available and the income from any educa-

---

[1] Bengal Act No IV of 1919.

tion cess that may in future be levied: and (6) the amount of grant or assistance from the Government which the Municipal Commissioners consider would be necessary to enable them to provide for primary education within the municipality, or any part thereof.

(*c*) If after complying with the directions of the Government, the Commissioners are of opinion that the primary education of all boys, not being less than six or more than ten years of age, should be made compulsory within the municipality, or any part thereof, they may apply to the Government for permission to *introduce therein compulsory primary education for such boys;* and if the assent of the Government be received primary education shall be compulsory for all such boys.

(*d*) The Municipal Commissioners shall appoint a School Committee and shall with the previous sanction of the Government make rules prescribing the manner in which it shall be constituted, the number of its members and its duties, and the steps which it may take to secure the attendance of boys at school.

(*e*) Primary education in Bengal, shall not ordinarily be free, but when it has been made compulsory in any area if a guardian satisfies the school committee that he is unable to pay the fees or any part of the fees payable for his ward, then such boy shall be admitted to a recognised primary school free of charge, or at such reduced fees as the School Committee may determine.

(*f*) If the existing resources of any Municipality including any grant from the Government are not sufficient to cover the cost of primary education within its area, the Commissioners may, with the previous sanction of the Government, impose a tax, to be called the Education Cess; the cess so levied shall be a rate amounting to the sum required, after deducting the Government grant and the receipts from the school fees, endowments and contributions, to meet the expenditure on primary education, together with ten per cent. above such sum to meet the collection charges and the probable losses due to non-realisation from defaulters; the Government may make rules prescribing the manner in which the education cess shall be levied.

The Bengal Primary Education Act was passed in 1919 to provide for the extension of primary education in Municipalities constituted under the Municipal Acts and in Unions constituted under the Bengal Local Self-Government Act[1] of 1885. In the same year the Bengal Village Self-Government Act[2] was passed to develop self-government in the rural areas of Bengal. In 1921, the Bengal Primary Education Act of 1919 was amended[3] to permit of its application to Unions constituted under the Bengal Village Self-Government Act, authorising the

[1] Bengal Act No. III of 1885.
[2] Bengal Act No. V of 1919.
[3] Bengal Act No. III of 1921.

Union Boards to exercise and perform all or any of the powers and duties conferred on the municipal commissioners by the Primary Education Act, subject to such control by the District or Local Board as the Government of Bengal may prescribe.

In August 1920, the Government of Bengal placed Mr. Evan E. Biss on special duty to draw up a scheme for the expansion and improvement of primary education in Bengal. He submitted two reports, one in 1921 and the other in 1922, in the first of which he pointed out that "Bengal is very far behind Madras and an immense distance behind Bombay in the direct part taken by Government and local bodies in providing schools for the people. The percentages of public institutions are in Bengal 6·9, Madras 26·9 and Bombay 80·7 per cent".[1] He therefore suggested that the existing system should be re-organised on the following lines[2] :—

(a) *The proper distribution of Schools*—"The schools at present cluster and compete where teachers can secure fees, other areas being left unprovided. In the new system each municipal or union area is to be mapped out, the parts that are uninhabited owing to the existence of water, cultivation, jungle or other causes, being shaded in the map and then left out of

[1] Biss—First report on Primary Education in Bengal, p. 58.

[2] Biss—Second report on Primary Education in Bengal, pp. 1 and 2

account. The populated areas are then covered with circles of half a mile radius, a publicly managed school being placed at the centre of each such school area. The result would be that each household would have a good permanent school within half a mile in the direct line, and there would be no mutually debilitating competition between schools in the same locality. All the funds that can be made available in the locality are to be developed to the highest point possible within the limits of the elementary system."

(*b*) *The concentration of the children*—"Within each half-mile school area will be found a certain number of boys of primary school-age. When the time comes for compulsion to be enforced these will all have to enter the school, but in the meantime they will form a rough guide as to the size of the school building. If 400 boys are found within the circle it will be safe to arrange for accommodation of 300, if the number is only 65 a school for 50 wil be built. The schools being truly national it is hoped that children of all classes and creeds will be able to attend them, provision being made in parallel sections of classes for the special needs of each community. The larger the schools up to a limit of 300 boys, the greater will be the economy and efficiency with which they can be conducted."

(*c*) *Popularisation*—"The schools are to provide the teaching that is needed and desired by the people of the locality. For instance,

Muhammadan boys will be taught their prayers and the Holy Koran, while Hindu boys receive instruction in their great classics such as the Mahabharata and the Ramayana. In the same way, wherever possible, some elementary English will be taught if the people desire it."

(*d*) *Co-ordination*—"As the schools become established on these lines they will take part in a public primary school examination which is much desired by the people. Through this examination they will be linked with schools for giving more advanced instruction on the cultural, and vocational sides. These higher schools will be organised in a way that will best serve the largest possible population, and so as to give the best boys every chance of developing their powers to the full for the benefit of their people."

Regarding educational finance in Bengal Mr. Biss made the following observations[1]—

(*a*) "That the existing expenditure on primary education, low though it is in India as a whole, is deplorably low in Bengal as compared with other provinces. The average annual cost of educating a boy is Rs. 3·5 in Bengal as against Rs. 15 in Bombay;"

(*b*) "that the people of Bengal are nevertheless, paying directly and voluntarily more than those in other provinces, for the fee rate in Bengal is the highest, averaging Re. 1-11-0 per annum,

---

[1] Biss—First Report on Primary Education in Bengal, page 58.

no other province, except Bihar and Orissa, coming up even nearly to one half of that;"

(*c*) "that the expenditure from public sources in Bengal is small, and the proportion from provincial sources is very small when compared with that in other provinces; if the cost of educating the boy, which is met from provincial resources, is distributed over the whole population, it averages ·029 (rupee) per head in Bengal and ·265 (rupee) in Bombay."

On the data furnished by the Government and the local authorities, Mr. Biss calculated that the total cost of the scheme to make complete provision for primary education in municipal (excluding Calcutta) and non-municipal areas in Bengal on a free basis would be Rs. 1,73,06,205 (Rs. 28,66,205 plus Rs. 1,44,40,000) capital and Rs. 1,76,79,051 (Rs. 10,73,051 plus Rs. 1,66,06,000) per annum recurring. Hence if Calcutta be included the ultimate cost of primary education for the whole of Bengal would be roughly 2 crores of rupees (Rs. 2,00,00,000) non-recurring and 2 crores per annum recurring.

The scheme formulated by Mr. Biss was partially accepted by the Government of Bengal and made applicable in several areas, as a result of which in nearly every direction primary education made a certain degree of progress in Bengal. Every year more than two millions of pupils attended primary schools numbering nearly sixty thousand. Of these the Muhammadans formed nearly 54 per cent of the roll strength and the Hindus and other communities together formed only 46 per cent. In the whole presidency there was one primary school to every 2 square miles and to 2·2 villages. India is essentially a land of small villages; and Bengal is principally a land of one-teacher schools. For a few years Bengal spent nearly Rs. 84,00,000 every year on primary education, of which a sum of Rs. 26,00,000 was contributed by Government, Rs. 18,00,000 by District Boards and Municipalities and the balance viz: Rs. 40,00,000 by guardians of pupils and benefactors in the shape of fees and donations.

The above figures appeared to be encouraging. But on closer examination it was seen that few of the pupils enrolled in primary schools remained for more than one year under instruction. The expenditure and care bestowed upon these pupils were almost entirely wasted, for in no sense of the word, could they be considered to be literate. The enormous preponderance of pupils in the lowest class revealed the proportion of wastage. Of 100 boys in the Infant Class, only 30 reached Class I, 20 passed to Class II, 10 to Class III and 8 to Class IV. Here was something to make one pause and think. Primary education too often meant merely a year in the lowest class. In the case of girls also, an overwhelming majority left school after the first year and soon relapsed into ignorance. The above figures therefore revealed not only lamentable waste but also the deplorably backward state of primary education in Bengal and the great need of keeping children in the primary schools after the Infant Class. Several authorities had discussed this question of waste of money and human materials. All of them agreed that the only way to avoid it was to have a widespread system of compusion so that boys could be retained at school for a sufficient number of years to enable them to get a firm grasp of the elements of literacy. To remedy the above state of affairs, some attempts were made in recent years. The Bengal Primary Education Act was passed in 1919, but it remained practically a dead letter, except in Municipal areas of Chittagong and Calcutta, because the ways and means of finding funds were left to the option of the local bodies. No special provision was made in the Bengal Primary Education Act of 1919, to enforce its provisions in any area whose local authority did not fulfil in any of the requirements of Act.

The principal Municipal Acts, *viz*: the Bengal Municipal Acts of 1884 and 1932, and the Calcutta Municipal Act of 1923, constituting the municipalities, no doubt empowered the local authorities to spend money on primary education; but they did not compel those authorities to provide complete primary education in their respective areas. For example there was no provision in the Calcutta Municipal Act making the Corporation liable for primary education beyond a clause providing that "the Corporation shall spend annually a sum of not less than a lakh of rupees for the purpose of promoting primary education among boys between the ages of six and twelve years and girls between the ages of six and ten years residing in Calcutta." The above mentioned substantive Acts needed to be so amended that the local authorities could be charged with and made responsible for giving effect to the provisions of the Bengal Primary Education Act, in particular for the maintenance and management of all schools that might be set up under the provisions of the Act. It should however be stated that the Corporation of Calcutta had been spending for some years nearly Rs. 9,00,000 per year for the maintenance of 240 free primary schools for boys and girls in Calcutta and giving away more than Rs. 1,50,000 every year as grants to non-Corporation primary schools and primary departments of secondary schools. So far only the Chittagong Municipality introduced the Bengal Primary Education Act of 1919 throughout the city and the Corporation of Calcutta introduced compulsion in a few of its wards in accordance with the procedure laid down in the Act. As the Chittagong Municipality was also anxious to introduce compulsory education for girls within its area, the Bengal Primary Education Act of 1919, was amended[1] in 1932 to permit of its application to girls residing within a municipal area in Bengal.

[1] Bengal Act VII of 1932.

The Chandpur Municapality also opened a large number of free primary schools within its jurisdiction although it did not introduce compulsion. The two towns, Chandpur and Chittagong, spent 42·9 and 36·7 per cent of their ordinary income on primary schools during the year 1938-39. The Commissioner of the Chittagong Division observed that the proportion in each of the two cases was a disproportionately large item, depriving the rate-payers of other things to which they had a right. While publishing the Resolution on the Working of the Municipalities in Bengal during 1938-39, the Government of Bengal concurred* with the above view of Commissioner of the Chittagong Division. Perhaps the Government indirectly hinted that an education rate should be levied by the municipal authorities if they wanted to spend a fairly large sum on primary education.

Under the present system of voluntary education the pay of the primary school teacher in Bengal was such that it could not even be called a living wage. The Seventh Quinquennial Review on the progress of Education in Bengal for the years 1922-27, revealed that there had been a small incrase in the average rate of pay of the primary teachers. In some districts there had been a positive decline. Some of the figures were so low as to be almost incredible—for instance, in

* *Vide* Supplement to the Calcutta Gazette, September 26, 1940, page 1400.

the Chittagong Division the average monthly emoluments of a teacher in an unaided school was Rs. 33. Even in an aided school it was so low as Rs. 6.

In rural areas the poverty of the local authorities and their natural reluctance to introduce coercive measures were usually the causes for the Bengal Primary Education Acts of 1919 and 1921 remaining so ineffectual. Not only compulsion is necessary to bring children to and keep them at school for a sufficient time to make them literate but far larger funds are necessary for the upkeep of the schools and adequate payment of teachers With a view to remove the defects in the Primary Education Act of 1919 and to improve the pay of primary school teachers a comprehensive Primary Education Bill for rural areas in Bengal was passed in 1930. This Bill had been hanging fire for four years from 1926. It moved through various stages and phases and was ultimately passed by the Bengal Legislative Council on the 26th August, 1930. The assent of the Governor General was obtained in 1931. The objects of the new Act were to provide a central authority for each district to control primary education and to raise funds necessary for the launching of a scheme which would ultimately develop into universal compulsory primary education.

It has already been mentioned that the Bengal Primary Education Act of 1919 was amended in 1921 to permit of its application to Unions constituted under the Bengal Village Self-Government Act, authorising the Union Board to exercise and perform all or any of the powers and duties conferred on the Municipal Commissioners by the Primary Education Act, subject to such control by the District or Local Boards as the Government of Bengal might prescribe. *But this Act practically remained a dead letter on the Statute Book so far as rural areas were concerned.* Several authorities felt that the initative in the matter of compulsion ought to come from the Provincial Government. The question was discussed by the Government in 1926, and a Resolution, embodying the Education Department's proposals to levy an education cess and to constitute special district school boards for the administration of primary education, was published in September, 1926.

As a result of conferences held at various places and the views received from the District Officers, Mr. Lindsay (Secretary to the Government of Bengal, Education Department) drew up a draft of the Bengal (Rural) Primary Education Bill in 1927. In July of that year Mr. B. Chakravarty as Minister-in-charge of Education sought permission of the Government of India to introduce the Bill in the August session of the Bengal Legislative Council. The permission was received: but before he could introduce the Bill in the Council, Mr. Chakravarty had to resign as the whole Ministry fell on a motion of no confidence in them.

Nawab Musharruf Hossain became Minister of Education in October 1927, and at his request the Director of Public Instruction in April 1928, issued a Circular to all inspecting officers of the Education Department and requested them to explain, in the course of their tours, to the educated member of the public, the main features of the Bill including the necessity for levying a cess on land for the improvement and expansion of primary education in the rural areas of Bengal.

Thousands of copies of two leaflets (one on Promotion of Primary Education in Bengal and the other on Promotion of Primary Education among the Muslims of Bengal) both in English and in Bengali, were distributed in rural areas of the province. As a result of these steps taken by the Education Department hundreds of meetings were held all over the province and the response was remarkable. The Director of Public Instruction assured the members of the Legislative Council that "far from being opposed to the introduction of the Bill, a very large majority, if not an overwhelming majority, of the people present at the meetings that were held, unanimously demanded and supported the introduction of this Bill; there was also practically no opposition to the introduction of the cess."

In August 1928, Nawab Musharruf Hossain introduced the Bengal (Rural) Primary Education

Bill, 1928, in the Legislative Council, which referred it to a Select Committee of 32 members. Their report was published in March, 1929. But before the publication of the report of the Select Committee, a no confidence motion against Nawab Musharruf Hossain was carried in the Legislative Council in February, 1929. The Council was also dissolved by the Governor in April of the same year, and the Bill, as amended by the Select Committee, automatically dropped.

After the General Election no Ministers were appointed for several months. It was, therefore, left to the Hon'ble Mr. McAlpin (Member-in-charge of Education), on the 5th August, 1929, to introduce the Bengal (Rural) Primary Education Bill, 1929. This Bill was drafted mainly on the basis of the recommendations of the Select Committee appointed in 1928 with a few modifications which Government thought necessary. The 1929-Bill was also referred to a Select Committee consisting of 45 members. Their report was published in January, 1930. In the meantime the Hon'ble Mr. K. Nazimuddin was appointed as Minister of Education by His Excellency the Governor of Bengal. On the 31st March, 1930, the Hon'ble Minister presented the report of the Select Committee on the Bengal (Rural) Primary Education Bill, 1929, and then moved for the withdrawal of the Bill on account of radical changes made therein by the Select Committee composed mainly of the *Swarajist* members of the

Legislative Council. This motion for withdrawal was very keenly opposed and was ultimately carried by a narrow margin of 3 votes only (51 against 48). The Hon'ble Minister, while moving for the withdrawal of the Bill as it had emerged from the Select Committee of 1929, also promised to introduce a new Bill, which was published in the *Calcutta Gazette* of the 10th April, 1930.

In July, 1930, the Hon'ble Minister went out into the country to explain the main features of the Bill to all classes of people and to seek their support and ensure their mandate in this respect to their representatives in the Bengal Legislative Council. He toured through the districts of Chittagong, Noakhali, Faridpur, Jessore, Bakerganj, Dacca and Mymensingh. His tour had the effect of rousing the country to what Mr. Fazl-ul Huq described in the Council on the 4th August, 1930, as "fever heat."

On the 13th August, 1930, the Hon'ble Minister moved the Council for permission to introduce the 1930-Bill. Permission being granted attempts were made to postpone consideration of the Bill in that session of the Council, first, by moving for its circulation for eliciting public opinion by December, 1931, and, secondly, by moving for a reference to a Select Committee. When all these motions had been successfully opposed, most of the Hindu Members of the Council made a grievance of their being treated in a cavalier fashion by the Hon'ble Minister and walked out of the Council as a protest. Immediately preceding this 'walking out' came the unexpected news of the resignation of one of the Ministers (the one in charge of the Local Self-Government Department) on the issue of the Primary Education Bill. The Hon'ble President of the Legislative Council characterised the walking out of the majority of the Hindu members as a crisis and adjourned the House. A respite of ten days was given by the Hon'ble President to the various groups in the House to come to a compromise, and this being found impossible, the Council sat on the 25th and 26th August, even in the absence of the majority of the Hindu Members, to consider the Bill, clause by clause, and passed it on the 26th August, 1930.

The foregoing seven paragraphs give a history of the passing of the Bengal (Rural) Primary Education Act through the Legislative Council. Its passage through the Bengal Legislative Council was almost as controversial as the insertion of an Education Clause by the British Parliament in the East India Company Act of 1813. A summary of the main provisions of the Act[1] as passed on the 26th August, 1930, is given below:—

The preamble says that the Act is intended to make better provision for the progressive

---

[1] Bengal Act VII of 1930, called Bengal Rural Primary Education Act.

expansion and for the management and control of primary education in rural areas in Bengal, so as to make it available to all children and with a view to make it compulsory within ten years. It extends to the the whole of Bengal, except town of Calcutta and other municipal areas. Hence the Act is intended for rural areas only, and all children who are not less than six and not more than eleven years of age or other prescribed age will come within its scope when it is enforced.

The Act of 1930 creates in each district a controlling body, viz, the District School Board. Subject to conditions prescribed by Government the District School Board has full power to manage, maintain and give grants-in-aid to all primary schools within its administrative jurisdiction. The District School Board will consist of:—(A) Officials—(*a*) the District Magistrate for the first eight years; (*b*) the Sub-divisional officers; (*c*) the District Inspector of Schools. (B) Non-Officials (Ex-officio)—(*a*) the Chairman and the Vice-Chairman of the District Board; (*b*) the Chairmen of the Local Boards. (C) Non-Officials (Elected)—(*a*) as many members as there are sub-divisions in the district to be elected by the members of the District Board provided that the number shall in no case be less than two; (*b*) one member from each sub-division to be elected by the members of the Union Boards, Union Committees and Panchayats within the sub-division: provided that the number shall in no case be less than two; (*c*) one teacher of a primary school to be elected by the teachers of primary schools: provided that for the first four years he shall be appointed by the Government. (D) Non-Officials (nominated)—(*d*) as many members as there are subdivisions in the district to be appointed by the Local Government: provided that the number shall in no case be less than two.

The majority of the members of the District School Board will thus be non-officials. Every Board shall be a body corporate and shall do all things necessary for the purposes of this Act. Subject to conditions prescribed by the Government of Bengal, every District School Board shall prepare schemes for the extension of primary education, maintain all primary schools under public management in the district, appoint and fix and pay the salaries of teachers in all primary schools, grant recognition to schools, make grants for scholarships and stipends, make grants to primary schools under private management, and to form and manage a provident fund or annuity fund for teachers in primary schools. If ordered by the Government the District School Board shall delegate all or any of its powers of construction, repair, supervision and management of primary schools to Union Boards, Union Committees or Panchayats. The last named bodies shall also be considered corporate bodies for purposes of the Act.

The greatest difficulty in connection with the

advance of primary education has been the want of funds. The Act proposes to provide this by the levy of a Primary Education Cess similar to the Roads and Public Works Cesses. The Education Cess will be at the rate of five pice in the rupee, of which the cultivator will pay three and a half pice and the landlord one and a half pice. As the cess does not touch those whose income is derived from trade, business or profession a special section empowers each District Magistrate to assess a tax upon persons whose incomes are derived from sources other than the cultivation of land. On the 21st August, 1930, the Minister of Education in reply to a question in the Legislative Council, stated that the total annual contributions by the holders of estates and holders of tenures would be Rs. 28,67,000 approximately, and the total annual contribution by the cultivating *raiyats* would be Rs. 83,08,000 approximately.[1] The amount of Government contribution has been statutorily fixed by the acceptance of the following clause, viz., "In addition to the sums, which may be appropriated from the provincial revenues in any year for the purpose of primary education, the Local Government shall every year provide a sum of Rs. 23,50,000 for expenditure on primary education in rural areas." It may be here be added that *the whole of the expenditure required on account*

---

[1] Proceedings of the Bengal Legislative Council, Vol. XXXV (August 1930) p. 600.

of the training of teachers shall be met from provincial revenues and not from the resources provided by the new taxation or from the Government grant mentioned above. The whole cost of the inspecting staff shall also be met from provincial revenues and not from the District Primary Education Funds. The cess realised from a district shall be spent solely for the promotion of primary education of the same district.

The Local Government after consulting the District School Board may declare that primary education shall be compulsory within a specified area. No fee shall be charged by any primary school under public management in any area in which primary education has been declared compulsory, and also from the time provisions of the Act have been extended and cess imposed in the area, even if the primary education be not declared compulsory. Only for well-defined reasons exemptions to children from compulsory attendance at a primary school will be granted by the District School Board. In response to a widely expressed public demand, provision in the Act has been made for the imparting of religious instruction, if possible, during school hours.

For the purpose of advising the Bengal Government on all questions affecting *control* over the District School Board, *supersession* of the Board, *delegation* of the Board's powers to Union Boards, Union Committees and Panchayats, *notification* regarding the introduction of compulsory education, curricula and syllabuses of studies to be prescribed for rural primary schools and conditions to be framed under the Act, a Central Primary Education Committee will be formed for Bengal. The Committee shall consist of:—(*a*) The Director of Public Instruction; (*b*) ten members of whom two shall be elected from each of the five divisions of the province by the members of the District School Boards of each division, one to be a Muhammadan and the other a Hindu; (*c*) five members to be appointed by the Bengal Government, of whom two shall be representatives of the depressed classes.

Besides the items mentioned in the previous paragraph, the Bengal Government may refer any other matter affecting primary education in rural areas to the Central Primary Education Committee for their opinion. Such, in brief, are the provisions of the Bengal (Rural) Primary Education Act as passed by the Legislative Council on the 26th August, 1930.

On account of financial difficulties of the Government of Bengal all the provisions of the new Act have not yet been enforced in all the districts. But the Education Department enforced some of the provisions of the Act by creating District School Boards in sixteen districts in Bengal. The District Boards made over the sums which they were spending on primary education in their respective areas to the District School Boards as soon as they were formed by Government. The Government grants for primary education in those areas were also made over to the District School Boards. In a few of these 16 districts the Education Cess has not yet been imposed. As the Act contemplates full control over all primary schools by the District School Board it has been laid down that the Board shall appoint and fix and pay the salaries of teachers in all primary schools whether under public or private management. Hence unless means are found for crediting the fee income of all primary schools in the District Primary Education Fund it may be difficult for the District School Board to operate the Act *either* till the time comes when the Education Cess can be levied and enough funds obtained *or* till the Bengal Rural Primary Education Act is further amended absolving the District School Board from exercising some of the obligatory duties at present imposed upon it.

A Government Resolution on Education was issued by the Ministry of Education, Bengal, on the 27th July 1935, reviewing the process of expansion of education that had been going on in Bengal since 1835, the year in which the famous Resolution of the Government of India was issued by Lord William Bentinck. The Government Resolution of 1835 gave a new direction to education in India. On account of the passing of the new Government of India Act, the year 1935 was considered as the threshold of a new area of provincial autonomy. The time was ripe for a review of the whole position, especially of primary education, in which Bengal lagged behind most of the other provinces of India. The Resolution of July 1935 pointed out the defects of the educational system in Bengal and attempted to state clearly how the present system and conditions of education, particularly of primary education, could be reorganised. The Resolution made the following suggestions* in regard to improvement of primary education in Bengal:—

(1) The Primary Course should last for four years and not for five years as at present.

(2) All those who are poor should be exempt from payment of fees for primary education; only those who are able to pay should pay fees.

(3) Once a boy joins a primary school he should be compelled to remain at school up to the end of the primary standard, subject to this proviso that no boy should be allowed to remain in the same class for more than two years.

(4) The curriculum in the primary stage should be so framed as to be suitable to village needs; it should aim at literacy, viz Reading Writing, Arithmetic, and should include instruction in the elementary needs of village life and in matters such as personal and village hygiene, home geography and village organisation.

(5) There should be four teachers to each four-class primary school.

* The suggestions have been summarised in this book under 32 categories for the convenience of the readers.

(6) The immediate aim should be 16,000 primary schools of the new type—so located that each school will serve a population of 3000 people or alternatively an area of 4 or 5 square miles.

(7) Owing to the financial condition of the province, it is not possible to aim at any higher number of primary schools now, but when money is available more schools could be established.

(8) Local adjustments and special considerations will be necessary in areas with special geographical features.

(9) A survey should be undertaken of the location and standard of existing schools and the possible location of future schools.

(10) These 16,000 schools with 64,000 teachers working in double shifts, are expected to meet the needs of rural areas in the matter of primary education.

(11) The whole of Bengal is to be divided into 16,000 primary school areas distributed in various districts according to population.

(12) There shall be one school with four classes—I, II, III, IV—located in a central place within the area with a staff of four teachers.

(13) The central primary school shall sit for 4 hours in the day-time and will consist of 30 pupils in Class I, 20 pupils in Class II, 30 pupils in Class III and 30 pupils in Class IV.

(14) Each teacher will have only four hours' teaching work in the central primary school and will be able to work another two hours in the

morning or in the evening. Two other villages shall, therefore, be selected conveniently situated within the area. Little boys and girls of the two lowest classes (Classes I and II) may find it difficult to walk the distance to the central primary school and these are the classes where the largest enrolment may be expected. These two outlying villages will therefore each have a feeder or subsidiary school, each with the two lowest classes —Classes I and II. The four teachers will be divided in two groups, each working for two hours a day in the feeder schools.

(15) The number of students in each of the classes of the feeder schools shall be as in the central school, viz., 30 in Class I, and 20 in Class II.

(16) The total number of students in each primary school area with one central school and two feeder or subsidiary schools will thus be:— 90 in Class I, 60 in Class II, 30 in Class III, and 30 in Class IV (Total—210).

(17) The total number of students that could be taught in 16,,000 schools as organised above will be 33,60,000, as against the existing roll streagth of 21,00,000 distributed in nearly 64,200 primary schools.

(18) The salary of head masters of primary schools should be Rs. 20 per month and of other teachers Rs. 15 per month.

(19) Provision should be made to train the primary school teachers and for this purpose short

training courses in district camps should be organised.

(20) In any scheme of reorganisation of schools the needs of areas which are deficient in schools should be specially considered so that the requirements of educationally backward communities may be satisfied.

(21) The primary school curriculum should be so devised as to be suitable to both primary schools and maktabs and so organised as to provide the necessary variations in studies between primary schools and maktabs.

(22) Provision should be made in all schools attended by Muslim students for religious instruction and the teaching of Islamic subjects. Similar provision should also be made for Hindu students.

(23) All primary schools attended by a majority of muslim pupils might be named maktabs and it may be necessary in places to have maktabs as separate schools for Muslims only.

(24) Where the number of students justifies it there should be separate schools for boys and for girls.

25) No girl will however be compelled to attend a school where there are boys only or both boys and girls.

(26) There should be at least one middle vernacular school, gradually increased to five, to every 25 primary schools, i.e., from 640 rising up to 3,200 middle vernacular schools.

(27) At these middle vernacular schools

along with the other usual subjects English will be an optional subject as an alternative to agriculture and rural science (viz., natural science, village sanitation, co-operative principles, and elementary civics), the course covering three years or being reduced to two years, if feasible.

(28) The usual type of Middle English schools will remain to serve the needs of those who wish to join later High English schools for completing the Matriculation course.

(29) A large number of free studentships should be offered to boys of rural primary schools on the results of Primary Final Examination.

(30) There should be one sub-inspector of schools to every 100 primary schools. One fourth of the total number of sub-inspectors should be recruited from head masters of primary schools and one fourth from teachers of middle schools and they may be paid at a lower scale than the present pay of sub-inspectors.

(31) The primary school inspectorate should make it their business to educate the villagers in rural uplift.

(32) There should be village halls with libraries containing books suitable to village needs and requirements.

It was further stated in a Memorandum issued in August 1935, that the Government of Bengal were genuinely anxious to expand the opportunities of real education and to improve the standard so that the dangers of wastage and of lapse into illiteracy might be avoided.

In pursuance of their Resolution mentioned above, the Government of Bengal appointed in March 1936, a committee to consider the curricula suitable to the needs of primary schools and maktabs, and the question of religious instruction in those institutions. The Committee completed their work in November 1936 and submitted their recommendations to Government early in December 1936. The curricula as recommended by them and approved by Government in March 1937, will be found in Section II of the last chapter of this book.

The Resolution of July 1935 made only tentative proposals for the reorganisation of education in Bengal. After considering the criticisms and suggestions from individuals and public bodies, the Government of Bengal issued a fresh Resolution[1] in March 1937, laying down the policy and programme which should be followed in future in regard to primary education. The new Resolution outlines a scheme which in the main falls under three heads:—

(1) A distribution of schools throughout the province which will place educational facilities within reasonable reach of every child.

(2) The prevention of the present wastage by

---

[1] Government of Bengal, Ministry of Education, Resolution No 1037-Edn., dated 9th March 1937, published in the Calcutta Gazette of the 18th March 1937.

ensuring that as far as possible children shall attend primary schools for a minimum period of four years and shall not leave before the end of that period.

(3) The provision of a well trained and reasonably well paid body of teachers who will regard primary school teaching as their vocation.

The Resolution then discusses the above three aspects. As regards distribution of schools it says that there are now 64,200 primary schools, of which 9,853 are of the upper primary standard. These 9853 schools are located in 8500 villages. The remaining 54,347 lower primary schools are located in 28,631 villages. There are approximately 1,00,000 villages in Bengal. It follows, therefore, that there are nearly 65000 villages in the province without a school of even the lower primary standard and there are only 8500 villages with upper primary schools, i.e., with schools which, if well staffed and well attended up to the end of Class IV, would help to remove illiteracy. The scheme previously set out by Government contemplated a system of central and feeder schools, but there has been considerable criticism of the feeder system and Government after consideration of these objections agree that it is probably not satisfactory to have the same staff of teachers working in both a feeder and a central school. Such a system would probably lead to very considerable difficulties. Government have therefore abandoned the proposal of central-cum-feeder schools. It is therefore proposed to establish primary schools up to the upper primary standard in every "unit of school area" and so located that no child may be required to walk more than one mile. It will obviously not be possible immediately to establish all the schools under the new system, nor is it probably desirable to do away with any great number of the existing schools all at once. A lengthy period of transition is inevitable; in any case, as a preliminary to the reorganisation and redistribution of schools prior to the establishment of new schools or the replacement of the old ones, a careful survey will be needed to ascertain the nature of the existing schools and the location of the schools of the new type.

As regards wastage in primary education the Resolution mentions that although there are over 64,000 primary schools in Bengal most of them are ineffective and contribute little towards the removal of illiteracy. It has already been mentioned that of these primary schools, only 9,853 are of the upper primary standard and over 54,000 are of the lower primary standard. A lower primary school has an average of 32 pupils distributed as follows:—

Infant Class..........21·0
Class I...............6·5
Class II..............4·5

The figures show that very few of the pupils attending a lower primary school do so for more than one year. The teaching in these schools is neither good nor sufficiently prolonged to ensure literacy. A lower primary school is thus contributing practically nothing towards the solution of the problem of primary education. Its only value is to the four or five children who after leaving Class II go up for further education to an upper primary or a secondary school. But even in the case of the 9,853 upper primary schools there is an enormous wastage as is shown by the following pupil distribution:—

Infant Class	21·0
Class I	6 5
Class II	4 5
Class III	2 0
Class IV	1·5

It is generally and correctly assumed that in the present condition of primary education, literacy can only be assured to a pupil who has passed through Class IV and it therefore follows that only 1 5 out of 21 or about 7 per cent of the pupils receive any material benefit from primary education. The contribution of the existing primary school towards literacy is practically nil. The actual position is that apart from a few primary schools controlled by local authorities, mission schools and the primary classes of secondary schools, the primary school organisation of to-day is of very doubtful value. Far from there being 64,000 useful primary schools in the province, it is safe to say that the number of schools which are effectively contributing towards the removal of illiteracy is not more than 5,000 at a generous estimate. The remaining schools numbering nearly 60,000 are valueless so far as their educational merits are concerned. If this wastage continues, no scheme will be satisfactory or can be successful. Effective compulsion in Bengal will have to be introduced if the wastage is to be materially reduced.

As regards provision of qualified teachers the Resolution mentions that the unsatisfactory nature of the teaching provided is one of the reasons for the failure of the present system of primary education. Success in a primary school depends mainly upon the teacher. It is absolutely essential that the teachers who are to be responsible for primary education should regard their work as a life's vocation, should be reasonably well satisfied and should be effeciently trained for their duties. The present position is deplorable. The total expenditure upon 64,000 primary schools is approximately Rs. 80,00,000.* The total number of teachers engaged in primary schools is 88,000. It works out as an average of Rs. 7-8-0 per month per teacher. But this sum includes the teachers' income from fees and other sources. The only assured income which a primary school teacher receives is what is paid from public funds, i.e. by Government, District Board and Municipality—a total sum of approximately Rs. 47,00,000, i.e., an

* Prior to 1932 the expenditure was Rs 84,00,000.

average of Rs. 4-8-0 per month. But the salaries drawn by teachers in municipal areas and in Board primary schools are higher than the emoluments of the average teacher in an aided rural school. The average grant received by a primary school teacher in rural areas from public funds works out at only Rs. 3-8-0 per month. It is said that he receives in addition a sum of Rs. 3-0-0 per month from fees and other sources, but whether this is actually received by him is doubted by all who are familiar with the state of affairs in village schools. But even assuming that the full amounts are available for him his emoluments amount to only Rs 6-8-0 per month Naturally it is not possible to get either a qualified or a contended teacher on this small amount. It is not possible to expect any radical betterment in the conditions of primary education, unless the teachers trained and qualified under the newly proposed scheme receive a reasonable wage, and the following scale of salaries cannot in any way be considered as extravagant for the purpose :—

Head Master.........Rs. 25-½-30
Other teachers........Rs. 20-½-25

This would however mean an immediate annual expenditure of over Rs. 2,50,00,000, on salaries alone, even if Bengal is to have only 20,000 schools. Such a large sum is not now available. For the time being the salaries of primary teachers will have to be more in keeping with the money available for the purpose. The Resolution therefore suggests[1] that the following should be laid down as minimum salaries for teachers in Bengal:—

Trained Head Master	Rs. 16	per month
Trained Teacher	Rs. 12	„ „
Untrained Assistant Teacher	Rs. 10	„ „

Ordinarily each school will have three teachers, and not four suggested in the earlier Government Resolution of 1935, although in more sparsely populated areas there may be only one or two teachers in schools teaching the full primary course. According to the Resolution of 1937, Bengal cannot afford to have one teacher for each class and the three teachers of a school shall be expected ordinarily to teach pupils not exceeding 135 in number, distributed approximately as follows:—

Class I	40	pupils
Class II	35	„
Class III	30	„
Class IV	30	„
TOTAL	135	„

If the roll strength goes substantially beyond this figure, an additional teacher shall be appointed for every 40 additional pupils.

[1] In July 1936, Government notified that the pay of a Head Master should be Rs 20 per month and of a Trained Teacher Rs 15 per month. After the issue of the Resolution of 1937, the pay of the teachers was revised and in Notification No. 877-Edn. of the 8th April 1941, Government laid down that the Head Master and the Trained Teacher of an aided primary school under private management coming under the new scheme should get Rs. 16 and Rs. 12 per month respectively.

Although the Resolution of 1937 practically negatives some of the proposals and modifies most of the proposals tentatively made in the Resolution of 1935, still it must be said that it clearly lays down the principles which should be followed in future in regard to the development of primary education in Bengal. About organisation and programme, the Resolution of 1937 enumerates the following conclusions of Government:—

(1) *Unit School area*—Subject to local adjustments and special considerations, particularly in areas with special geographical features, every district should be divided into a suitable number of school units ordinarily on the basis of an average population of 2,000 or alternatively an area not exceeding 3·14 square miles. If a school is situated in the centre of an area of 3·14 square miles, the maximum distance that a child will have to cover will be only a mile.

(2) *Organisation*—(*a*) Every School Board shall organise one primary school in each unit of school area and for this purpose the existing schools including maktabs and special girls' schools may, wherever possible, be utilised for development.

(*b*) The School Board shall either themselves organise such schools or, without prejudice to the main features of the scheme, encourage private and local efforts in the establishment of such schools.

(*c*) Every School Board shall be competent to arrange for more than one school in a unit of school area if in their opinion one school does not adequately serve the unit. For this purpose such local authority will be competent to recognise primary schools started through private enterprise so long as such schools satisfy the general outline of the scheme and to give such financial assistance as it may decide.

(*d*) The School Board shall also be competent to recognise other primary schools within a school unit organised and maintained through private enterprise, as long as such schools satisfy the general outline of the scheme and do not require any financial assistance from any public fund.

(*e*) In the organisation of primary schools, primary classes of middle and high schools and of junior and high madrasahs may be taken as primary schools and, subject to the main feature of the scheme, it shall be open to the School Board to recognise them as primary schools and to give grant-in-aid, if and where necessary.

(3) *Duration of primary course*—A primary school shall consist of four classes, and for this purpose, the classes shall be known as Class I, II, III, IV. Primary education shall thus ordinarily last for four years.

(4) *Staff*—Each school should ordinarily have three teachers—one head master and two assistant teachers; at least two of the three teachers shall be trained teachers.

(5) *Religious education*—Provision shall, so far as possible, be made in every primary school

for religious instruction during school hours of every child attending the school in the religion of the guardian of such child, provided that at the request in writing of the guardian of any child, such child shall be exempted from religious instruction.

(6) *Holidays*—Every School Board shall arrange holidays in primary schools in such a manner as to be suitable to local needs, but the total number of holidays excluding Sundays shall not exceed 75 days.

(7) *Compulsion*—Steps should be taken to introduce free and compulsory education for boys in accordance with the provisions of Primary Education Act. There will be no compulsion for girls at the beginning, but it will be left to local option to demand compulsion for girls. For the purpose of primary education the following shall ordinarily be the school age:—

Age 6 to 7 years.......Class I
Age 7 to 8 years.......Class II
Age 8 to 9 years.......Class III
Age 9 to 10 years:......Class IV

(8) *Fees in primary schools*—If a School Board in any district before the levy of the Primary Education Cess desires to levy fees in any primary school, such fees should not exceed two annas per month in any class, and children who are poor, should invariably be exempted from payment.

(9) *Separate schools for girls*—Where the number of pupils justifies, there may be separate

schools for boys and for girls, but otherwise all primary schools will be open to both boys and girls. No girl will, however, be compelled to attend any boys' school.

(10) *Honorary Inspectors*—The Director of Public Instruction, Bengal, may from time to time appoint Honorary Inspectors of Primary Education with authority to inspect such schools in such areas as the Director may decide in this behalf.

Before closing this Section it should be mentioned that the Government of Bengal have not yet passed any orders about the reduction of the primary course in municipal areas. In such areas the primary education extends over a period of five years. Even in rural areas of districts where the School Boards have not been formed the primary course lasts for five years.

Increased accommodation, satisfactory location, properly trained and contended teachers, efficient control and finally compulsion in regard to attendance are the most important steps in formulating schemes for removal of illiteracy in Bengal. It is hoped that enforcement of the Bengal Rural Primary Education Act in the light of the instructions issued in the Government Resolution of March 1937, will enable the local authorities to tackle the above mentioned problems efficiently.

SECTION II

—THE MADRAS PRIMARY EDUCATION ACT

The Madras Elementary Education Act was passed in October, 1920. Its provisions are more definite than those of the primary education Acts in Bengal, Bihar and Orissa, the Punjab, the United Provinces, and the Central Provinces. In the Madras Act the school-age, however, has not been definitely fixed, but has been left to the discretion of the Governor in Council to prescribe in respect of children of either sex in any local area or of any particular community. The main provisions of the Madras Elementary Education Act[1] can be summarised as follows:—

(*a*) For every district in which this Act is brought into force there shall be constituted a District Educational Council consisting of a president and such number of members as the Government may prescribe. The following shall constitute the District Educational Council—(1) a president nominated by the Governor or elected by the Council from among its own number, (2) the District Collector, (3) the inspector and assistant inspector of schools of the area, (4) the president of the district board, *ex-officio,* and a representative of the members of the district board, (5) such number of persons as may be prescribed to represent every local authority

[1] Madras Act No. VIII of 1920.

within the district, (6) one or more persons determined by the Governor in Council to represent any recognised private educational body maintaining elementary schools or any association of managers of elementary schools, and (7) such other members as may be appointed by the Governor in Council, especially to represent the Muhammadans and other minorities; provided that the number of persons appointed by the Governor in Council shall not exceed one-fourth of the total number of members excluding *ex-officio* members.

(*b*) As regards the working of the District Educational Council the Act lays down that (1) the term of office of the members of the Council shall be three years, (2) no member of a District Educational Council shall receive any salary or other remuneration from the funds at the disposal of the Council, (3) all meetings of a District Educational Council shall be open to the public, (4) the minutes of the proceedings of each meeting shall be published in the district gazette in English and in the vernacular language of the district, and (5) the resolutions of a District Educational Council shall be carried into effect by the President in whom the entire executive power of the Council shall be vested.

(*c*) Besides preparing and maintaining registers showing the number of elementary schools and school places, and an estimate of the further provision necessary to place elementary education within the reach of all children of school-age, it shall be the duty of every District Educational Council (1) to grant recognition to schools, (2) to consider and pass orders on all applications for grants-in-aid on behalf of elementary schools under private management, (3) to disburse all sanctioned grants-in-aid from funds placed at its disposal by the Governor in Council, (4) to maintain a register of all recognised institutions in the district which provide for the training of elementary school teachers, and of all trained and certificated teachers employed in elementary schools in the district, and (5) to prepare and transmit to the Director of Public Instruction proposals for increasing the supply of trained teachers; and to advise upon all matters relating to elementary education referred to the Council by the Director.

(*d*) For each local authority there shall be constituted an elementary education fund to which proceeds of any tax levied, Government grants, fees (if any), fines and penalties, endowments and contributions shall be credited. With the previous sanction of the Governor in Council any local authority may levy within its area an education rate not exceeding twenty-five per cent. of the taxation leviable under all or any of the following heads, *viz.*, property tax, tax on companies, profession tax and land cess.

(*e*) The Government shall contribute to any local authority a sum not less than the proceeds of the education cess levied in the area; such contribution shall be in addition to, and not in lieu of, the amount of recurring expenditure incurred from provincial funds, during the financial year before the coming into force of this Act, on education in elementary schools under public management situated within the area for which such elementary education fund has been constituted.

(*f*) Any local authority may resolve to make education compulsory within the whole or a specified part of the area under its jurisdiction, for all children, or for boys, or for girls of school-age. If the resolution be accepted by the Government and so notified, then it shall come into operation within such area and from such dates as may be specified in the notification. No fee shall be charged where the elementary education has been made compulsory. The Government may, however, exempt any person or class of persons from compulsory attendance. The local authority shall for the purpose of enforcement of the attendance clause appoint one or more attendance committees.

(*g*) There shall be no bar to religious instruction being given at an aided elementary school under private management. But if not less than ten guardians of children attending such school, in any area where compulsory elementary education has been introduced, apply to the District Educational Council to exempt their wards from being present during religious instruction based on distinctive doctrines or creed of any particular religion, sect or denomination, then the Council on being satisfied that the requisite provision for such exemption does not already exist in some other neighbouring elementary school shall ask the manager of denominational school to excuse attendance during religious instruction of all children whose guardians have made such a request. If within a prescribed time the manager of the denominational school fails or refuses to give such exemption, the District Educational Council shall arrange with the local authority concerned to open a new school within one mile from the residence of every child in respect of whom alternative educational facilities are required. Nevertheless the denominational elementary school, the manager of which refuses to give exemption to children from being present during religious instruction, shall be eligible for such grants-in-aid as may be admissible under the Departmental rules if it contiuues to comply with the conditions on which recognition has been granted.

The principle laid down in the above paragraph concerning the eligibility for grants-in-aid of recognised schools where religious instruction is compulsory will help the Christian Missions and other religious bodies to carry on their educational work as before. In the previous section of this Chapter it has been noticed that not content with the provisions of the Bengal Primary Education Act of 1919, the Government of Bengal passed the Bengal Rural Primary Education Act of 1930 to give further impetus to the local authorities to introduce compulsory primary education. The Government of Madras have not yet amended the Madras Elementary Education Act of 1920, but have been considering the proposals for its amendment for some years. They at first convened two Elementary Educational Conferences on the 24th July and the 13th August, 1924, over which the Minister of Education presided and the following resolutions were passed:—

1. "The ultimate aim is to entrust the management of schools under public management to properly constituted panchayats whenever circumstances permit.

2. "The Taluk Board shall be the Taluk Educational Council for the Taluk Board area, and when the Taluk Board acts in this capacity it shall have on it co-opted members representing private agencies engaged in the field of education.

3. "For each prescribed area under a Taluk Board's jurisdiction there shall be constituted an Elementary Education School Board or Boards, the functions of which will be the following— (*i*) they will take up the management of all schools under public management in the area and transfer the immediate management wherever possible to village panchayats under such conditions as may be arranged in each case; (*ii*) they will supervise

all schools; (*iii*) they will open new schools either departmentally or through private agencies according to local circumstances; (*iv*) they will make recommendations to the Educational Council as regards the recognition of schools, grants to be paid to private schools, etc. Separate Boards may be formed wherever necessary for the elementary education of Muhammadans and the depressed classes and for the education of girls.

4. "The functions of the Taluk Educational Council shall be—(*i*) to form school boards in the manner described, (*ii*) to regulate school hours, select courses of study and text books, and assist in the provision of school buildings, equipment, etc., according to local conditions; (*iii*) to appoint supervisors, or inspecting school masters who will be under the direct control of school boards; (*iv*) to disburse from the Taluk Educational Fund, subsidies to school boards and panchayats, for the maintenance of schools; (*v*) to disburse grants to schools under private management from the funds placed at their disposal by the Government; and (*vi*) to do such other acts as are enumerated in the Elementary Education Act of 1920.

5. "A Taluk Education Fund shall be constituted for each Taluk Board area and will consist of (*i*) a fixed contribution entered in the normal budget of the Taluk Board for elementary education, (*ii*) the proceeds of education cess, (*iii*) the contribution made by the Government for elementary education under the Elementary

Education Act, (*iv*) the contribution made by the Government towards the payment of grants-in-aid to schools under private management, (*v*) all income derived from fines or any endowment or any property owned or managed for the benefit of elementary education."

In spite of the provisions made in the Elementary Education Act of 1920 enabling the local bodies to augment their resources for expanding primary education it was found that in most cases they were not willing to levy the education cess mentioned in the Act. Hence no appreciable advance was made in the expansion of primary education. Still by the end of 1925, compulsory primary education was introduced in about 23 municipalities out of a total of 81 in the province. The Government then endeavoured to secure expansion of primary education in rural areas by subsidising the local bodies and giving revised scales of grant-in-aid to the private agencies. They encouraged expansion of such education through aided agencies as far as practicable. Under the Elementary Education Act of 1920 there were two agencies to secure expansion of primary education; one was the local body which was entitled to raise an education cess so that an Elementary Education Fund might be formed separately in the local area; the other was the private aided agency which consisted of Christian Missions and non-mission agencies including teacher-managers of schools. Adequate supervision was provided for each class of schools and a programme was worked out by which every village with a population of 500 and above would have a school in the near future and thereafter villages with a population between 200 and 500 would be taken up.

The Elementary Education Act laid down that the Government should contribute an amount equal to the Education Cess raised by the local body. But the provision for the contribution of a sum not less than the proceeds of the Education Cess levied in the area and that such contribution should be in addition to and not in lieu of the amount of recurring expenditure incurred from provincial funds during the financial year before the coming of the Act into force, was very elastic. Therefore whenever the Government were satisfied that a local body had done its best to levy the Education Cess under the Act, it was given a subsidy of an amount sufficient to secure full expansion of primary education by opening new schools in school-less areas. In many cases the Education Fund of the local body was not sufficient to cover the whole area with schools under the scheme. Hence several such local bodies were assisted from the provincial funds for purposes of expansion of primary education . By adopting this method the Government were able to persuade some of the local bodies to take up the responsibility of providing free and compulsory primary education within their respective areas.

During the year 1924-25, a survey of the condition of primary education in the Madras Presidency was conducted by the Director of Public Instruction with the help of Mr. Damodar Mudaliar who had been appointed as Special Officer for the purpose. The report on the Elementary Education Survey stated that the income of the aided schools consisted of the teaching grants, fees and subscriptions or donations from private individuals in kind or cash. The rates of fees levied in these schools were generally higher than the standard rates prescribed in the Madras Educational Rules. With the opening, however, of a large number of board schools in many of which no fees were levied, the aided school masters were not able to realize any appreciable income from fees or subscriptions or donations and had to depend mainly on the teaching grants for the maintenance of their schools. The villagers were unwilling to pay fees and they thought that if the aided schools were closed for want of local support their villages would be supplied with board schools. In these circumstances, it seemed expedient, in the interest of educational expansion, to increase the rates of teaching grants so as to enable the private agencies to keep their schools in an efficient condition and to open new schools in centres which were devoid of educational facilities.[1]

[1] Report on the Elementary Education Survey of the Madras Presidency (1924-25), page 16.

Hence after the report was published the Government revised the system of capitation grants given to aided private agencies so that expansion might be secured in non-cess-levying areas.

In 1927, Mr. R M. Statham submitted a report to the Government of Madras on the development of primary education in the Madras Presidency with proposals for the reorganisation of the controlling agencies and for the amendment of the Elementary Education Act of 1920. The full report was not made available to the public. Only extracts from it were published in July 1927. After making a careful survey of the working of the District Educational Councils in the Madras Presidency Mr. Statham mentioned that experience had shown that no District Educational Council had fulfilled all that was expected of it under the Act. This was chiefly due to the fact that the District Educational Councils had no authority to open or improve schools with the result that progress was mainly dependent on the chance of local bodies being in agreement with the schemes prepared by the District Educational Councils and being willing to finance such schemes with the help of grants from the Government. Mr. Statham recommended the abolition of the District Educational Councils as they had not fulfilled all their duties satisfactorily, formed no logical part of a scheme for progressive Local Self-Government, could not be expected to prepare schemes which they could neither finance nor control, and did not exist elsewhere in India in provinces which were faced with almost identical problems.

Besides recommending abolition of the District Educational Councils formed under the Madras Elementary Education Act of 1920, Mr Statham made several other recommendations, the most important of which were the following:—(*a*) the institution of school committees of district boards and municipalities to control and finance all elementary education, (*b*) the restoration of the power of granting recognition to the Education Department of the Government, (*c*) the reorganisation of the inspecting agency so as to provide for an Inspector of Elementary Education and three Divisional Inspectors of Schools, (*d*) the protection and development of aided agencies, (*e*) an increase in the rates of grants-in-aid, (*f*) the gradual elimination of single-teacher schools, (*g*) the adoption in every district and municipality of definite programmes of consolidation and expansion limited to a set period of years, (*h*) consolidation before expansion and compulsion, (*i*) the taking of power by the Government to enforce the introduction of compulsion where necessary, (*j*) the fixing of minimum pay for all teachers, trained and untrained, (*k*) the ultimate staffing of all schools by trained teachers, (*l*) the grading of local bodies according to their relative wealth and poverty for purposes of granting Government subsidies, (*m*) the adoption of a policy which will recognize the financing of elementary education as the first charge on provincial and local revenues, (*n*) the insistence of a minimum percentage of expenditure by local bodies on elementary education, (*o*) the treatment of girls' education generally as a separate problem needing a special survey and investigation, (*p*) the adaptation of the instruction given in rural schools to the life and needs of the rural community, (*p*) the co-operation of all departments in rural community work.

The report on the Elementary Education Survey of 1924-25 and the recommendations made by Mr. Statham in 1927, practically precipitated the question of revising the Madras Elementary Education Act of 1920. Subsequently a Bill was prepared and referred to District Educational Councils, District Boards and Municipalities for their opinion. The main changes contemplated in the Bill are the following:—(*a*) The District Educational Councils are to be abolished and school committees of district boards and municipalities established which will be responsible both for preparing programmes of expansion and development and for controlling elementary education funds. The management of elementary schools now directly maintained by taluk boards and municipal councils will be transferred to the proposed school committees of district boards and municipalities respectively. These committees will also do the work of sanctioning and disbursing grants-in-aid to elementary schools under private management, which is now performed by the District Educational Councils. (*b*) The school committees will make a survey of the educational needs of the areas under their jurisdiction, frame programmes for the improvement of existing educational facilities and for the expansion of elementary education, formulate proposals for expenditure which will effectively carry out the programmes already framed and distribute equitably grants-in-aid to aided institutions. (*c*) The Government are to be given power to compel the school committees to submit schemes for making elementary education compulsory in cases where the Government are satisfied that a local area is sufficiently well equipped with schools and trained staffs to render the application of compulsion both necessary and desirable. (*d*) The Government are also to be given power to compel a local authority to levy the education cess.

The opinions of the District Educational Councils, District Boards, Municipalities and other public bodies were obtained. But Government did not not introduce the Bill in the Legislative Council. Many factors, mostly political, prevented the introduction of the Bill as outlined above at that stage. Since then no fresh attempt has been made for its introduction or further modification. The policy concerning compulsory primary education in the Madras Presidency is still governed by the Elementary Education Act of 1920. So far the scheme of compulsory primary education has been working in 27 towns (including areas in which the scheme has been partially introduced) and 104 villages included in 7 rural areas[1] only.

SECTION III

—THE BOMBAY PRIMARY EDUCATION ACTS.

The Bombay Primary Education (District Municipalities) Act[2] passed in February 1918, laid down that—

(*a*) Its operation should be limited to municipal districts in the Bombay Presidency other than the City of Bombay.

(*b*) The primary education of boys or of girls or of children of both sexes could be made compulsory in any municipal district from a date to be mentioned in the notification by its local authority with the previous sanction of the Government.

(*c*) The age of compulsory attendance of a child was not less than six and not more than eleven years.

(*d*) The municipality was to make provision for compulsory primary education after a resolu-

---

[1] Quinquennial Review on the Progress of Education in India, 1932-37, (Government of India publication 1940), page 141

[2] Bombay Act No. I of 1918. This Act was repealed by the passing of a new Act called the Bombay Primary Education Act, 1923 The new Act contains all the important provisions of the 1918 Act, and more definite provisions to give further impetus to the local authorities to introduce compulsory primary education in the Presidency of Bombay.

tion had been passed at a general meeting specially called for the purpose and which had been supported by at least two-thirds of the councillors present at the meeting and by one-half of the whole number of councillors.

(*e*) No fee could be charged in any municipal school in respect of the primary education of any child of less than eleven years of age.

(*f*) Where the Act came into operation the municipality was to appoint a school committee to enforce the provisions of this Act respecting the attendance of school children at school and the employment of children.

(*g*) The local authority could exempt by notification any particular class or community from the operation of this Act.

(*h*) To meet the cost of education the municipality could impose any fresh tax or increase any tax which was already levied in the municipal district.

(*i*) The Bombay Government could make rules determining the extent to which the cost of providing free and compulsory primary education should be met from the provincial revenues.

Not content with the provisions of the 1918 Act the Bombay Government set up, in July 1921, a committee of two officials and eight non-officials to consider further the question of compulsory education. The Committee urged that the extent of financial responsibility of the Government regarding additional recurring and non-recurring annual cost of the scheme of primary education prepared by any local authority should be clearly stated in the Act. The committee also recommended the setting up of a School Board for every local authority. On receipt of the report of the Committee, legislation was undertaken in 1922 on the basis of their recommendations. An Act called the Bombay Primary Education Act, 1923, was passed repealing the 1918-Act. It was however stated in the Act passed in 1923, that in any municipal area where the 1918-Act had already been enforced the provisions of the new Act should have effect in the area from the date of repeal of the old Act as though the municipality had followed the procedure laid down in the new Act. The old Act, viz., the Bombay Primary Education Act of 1918, was enforced in four municipalities (urban areas), before the passing of the new Act in 1923. The last named Act after having received the assent of the Governor General was published on the 22nd February 1923. A short amending Act was also passed in 1927.

The Bombay Primary Education Act[1] of 1923 as amended in 1927 lays down that—

(*a*) Its operations shall extend to the whole of the Bombay Presidency except the City of Bombay.

(*b*) For every local authority (a district local board or a municipality which is authorised by the

[1] Bombay Act No IV of 1923.

Government to manage its own schools) there shall be a School Board.

(*c*) The School Board shall consist of not less than seven and not more than nine elected members (persons experienced in education, women, representatives of minorities, and of backward and depressed classes) if the local authority is a municipality, and not less than nine nor more than sixteen elected members (persons experienced in education, women, representatives of minorities, and of backward and depressed classes, and representatives of municipalities in the district which are not local authorities) if the local authority is a district local board. Members of the school board shall not necessarily be members of the local authority. The Government may appoint on the School Board not more than three additional members if the local authority is a municipality and not more than four if the authority is a district local board. The School Board shall elect a Chairman from amongst the members of the Board.

(*d*) The School Board shall exercise the powers and perform the duties of the local authority for which it is constituted in respect of primary education; the Board shall enforce the provisions of this Act; it shall however submit its annual budget and all alterations therein for the sanction of the local authority.

(*e*) The School Board may from time to time delegate any of its powers and duties to any subcommittee or member or honorary or stipendiary officer of the Board. The Local Authority shall after inviting and considering the suggestions of the School Board and with the approval of hte Government, appoint an officer who shall be called the School Board Administrative Officer.

(*f*) A Local Authority shall take over and employ such primary school teachers employed under the Education Department of the Government as the Government may direct, on the same terms and conditions on which such persons were employed under the said department.

(*g*) A Local Authority may by resolution declare its intention to provide compulsory primary education for children of either sex or both sexes who are at the beginning of the school year not less than six and not more than eleven years of age, in the whole or any part of the area under its jurisdiction, and shall submit its proposals to the Government in the form of a scheme. A Local Authority, if called upon by the Government so to do, shall within a time to be specified by the Government submit a scheme to provide compulsory primary education for children of either sex or both sexes as the Government may specify and in such area as the Government may direct. Every Local Authority shall, within a prescribed period, prepare as complete a programme as possible for the universal introduction of compulsory education within the area under its jurisdiction.

(*h*) The Government may after such enquiry as shall seem necessary sanction such scheme with or without modification.

(*i*) If the scheme is sanctioned, without affecting the claim of any Local Authority to any annual grant which at the time this Act comes into operation is being paid to it by the Government for purposes of primary education, the Government shall bear half of the additional recurring and non-recurring annual cost of the scheme if the local authority is a municipality, and two-thirds of the said cost if the local authority is a district local board.

(*j*) When a scheme has been sanctioned the Local Authority shall make adequate provision for compulsory primary education within the area of compulsion, and such education shall be free.

(*k*) Compulsion shall only be resorted to in the case of children who are not under six and not over eleven years of age at the beginning of the school year; the Government may however exempt children of either sex of any particular class or community, in any area of compulsion or part thereof, from the operation of this Act.

(*l*) If a Local Authority when called upon makes default in preparing a scheme or after a scheme has been sanctioned omits to make adequate provision for compulsory primary education in accordance with the scheme as sanctioned and to bring into operation or continue to keep in operation such scheme, the Government may after due enquiry appoint a person to prepare the scheme or bring it into operation or to continue to keep it in operation as the case may be, and the expense thereof shall be paid by the Local Authority to the Government. If the expense is not so paid the Government may make an order directing any person who has, for the time being, custody of any money on behalf of the Local Authority, either as banker or in any relation, to pay such expense from such moneys as he may have in his hands or may from time to time receive and such person shall be bound to obey such order.

In Bombay all district local boards, except two had taken over control of primary education and, inspite of difficulties of various kinds the Director of Public Instruction reported that on the whole the administration of the Primary Education Act of 1923 was proceeding with increasing smoothness and harmony.[1]

The City of Bombay was excluded from the operations of the Act of 1918. It has also been excluded from the operations of the Act of 1923. A special Act for the city called the City of Bombay Primary Education Act[2] was passed in 1920. It lays down that—

(*a*) The Corporation of the city shall first satisfy the Governor in Council that they are in

---

[1] Education in India in 1930-31 (Government of India Publication, 1933) page 29.

[2] Bombay Act No XV of 1920.

a position to make and will then make adequate provision in municipal or other recognised schools for free and compulsory primary education of boys or of girls or of children of both sexes whose age is not less than six and not more than eleven years.

(*b*) The other provisions of this Act are practically identical with those made in the Bombay Primary Education (District municipalities) Act of 1918, except in the case of the formation of the school committee; on this committee there shall be sixteen members, twelve of whom shall be municipal councillors and the remaining four, of whom two shall be women, shall be persons, not being councillors, resident in the city of Bombay.

Compulsory education in accordance with the City of Bombay Primary Education Act of 1920, has been introduced in a number of wards of the city and the progress has been satisfactory.

A committee was appointed by the Government of Bombay in October 1927, to consider and report on the reorganisation of primary and secondary school courses with a view to their co-ordination and introduction of vocational and industrial training in primary and secondary schools. The Committee reported in November 1929 that "for various reasons mainly financial, little progress has been made towards introducing compulsion...... There is no doubt that the wastage in primary schools is great, and that a comparatively small proportion complete the elementary course. *The mere fact of placing a child at school does not ensure his eventual literacy.* He may either stagnate in one class for a number of years, or he may be withdrawn after a short period of study...... Withdrawls are partly due no doubt to economic reasons. However anxious a parent may be to keep his child in school he is at times compelled to remove his child from school either for service in the field or for service at home But the main cause is the ignorance and apathy of the parent. *Compulsion appears to be the chief remedy,* but it will not solve the difficulty completely, unless part-time and short-term schools are established at the same time...... *Stagnation is due primarily to ineffective teaching.* Nearly fifty per cent of the primary schools are one-teacher schools and the majority of them are in charge of untrained teachers. The work done also does not emphasise sufficiently the child's life and environment and the whole school and village atmosphere is such that the child does not realise what bearing education has on the life he is familiar with...... At the present time roughly 63 per cent of the boys of school-going age and 89 per cent of the girls do not attend school. Of those who are at school, nearly 80 per cent are in the elementary stage. It does not appear to be possible at present to attempt anything higher than the acquirement of literacy for the majority of pupils, but *ultimately a more extended education should be the aim*".[1]

So far compulsion has been introduced in 9 urban areas (towns) and 143 villages[2] in the Presidency of Bombay (excluding Sindh) in accordance with the rules framed under the Bombay Primary Education Act of 1923, as modified up to March 1936.

It should be noted that Sindh was made into a separate province under the Government of India Act of 1935. The Bombay Primary Education Act of 1923 operates in the new province of Sindh. And in this province 1 urban area and 613 villages[3] included in one rural unit only are already under compulsion. But the provincial report is not encouraging as regards further expansion of the scheme.

SECTION IV

—THE PUNJAB PRIMARY EDUCATION ACT.

The Punjab passed its Primary Education Act[4] in 1919. Its main provisions can be summarised as follows:—

(*a*) Part I of the Act, namely submission by the local authority to the Provincial Government, of a statement showing the school accommodation, equipment and education staff required

---

[1] Report of the Committee on Primary and Secondary Education, Bombay, 1927-29 (Bombay Government Central Press, 1930), pages 11, 16, 17 and 20

[2] Quinquennial Review on the Progress of Education in India, 1932-37 (Government of India Publication, 1940), page 141.

[3] Ibid

[4] The Punjab Act No. VII of 1919.

for introducing compulsory system of education and the amount or part of expenditure thereon it is prepared to supply, shall extend to the whole of the Punjab: Part II of this Act dealing with compulsion shall extend only to those local areas to which it may be applied in accordance with the provisions of Part I when the proposals and the statement have been sanctioned by the Government.

(*b*) Compulsion shall only be resorted to in the case of boys who are not under six and not over eleven years of age; but the local authority with the previous sanction of the Government may substitute "seven" for "six" and "twelve" for "eleven" in the area under its control.

(*c*) The local authority shall provide and maintain such school accommodation and equipment, and shall employ such educational staff as the Director of Public Instruction may consider necessary.

(*d*) The local authority shall charge no fees in any recognised school maintained by itself; and if required by the managers of any school within its local area not maintained wholly out of provincial or local funds, the local authority shall pay from its own funds the whole or part of any fees payable for primary education in respect of any boy or boys attending such school.[1]

---

[1] This power to contribute towards fees payable by boys attending schools not maintained by the local authority, is not given in the Acts of other provinces.

(*e*) The local authority shall appoint one or more school attendance committees to be constituted in such manner as may be prescribed by bye-laws made by such authority in this behalf.

(*f*) The Government may by notification exempt particular classes or communities from the operation of this Act; the Government may also by notification suspend or cancel the application of rules regarding compulsory attendance in any local area.

(*g*) Subject to any rules which the Government may make in this behalf, the local authority may impose an additional tax towards meeting the cost of providing primary education for boys residing in such area.

(*h*) The Government may, however, by notification direct that any additional taxation imposed for education shall be reduced or discontinued from such date as it may fix.

The Director of Public Instruction in his report on the progress of education in the Punjab for the year 1924-25, stated—"The main principles which have guided the educational policy are those of *Expansion, Economy, Efficiency and Equality*. The mere fact that, four years ago, only 27 per cent (instead of the required 15 per cent) of the total population was receiving instruction, has demanded a speedy *Expansion*. The very urgency of that expansion, allied with the serious financial shortage, has demanded the exercise of drastic *Economy* so that every rupee saved should be made available to the much needed expansion. The depressing statistics showing that a very large proportion of the pupils have been congregated in the lowest class and thus rarely reach even the fringe of literacy, have demanded a large measure of *Efficiency.* The alarming backwardness of several areas and communities have demanded a nearer approach to *Equality* in the advance that is being made".[1] The Punjab Government realised that expansion and efficiency could not be attained simultaneously unless primary education was made compulsory. The Government therefore enforced the provisions of the Punjab Primary Education Act in many areas.

The economic condition of the people of the Punjab is fairly satisfactory on account of large tracts of lands being brought in under cultivation by means of proper irrigation. Twenty thousand miles of canals and distributaries, all made since 1870, have made the province practically free from famine. The climate is dry but irrigation has made the soil fertile. "But its greatest blessing is that it is a land of peasant proprietors. In the west there is a movement, which has grown in strength since the war, to substitute the peasant proprietor for the landlord, in the belief that the welfare of a country is closely linked with this form of agricultural organisation. In the Punjab

[1] Report on the Progress of Education in the Punjab (1924-25), page 1

the problem does not arise, for, except along the outer marches, the peasant proprietor is everywhere predominant".[1] The peasants of Montgomery, Lyallpur and many central districts are very prosperous. But in the districts of Dera Gazi Khan, Muzaffargarh, Multan and Jhang there are very poor tenants and big land holders (known as Tumundars). There are also some big Tumundars in the districts of Attock and Shahpur. The people of the Multan district are not very enterprising and they are the most home loving people in the Punjab. The people of the districts of Rawalpindi and Jhelum are very keen on education. They served in the Great War (1914-18). By their travels abroad their outlook on life has widened. They therefore appreciate the value of education and heartily support all schemes for the introduction of compulsory primary education in their areas.

The irrigation scheme is converting dry and dreary lands into arable plains and thereby bringing in more revenues into the provincial treasury. The Punjab Government can therefore spend an increasingly large sum of money every year on education, public health and other nation building departments without levying any special cess like the Education Cess.

The organisation of the Primary education in the Punjab is simple. As in Bombay the work is

[1] Malcolm Darling—'The Punjab Peasant in Prosperity and Debt' (1925), page xii.

done through local authorities (district boards and municipalities). In the Punjab there is an Inspector of Vernacular Education attached to the office of the Director of Public Instruction. Owing to the fact that the Divisional Inspectors have so much else to do, much of the correspondence in the office of the Director of Public Instruction regarding primary education is done by the Inspector of Vernacular Education direct with the district boards and district inspectors of schools.

The provisions of the Punjab Primary Education Act were first applied in selected areas in 1923 and 1924. It was noticed that even in a prosperous village a board primary school staffed by two teachers (for four classes) would not be attended by more than 30 boys voluntarily though there might be accommodation in the school for 100 boys. The Education Department then suggested to the local authority concerned that if compulsion were introduced in the area lying within a radius of two miles from the Board School then 60 boys would certainly come to the school. The two teachers could easily manage 60 boys. No extra teacher was required and hence the cost of educating each pupil of that village became cheaper after introduction of compulsion in the area. When the number increased to about 80 or 90 an extra teacher was given. The plan was therefore, to start board primary schools first and then see to what extent they were attended voluntarily. If the accommodation in a particular school was for about 100 boys and the local authority found that 40 or 50 per cent of the seats remained vacant then these seats were filled in by enforcing the provisions of the compulsory Primary Education Act. The principle followed in the Punjab might be called *the doctrine of filling in the vacant places.*

Compulsion also enabled the boys to stay in the school for 3 or 4 years and gave them less chance of relapsing into illiteracy. It had been stated that *economy and efficiency were both attained by compulsion.* Compulsion also made no distinction between communities. Hence it gave scope for an approach to *equality for all communities* in the advance that was made. Sir George Anderson in his report on the progress of education in the Punjab for 1925-26 said—"compulsion is therefore, an economy and not a luxury which must wait for better times. Every effort should therefore be used to introduce it as rapidly as possible. But it is neither possible nor advisable to apply compulsion at one and the same time throughout the length and breadth of the province. Much time and money have already been wasted in the preparation of schemes which have been necessarily vague and obviously unreal. Equally inadvisable and unfair is the limitation of compulsion to those areas which can afford to contribute a fixed proportion of the additional expenditure involved; for this is tantamount to the encouragement of the rich at the expense of the poor. An imperfectly devised scheme of compulsion may easily result in widening the gap between rich and poor, between progressive and backward. In the Punjab the expenditure on compulsion is included in the ordinary accounts for vernacular education, and the Government assistance is regulated by the *grading* of each board".[1]

When compulsion had once been introduced in a particular area, the people of the neighbouring areas also demanded it. It has already been stated that the Punjabi is keen after education and this keenness has spread from village to village The initiative for compulsion now comes from within and is not super-imposed from above. It is the villagers themselves who apply for the introduction of the provisions of the Primary Education Act and not the local authority which enforces compulsion on unwilling people. The application from the villagers is considered by the local authority at a meeting specially convened for the purpose. If a resolution for the enforcement of the Act is passed by at least a two-thirds majority then it is published locally. Any person objecting to introduction of compulsory education may within thirty days from its publication send his objection in writing to the local authority and the latter shall at a meeting convened for that

[1] Report on the Progress of Education in the Punjab (1925-26), page 13.

purpose take the objection into consideration. If no objection is sent within the said period of thirty days or if the objections received having been considered are deemed insufficient by a majority of a two-thirds of the members present at such meeting, the local authority submits its proposals to the Government, with the objections, if any, which have been sent in and with its decision thereon. The proposals are submitted to the Government through the Deputy Commissioner. On receipt of sanction of the Government the local authority applies the Act.

The Punjab Government have made it possible for the District Boards to enforce the Act by placing large grants at their disposals. In 1917 it was laid down that ultimately a board school should be established at every centre where an average attendance of not less than 50 children might be expected provided that a distance of not less than two miles by the nearest route should ordinarily intervene between two schools. Maps were prepared by the Inspector of Vernacular Education to serve as a permanent record showing the existing condition and the ultimate needs of each district on this basis. In 1919 the District Boards were graded in accordance with their educational needs and poverty and war service of the people inhabiting those districts. The grants given in 1918 were considered as basic grants for the districts and it was decided that all additional expenditure for the introduction of compulsory primary education would be borne by the Punjab Government to the extent indicated below:—

(*a*) *Districts in the Ambala Division*—Hissar 70 per cent; Rohtak 80 per cent; Gurgaon 80 per cent; Karnal 66 per cent; Ambala 60 per cent; Simla 100 per cent. (*b*) *Districts in the Jullunder Division*—Kangra 90 per cent; Hoshiarpur 60 per cent; Jullunder 60 per cent; Ludhiana 70 per cent; Ferozepur 60 per cent. (*c*) *Districts in the Lahore Division*—Amritsar 60 per cent; Lahore 70 per cent; Gurudaspur 60 per cent; Sialkot 80 per cent; Gujranwala 60 per cent; Sheikhupura 60 per cent. (*d*) *Districts in the Rawalpindi Division*—Gujrat 60 per cent; Shahpur 60 per cent; Jhelum 100 per cent; Rawalpindi 100 per cent; Attock 90 per cent; Mianwali 90 per cent. (*e*) *Districts in the Multan Division*—Montgomery 60 per cent; Lyallpur, 50 per cent; Jhang 60 per cent; Multan 60 per cent; Muzaffargarh 70 per cent; Dera Gazi Khan 80 per cent.

The offer of the Punjab Government for such liberal help had acted as a great incentive in enforcing the provisions of the Primary Education Act of 1919. Upto the end of March 1937, compulsion had been introduced in 10,450 villages included in 2981 rural areas and 63 municipalities.[1]

It has been noticed in Section I of this Chapter that in Bengal the greatest obstacle to

[1] Quinquennial Review on the Progress of Education in India, 1932-37 (Government of India Publication, 1940), page 141

progress in primary education is the persistence of inefficient one-teacher school. On an average only 36 boys attend a primary school in Bengal and 70 in the Punjab In the Punjab the Government followed the policy of providing an additional teacher in each of the one-teacher schools whose increased enrolment justified this extra support. In 1922, there were as many as 2754 of these schools; but in 1927 the number was reduced to about a thousand Here again compulsion was raising the tone of the school by providing an extra teacher. Mr. Arthur Mayhew forcibly brought the weakness of the one-teacher school to our notice. "We have tried to show generally the extravagance and ineffectiveness of the voluntary system, owing to irregular admission, attendance and school hours, the swollen lower classes and sparsely attended upper classes, and the prolongation of time required for completion of the course. But to bring out more clearly the defects, it is necessary to remind ourselves that India is essentially a land of small villages; it is in these small villages, inhabited mainly by castes and classes opposed to education, that the battle for literacy has mainly to be waged and that the wasteful methods of the present system are most clearly seen. A few figures will make this clear. We may assume that the economic attendance for a school is 100 and that, if these 100 were to attend regularly and receive effective instruction, a course satisfying the present needs of India could be completed in four years. Under a compulsory system, with precise regulations for the age of admission and leaving, this number of pupils would be grouped in four classes of 25 each, one class for each school year and one teacher for each class. At the present rate of salaries the annual salary bill for such a school would amount to about Rs. 1,500 per annum, and the annual number of pupils completing the course would be 25. Completion of a course on such a system ought to ensure life literacy. The cost per literate reckoned on teachers' salaries alone would then be Rs. 60. But we find that the average number of pupils per primary school in India is not 100, but only 42. And this very low average is obtained from schools situated mainly in towns and large villages, not in small villages where most of India's population lives and which are at present, most inadequately supplied with schools........ Taking, however, the present average of 42 pupils per school, and reminding ourselves of the conditions prevalent under a voluntary system, we may estimate the annual out-turn of pupils who have completed the course in such a school at 3. The three lowest classes would probably contain the remaining pupils, 20 of whom would be in the infant class. For the instruction of this number a staff of more than two teachers would be thought excessive. But their work distributed over, at least four years and disturbed by irregular attendance is ineffective. There is no guarantee that the three passed pupils will not relapse into illiteracy. Assuming hopefully that they will not, and estimating the annual cost of the two teachers at Rs 720, we find the cost per literate of a school, with the average enrolment provided under the present system, is Rs. 240, which is four times the cost per literate on the economic minimum of 100 under a compulsory system. This difference in cost is even more marked if we add to the teachers' salary bill such items as the cost of their training and the cost of erecting, maintaining, and equipping school buildings. When we consider the millions in India who have to be raised to literacy this difference in cost becomes appalling."[1]

Mr. Mayhew also suggested that "the only way to meet the problem of small villages is to group them for school purposes, making one central school with a full course for an area, and arranging feeder schools, which must serve as a rule more than one village, from which the central school is to be fed." This device of feeder schools or branch schools, as they are called in the Punjab, has been very successful in certain places, notably in canal areas. It has already been mentioned that compulsion is introduced within the zone of a circle of radius approximately two miles from the main school. The branch

[1] Arthur Mayhew—'The Education of India' (1926), pages 235-236.

school is started at a distance of about a mile from the main school. It meets the needs of young children living in the fringe area of the compulsory zone who find it too far to walk to and from the main school. Or, in others words the children find a school at a distance of about a mile from their homes. It comprises only two classes (in some cases only one), and can therefore be placed under a single teacher whose name is borne on the roll of the main school. A branch school has therefore no separate existence. It forms a part of the main school. The Head master of the main school visits the branch school about three times every week and supervises its work. Wherever compulsory education is introduced the local authorities are compelled to appoint one or more school attendance committees under the Act for their own areas. In large municipal areas one School Attendance Committee is appointed for each ward. Every big municipality also appoints a Superintendent of Schools. Generally he is a Government servant in the Subordinate Educational Service Hence the departmental policy is carried out easily throughout the Punjab.

Where compulsion had been introduced the vast majority of the parents, as a rule, did not object to send their wards to schools. It was easy to ensure the attendance of 80 per cent. of

[1] Arthur Mayhew—'The Education of India' (1926), page 237.

the boys of school-going age. The difficult problem was to bring prompt action against the few remaining defaulters. The Superintendent of municipal schools, Lahore, once stated—"Last year about 130 notices were issued against defaulters, but not more than 73 prosecutions were successful. This was due to defective procedure. The legal adviser to the municipality institutes all prosecutions on behalf of the municipality. Generally, it takes at least three months to obtain a hearing in court, and sometimes more. The report is normally made in mid-winter, but the prosecution is rarely heard until mid-summer. During this long interval a large number of defaulters have left the station. In some cases the boys have become over-age."[1] With regard to a rural area in Gujranwala, the District Inspector stated—"After the formation of the attendance committees, notices were issued to all the parents with the result that within a short period of time the roll was almost doubled. There are now over one hundred boys in the school, and with the exception of about a dozen all the boys of school-going age have been enrolled. The question therefore arises as to the action which should be taken against the defaulters. A recalcitrant parent pays no heed to the threats or persuasion of the committee. Delay in taking the necessary

---

[1] Quinquennial Report on the Progress of Education in the Punjab, (1922-27), page 8.

action creates in time a spirit of bravado."[1] In compulsory education areas the guardians are no doubt prosecuted for not sending their wards to school. But the prosecution is only launched against those who totally refuse to send their boys to school. The guardians who send their wards to a school for a year or two and then take them away from it although they are below eleven years of age are seldom prosecuted. This has created a feeling in the minds of the guardians that it is only necessary to send the boys to a school for a short period to avoid prosecution. It is more necessary to prosecute those guardians who after having sent their boys to school take them away from it before completion of eleven years of age.

In the Punjab there are only 4 classes in a primary school. Practically no fee is charged in a primary school even in a non-compulsory area in the Punjab Prior to the passing of the Primary Education Act, there were five classes in the primary school. The substitution of the four for the five-class primary school was made to meet the requirements of the Act, to relieve teachers in single-teacher schools from the impossible task of teaching five classes, to eliminate the three-class school and also to equalise the opportunities of urban and rural boys, the study of English being started in the fifth class. That

[1] Quinquennial Report on the Progress of Education in the Punjab, (1922-27), page 8

is to say English has been completely removed from the curriculum of the primary school. A new type of school, called the lower middle school, was created During the years 1922 to 1927 the Education Department annually converted about 300 to 400 primary schools into lower middle schools. Sir George Anderson in 1927 stated that "the Punjab is rapidly advancing towards the day when the lower middle school will be the ordinary elementary school of the country side with lower grade feeder schools grouped around it Moreover, this rapid increase makes possible the belief that a still greater day will come when the full vernacular middle school with eight classes will be the elementary school of the Punjab, and this would mean a well educated peasantry."[1] It should also be mentioned here that the fee rates in the middle schools in the Punjab are very low compared to the rates in Bengal. The fee rates in the former are about one-fourth of the rates charged in the latter.

In spite of the praise bestowed on the four-class primary schools in the Punjab, some people were not satisfied with the system. They thought that some readjustment was necessary to make the foundation of education strong. The Punjab University Enquiry Committee which was appointed by the Punjab Government in October 1932, with Sir George Anderson, former Director

---

[1] Quinquennial Report on the Progress of Education in the Punjab, (1922-27), page 8.

of Public Instruction, as Chairman, reported in June 1933, that the school foundations were not strong enough. The Committee noted as follows —"In spite of several meritorious qualities, the school foundations are not strong enough, particularly in organisation and adjustment. Every stage of education should have a clear objective, and as far as possible be self-contained. There is too much overlapping between successive stages. In consequence there is confusion of objective. The main objective of the *primary course* should be to make the masses literate and to give them that modicum of knowledge which all should possess; but many witnesses have pointed out that a primary school with only four classes is unlikely to fulfil even this limited aim, especially in rural areas, where the danger of relapse into illiteracy is very great. Many pupils have to attend the middle department for one or two years in order to accomplish what should be the end of the primary course. This practice is inconvenient and uneconomic in itself. It also confuses the function of the middle schools. There is much justification for the view held by many witnesses, that the primary courses should be extended to five years in order to ensure literacy within that stage The majority of pupils would then complete the modest degree of education which their parents have sought for them."[1]

[1] Report of the Punjab University Enquiry Committee, 1932-33, pages 299 and 300.

The Government of India in 1925 extended the Punjab Primary Education Act of 1919 to the province of Delhi. It may be mentioned that the province of Delhi comprises only the city of Delhi and its suburbs. The suburbs are considered rural areas for the purpose of the Act. So far compulsion has been introduced in the city of Delhi and nine rural areas in the suburbs.[1]

The Government of the North-West Frontier Province once thought of introducing the provisions of the Punjab Primary Education Act in their province. But the Director of Public Instruction of the North-West Frontier Province said to the Government of India in 1931 that "the general application of compulsion is not yet a practical problem."[2] The year 1932 saw the introduction of reforms in the North-West Frontier Province, with the consequent creation of a legislative council. In the Legislative Council of the Frontier Province education continued to receive attention though mainly by way of questions about matters of local interest.

The problems concerning introduction of compulsory education are almost similar in all provinces of India. As however the Punjab has made a satisfactory progress in introducing the scheme of compulsory primary education in nearly 3,000 rural areas and 63 urban areas, all aspects of the

---

[1] Quinquennial Review on Progress of Education in India, 1932-37, (Government of India Publication, 1940), page 141.

[2] *Ibid.*

scheme have been discussed in detail in this section of the chapter on Primary Education Acts.

SECTION V.—THE UNITED PROVINCES PRIMARY EDUCATION ACTS

It has been noticed in the previous section that the Punjab Primary Education Act of 1919 could be applied to the whole of the province. In the same year the United Provinces Primary Education Act was passed permitting only the municipalities to introduce compulsion within the areas under their control. The main provisions of this Act[1] are as follows:—

(*a*) It extends only to the municipalities of the United Provinces to enable them to introduce compulsory primary education in urban areas, for all children between six and eleven years of age.

(*b*) Primary education of male children shall first be made compulsory in the whole or any part of the municipality; later on, on the application of the municipal board the Government may notify that primary education of female children shall be compulsory.

(*c*) Such compulsory primary education shall be free of charge.

(*d*) The municipal boards are the educational authorities in their respective areas, but they shall

[1] United Provinces Act No. VII of 1919.

appoint school committees to enforce provisions respecting the attendance of children at school and the employment of children and shall determine their other duties, powers and responsibilities.

(*e*) The Government may exempt any particular class or community from the operation of this Act.

(*f*) The municipal board may impose a tax called the education cess, the proceeds of which shall be devoted solely to primary education; the board may levy the education cess by imposing a new tax or by increasing any tax which is already levied; and in the latter case, the income derived from the increase shall be deemed to be the proceeds of the education cess.

(*g*) The Government may make rules prescribing the range of instruction in primary schools, determining generally what shall be considered to be adequate provision for compulsory primary education free of charge, and defining the conditions on which the Government will bear a share of the cost of providing primary education.

Soon after the passing of the Primary Education Act of 1919, the Government of the United Provinces promised, if sufficient funds were available and granted by the legislative council, to give assistance to the extent of two-thirds of the extra cost involved, including the cost of remitting fees and also to meet the total cost of bringing the minimum pay of municipal teachers up to the minimum rates prescribed for district boards, provided that the total contribution made by the Government to any municipality on account of primary education should not exceed 60 per cent. of the total cost of the same. This generous offer of the Government had a great effect on the educational activities of the municipal authorities. No fewer than 32 municipalities soon expressed their willingness to enforce the Act, of which 24 actually introduced it either in the whole or in parts of their areas before the end of the year 1926-27. Subsequently the progress was slow and by the end of 1936-37 the number of urban areas under compulsion was 36.

In the municipalities of the United Provinces compulsion is not introduced all at once. A census of boys between the ages of 6 and 11 years is taken and a progressive three years' scheme is prepared. *It is considered that 20 per cent. of the boys will not read in any primary school.* Most of them will receive their education in secondary and anglo-vernacular schools and a few will get exemption under the provisions of the Act. Of the remaining 80 per cent. it is expected that 75 per cent. (*i.e.* 60 per cent. of the total number of boys) will be in primary schools in the first year of operation of the Act; 90 per cent. (*i.e.* 72 per cent. of the total number) will come in the second year; and 100 per cent. (*i.e.* the full 80 per cent. of the total number) in the third year. If the required percentage is not attained in the third year of the enforcement of the Act then prosecutions against the defaulting guardians are made in the following year. Or in other words *no prosecutions are made till the fourth year of the operation of the Act in any area.*

The three years' scheme mentioned above has not been unsuccessful, but it has not attained the degree of success that was possible. The Director of Public Instruction says—"There appear to be various reasons for this. The enthusiasm of some boards which introduced the scheme to the sound of trumpets died away when the opening fanfare ceased. Lack of success is also, in some measure, due to the lack of experience of the boards; failure to co-ordinate the duties of the superintendent of education and the attendance officer has been a contributory factor. The application of compulsion to part only, one or two wards, of the municipal area has sometimes resulted in the migration of boys to wards not affected by compulsion; this, of course, will cease when compulsion will be introduced into the whole of the municipal area. The main factor, however, appears to have been the inability or hesitancy of boards to apply the powers bestowed on them under the Act."

Expansion of primary education in rural areas is attempted through the machinery of the district board. Regarding the finance of the scheme of expansion in rural areas a definite contract is made by the district board with the Education Department of the Government of the

United Provinces. The main features of the contract scheme are the following:—

(1) "The Government prescribe for each board the minimum amount which it is bound to provide in its budget under each of five heads, viz.—(*a*) vernacular middle schools; (*b*) ordinary primary schools, including training classes; (*c*) Islamia schools and maktabs; (*d*) depressed class education and (*e*) female education.

(2) "Towards the total expediture by the boards under these heads the Government give a lump general grant.

(3) "Each board has, therefore, to provide in its budget an amount under each head not less than the minimum prescribed for that head. The difference between the amount provided in the budget and the amount actually expended is required to be credited to an education fund for each head; this fund can be used only for new buildings, equipment and similar non-recurring items of expenditure under the head for which these savings have accrued.

(4) "A board may not transfer, from the minimum prescribed expenditure, funds between the five heads specified, but may from funds at its disposal increase the provision under any of these heads, provided that it does not reduce the expenditure under any head below this prescribed minimum.

(5) "If a board decides in any year to increase its recurring expenditure under any head

over the prescribed minimum, it does so on the clear understanding that the board is committed to the increased recurring expenditure in future years, and that the minimum prescribed under the head will consequently be reckoned at the increased figure."[1]

The contract system worked fairly satisfactorily and during each of the years 1924-25, 1925-26 and 1926-27; the government contribution was Rs. 65,42,600 towards a total minimum expenditure by district boards of Rs. 95,86,000. For the year 1927-28, the government contribution was Rs. 68,62,600 towards a prescribed minimum expenditure of Rs. 1,01,78,180 by the district boards. It would therefore appear that the Government had been contributing since April 1924, nearly two-thirds of the expenditure incurred on vernacular education by the district boards of the United Provinces.

In 1925 the Government of the United Provinces with the help of a special officer examined the questions of securing better results from the present expediture on primary education and of introduction of compulsory primary education in rural areas. The special officer strongly recommended the abolition of the preparatory schools (with three years' course) and suggested that there should be only one type of school called the

---

[1] Quinquennial Report on Public Instruction in the United Provinces (1922-27), page 65

primary school (with a minimum of two teachers) which should contain all classes included in the primary stage. All preparatory schools should be converted into full primary schools during the next three years. The resolution of the education department on the special officer's report stated that "the Government will within the limits of the funds available, assist district boards to develop as many district board preparatory schools as possible into schools teaching the full primary course. In place of the existing preparatory classes A and B there will be one class called the Infant class. Admission to this class will ordinarily be made only twice a year in July and January. The standard of staffing should be as follows:—(*i*) A school will have only one teacher until the average attendance reaches 31; (*ii*) when the average attendance is between 31 and 60, inclusive, a second teacher should be provided; (*iii*) when the average attendance is between 61 and 90, inclusive, a third teacher should be provided; and so on, one teacher being provided for every 30 additional pupils in average attendance; (*iv*) a corresponding reduction in staff should be made if the average attendance falls."

The above resolution of the education department definitely encouraged the abolition of one-teacher schools, by providing extra teachers as average attendance increased.

We have seen that, up till 1926, the policy of the Government of the United Provinces was that universal free and compulsory primary education in rural areas should be reached by a definite programme of progressive expansion. The provisions of the United Provinces Primary Education Act of 1919 did not apply in non-municipal areas. After following for six years a policy of voluntary expansion, the Government passed in 1926, an Act to provide for compulsory primary education in rural areas under district boards in the United Provinces. This Act[1] is called the United Provinces District Boards Primary Education Act. Its main provisions are summarised below:—

(*a*) It extends to all areas under the jurisdiction of the district boards.

(*b*) On the application of the board the Local Government may declare, by notification, that the primary education of male children shall be compulsory in the whole of the board's area or in any part thereof, for example, in any tahsil area, thana area, school area or village area. No notification shall be issued unless (i) the board has, by special resolution passed by a vote of not less than one-half of the total number of members constituting the board, resolved that such primary education should be made compulsory, and (ii) the Local Government is satisfied that the board is in a position to make, and will make adequate provision in recognised primary schools for such compulsory primary education free of charge.

---

[1] United Provinces Act No. I of 1926

(*c*) Where a notification has been issued regarding enforcement of compulsory primary education, the board shall appoint one or more committees for the purpose of exercising the powers and performing the duties of the school committee established under the Act. This committee shall enforce the provisions of the Act respecting the attendance of children at school and the employment of children.

(*d*) If a parent without any reasonable excuse fails to send his child to a recognised school then he shall be liable on conviction before a magistrate to pay a fine not exceeding five rupees.

(*e*) Any person (other than the parent) who utilizes the services of any child, between the ages of six and eleven, whose parent is required to cause him to attend a recognised primary school shall, on conviction before a magistrate, be liable to a fine not exceeding twenty-five rupees.

(*f*) The Local Government may, by notification, exempt any particular class or community from the operation of the Act.

(*g*) Primary education shall be free in an area where it has been made compulsory.

(*h*) All fines realized under the provisions of the Act shall be credited to the board's fund.

(*i*) The Local Government may make rules for carrying out the purposes of the Act.

(*j*) With the previous sanction of the Local Government, a board in the area of which compulsion has been introduced may make regulations consistent with the Act, prescribing the supply of text-books and educational requisites to the children of indigent parents free of charge, and the manner in which the school committee shall be constituted, its jurisdiction, the number of its members, and their duties, powers and responsibilities.

The District Boards Primary Education Act was passed in 1926. Several District Boards prepared schemes for introducing compulsory primary education in selected areas early in 1927. In July of the same year the Government promised to pay the whole of the extra cost of the compulsory schemes until the total contribution from the Government reached two-thirds of the total prescribed expenditure including in that expenditure the extra cost of the compulsory schemes. Hence the enforcement of the provisions of the United Provinces District Boards Primary Education Act of 1926 did not mean a severe burden on the resources of the boards. Up to the end of the year 1936-37, the provisions of the above named Act were introduced in 1224 villages included in 25 rural areas[1] spread over the province.

It has already been mentioned that in compulsory areas primary education is free. In primary and preparatory schools in non-compulsory areas the ordinary fee does not exceed two annas

[1] Quinquennial Review on the Progress of Education in India, 1932-37 (Government of India Publication, 1940), page 141.

a month in the highest class, nor it is less than half an anna in any class where it is charged. It can therefore be said that like the Punjab, the United Provinces Government are slowly trying to make primary education free for all.

SECTION VI.—THE BIHAR AND ORISSA PRIMARY EDUCATION ACT

The Bihar and Orissa Primary Education Act[1] was passed in 1919. Its main provisions can be summarised as follows:—

(*a*) It extends to the whole of the province.

(*b*) The local authority by a special resolution supported by at least two-thirds of the members present at a meeting convened for the purpose and after satisfying the Local Government that it is in a position to make adequate provision in schools, shall introduce a compulsory system of education only for boys between the ages of six and ten years.

(*c*) Such education shall not be free in areas where no education cess has been levied; but in areas where a special cess has been levied no fee shall be charged.

(*d*) The local authority is the education authority, but it may appoint a school committee for the whole area under its jurisdiction, or separate school committees for separate portions of the said area, to enforce the provisions of this

[1] Bihar & Orissa Act No I of 1919

Act respecting the attendance at school and the employment of children. If the local authority does not appoint a school committee, it shall exercise all the powers conferred and perform all the duties imposed by or under this Act upon a school committee so appointed.

(*e*) The Provincial Government may, however, prescribe the manner in which the school committee shall be constituted, the number of members and the period of office of members of the school committee its duties and powers, its relations with the local authority and with the prescribed educational authority of the province, and the circumstances in which separate school committees may be appointed for separate portions of an area.

(*f*) The Provincial Government may also exempt the boys of any class of persons or any community from the operation of this Act, or may direct the local authority to make such separate provision for the education of the children of such class of persons or such community as they deem fit.

(*g*) If the resources, including grants from local authority, are inadequate to meet the cost of primary education, the local authority may with the sanction of the Local Government impose an Education Cess.

(*h*) The education cess shall (i) in a Municipality be such percentage not exceeding thirty-three and a third of the maximum tax or rate which can be imposed upon owners or occupiers of property in the said area, as the local authority may fix, and shall be recoverable in the same manner as if it were such tax or rate, (ii) in a Union be such percentage not exceeding fifty of the assessment imposed under the Self-Government Act, and shall be recoverable in the manner as if it were such assessment.

In Bihar and Orissa the primary schools were very unevenly distributed. Prior to 1926, "there was no settled policy or line of action and schools were opened more or less haphazard at those places from which requests for new schools were received without regard to the needs of the district as a whole....Many localities had more than one school while others had none, and complaints were made by the residents of the latter that it was not fair to give no schools to them while the other localities had been provided with a number of schools."[1] Since then the policy regarding distribution of schools has changed. But even now the schools are unevenly distributed. The powers enjoyed, whether by district, local or union boards, were unfortunately not always exercised with due discretion. Some local bodies were reluctant to carry out Government's instruction that each upper primary school should contain two trained teachers and each lower primary school one. Recently

---

[1] Bihar & Orissa Quinquennial Review on Progress of Education (1922-27), page 60

however some of the district boards had been making efforts to combat stagnation of pupils in the lower classes. The Gaya District Board *imposed a fine on primary school teachers* of eight annas for each pupil who failed to pass the annual examination at the end of the course for Class I after two years' study. But this led to the removal from the rolls of the names of several such pupils.

The Bihar and Orissa Primary Education Act authorises the municipalities and union boards which bring into operation the provisions regarding compulsory education to levy an education cess. The amount of cess that can be levied in urban and rural areas has already been mentioned.[1] No fees can be charged in any recognised primary school in areas in which the education cess has been levied. "For purposes of receiving subsides from Government, district boards are divided into three classes: Class I comprising boards with a cess income of less than Rs. 150 per thousand of the population; Class II, those with an income of not more than Rs. 250 per thousand of the population, and Class III, the remainder. The grants are 2 annas per head for boards in Class I, 1½ annas for those in Class II and 1¼ annas for the rest. The rules for municipalities are calculated on two scales, one for those who have introduced

---

[1] Vide item (*h*) of the summary of the Act given on pages 297 and 298 of this book

compulsory education and one for these who have not. *For municipalities which have introduced compulsion,* the recurring grant admissible is limited to two-thirds of the cost of educating 10 per cent of the male population of the municipality as recorded at the previous census, at Rs. 8 a head, and the municipality is required to find from its own funds half as much as is paid by the Government. *For municipalities which have not introduced compulsion,* the recurring grant admissible is limited to the sum given in 1922-23, or half the cost of educating 5 per cent of the male population of the municipality as recorded at the previous census, at Rs. 8 a head, whichever is greater; and as a condition of any increase in the grant sanctioned for 1922-23, the municipality is required to find from its own funds as much as is paid by the Government and to spend on primary education not less than 5 per cent of its ordinary income."[1] The offer of government grants to local bodies in Bihar and Orissa at the rates specified above was not so liberal as the rates offered by the Governments of the Punjab and the United Provinces of Agra and Oudh to their respective local bodies. Hence the progress of compulsory primary education has been insignificant So far the provisions of the Bihar and Orissa Primary Education Act relating to com-

[1] Review of Growth of Education in British India by the Auxiliary Committee appointed by the Indian Statutory Commission (September, 1929), page 268.

pulsory primary education have been enforced only in 1 urban area and in 1 village of a rural area in Bihar, and in 1 urban area and 14 villages included in 1 rural area in Orissa.[1] It should be noted that Orissa was made into a separate province under the Government of India Act of 1935.

SECTION VII.—THE CENTRAL PROVINCES PRIMARY EDUCATION ACT

The Central Provinces Primary Education Act[2] was passed in May, 1920. The Act states that—

(*a*) It extends to the whole of the Central Provinces.

(*b*) The local authorities may with the previous sanction of the Local Government introduce compulsory primary education, free of charge, in their respective areas for all children of not less than six and not more than fourteen years of age; the Local Government shall determine the ages between which attendance of a child shall be compulsory and may vary such ages; the provisions shall, in the first instance, be with respect to boys residing in such areas; later on they may be made applicable to girls.

(*c*) The local authority shall prepare and maintain in the prescribed form a register of

---

[1] Quinquennial Review on the Progress of Education in India, 1932-37 (Government of India Publication, 1940), page 141.

[2] The Central Provinces Act No III of 1920

children liable to compulsory primary education in its local area, and revise the same periodically, and keep it open to *inspection by the public.*

(*d*) The local authorities are the educational authorities in their respective areas; but the Local Government may make rules for the purpose of carrying out the provisions of this Act, and in particular may (1) lay down instructions for the guidance of the local authority in prescribing days, hours and time or times for the attendance of a child at a primary school, (2) prescribe the conditions as to school accommodation, equipment and staff and as to financial provision which must be fulfilled by a local authority, (3) prescribe the proportions in which the cost of providing primary education under this Act shall be divided between the local authorities and the Local Government, and (4) prescribe or provide for the constitution of the school attendance authority.

It will be noticed from the above summary that the Central Provinces Primary Education Act of 1920 makes no provision for the levy of any education cess. Such a provision was not necessary for we have seen in Chapter IV that the local authorities in the Central Provinces had the power of levying an education cess even before the passing of the Primary Education Act. No fees can be levied in any area in which compulsion has been introduced. In such an area if there be recognised schools under private management then their loss of fee income is compensated by the local authorities by giving them additional grants. Not much progress in introducing compulsory primary education was made in the Central Provinces prior to 1930. The Director of Public Instruction stated that what was wanted in the responsible bodies was a change of outlook which would make itself manifest in the greater apprecia-tion of the necessity of entrusting, subject to their general control, the administration of their educational systems to skilled and responsible committees or officers. Up to 1930 compulsory primary education was introduced in only 90 rural areas and 13 urban areas. But in 1931 considerable progress was made and at the end of the year the scheme of compulsory primary education was working fairly satisfactorily in 344 villages and 22 urban areas in the Central Provinces.

In 1933, the Central Provinces Primary Education Act of 1920 was amended. The amended Act clearly lays down that in every area in which a notification regarding introduction of compulsory education is in force no fees shall be charged in respect of a child of the sex specified in the notification in any primary school managed by a local authority or by Government. Fees may however be charged or remitted in any primary school not maintained wholly out of provincial or local funds, *provided* that, if fees have been remitted, the local authority shall pay to the authorities of such school compensation for loss of income caused by such remission or such portion thereof as the Provincial Government direct. By the end of March, 1937 the scheme for compulsory primary education was operating in 27 urban areas and 508 villages included in 8 rural areas in Central Provinces and Berar.[1]

SECTION VIII.—THE ASSAM PRIMARY EDUCATION ACT

The Assam Primary Education Act[2] to provide facilities for introduction of compulsory primary education in the province of Assam was passed in 1926. The Act states that—

(*a*) It extends to the whole of Assam.

(*b*) Any local authority may resolve, by a majority of two-thirds of the members present, at a meeting specially convened for the purpose, to apply the section regarding introduction of compulsory education to whole or any part of the area within its jurisdiction or to children (of not less than six and not more than eleven years of age) of either sex or both sexes resident in the area within its jurisdiction with or without the exemption of any particular community or communities.

(*c*) The local authority shall submit to the Government for consideration the resolution as

---

[1] Quinquennial Review on the Progress of Education in India, 1932-37, page 141.

[2] Assam Act V of 1926.

published, the objection or objections, if any, received, and the modification or modifications, if any, decided on.

(*d*) The local authority shall at the same time submit to the Government a statement showing all particulars relating to the proposal, including details concerning the total existing expenditure incurred by the local authority and by the Government on primary education in the area in question, and the additional cost that the introduction of compulsory primary education will entail, and the manner in which the total cost of the scheme is to be met.

(*e*) The local authority of any area which resolves to introduce a scheme of compulsory primary education shall, without diminishing its current expenditure on primary education in that area, provide one-third of the additional cost and shall for this purpose ordinarily levy an education cess.

(*f*) In the event of the proposal being sanctioned, the Government shall provide to the local authority the remaining two-thirds of the additional cost of the scheme.

(*g*) If a local authority fails to submit a scheme for introducing compulsory primary education within a reasonable time, the Government may at any time call upon the local authority to submit the scheme: provided that when the Government propose to take action it shall lay the question before the Legislative Council. If however the Legislative Council by a majority of votes disapproves of the proposal then no action shall be taken by the Government.

(*h*) The Government may by notification make rules, which shall be laid before the Legislative Council, to carry out the purposes of the Act, and in particular prescribe the incidence of the education cess and the manner in which the education committee of the local authority shall be constituted and the education funds shall be maintained.

(*i*) No fees shall be charged from any pupil for tuition in any recognised primary school maintained or aided by the local authority.

(*j*) The children of necessitous guardians too poor to buy books and writing materials may, if the education committee so recommend, be provided with the use of necessary books and writing materials free of cost by the local authority.

(*k*) The local authority and the education committee concerned shall be responsible for the enforcement of the provisions of the Act and shall provide and maintain such school accommodation and equipment and shall employ such educational staff as the Director of Public Instruction may consider necessary.

Although the Assam Primary Education Act was passed in 1926, it has not yet been enforced in any area.

In the Primary Education Acts of all the provinces there are provisions for prosecuting the guardian in case of failure to cause the child to attend a recognised school. The penalties, usually fines, prescribed for such an offence, are different in different provinces. In all the Education Acts, except that of the Madras Presidency, penalties have also been prescribed for employing a child of school-going age. But the legislative measures (embodying the draft convention and recommendations of the International Labour Organisation of the League of Nations in the form in which they were specially modified for India) passed by the Government of India in 1922, amending the factory laws have put a stop to employment of children below twelve years of

CHAPTER VII

EDUCATION UNDER THE NEW CONSTITUTION —CONTROL, CURRICULUM AND SOME GENERAL REMARKS

SECTION I—THE CONTROL AND ADMINISTRATION OF PRIMARY EDUCATION IN DIFFERENT PROVINCES

With the introduction of constitutional reforms in 1921 (under the Government of India Act of 1919) some of the provincial subjects were classified as "transferred subjects" and were placed under the charge of Ministers responsible to the provincial legislative councils. Indian education was one such subject. A complete change in the administration of the provinces was subsequently made under the Government of India Act of 1935. All provincial subjects were transferred under the control of ministers responsible to the legislature and wide powers were conferred on the legislative bodies. The new Act came into operation on the 1st of April, 1937, and that date might be considered as the beginning of an era of provincial autonomy in India. Time is not come to give a narrative of the progress made, if any, in the field of primary education during the last four years, i.e., since the new ministers took charge of their offices in 1937. Moreover from December 1939, the reformed constitution ceased to function properly in seven[1] out of eleven provinces in British India. At present there are no ministers in charge of education and other subjects in these seven provinces and their respective Governors are carrying on the administration with the help of the departmental officers. Only in four provinces[2] the ministers are managing their respective departments. All the same it may be worthwhile recording the characteristics and diversities in regard to the administration of primary education in different provinces of India.

The administration and control of primary education involve many activities which may be classified under four heads:—

(*i*) The school site, building, playground and quipment; location and need; recognition of schools.

(*ii*) Staff—appointment, salary, increments, transfer, dismissal. Compulsion and attendance.

(*iii*) Curriculum; methods of teaching and inspection; general policy and aim.

(*iv*) Finance—grants.

Generally, the local authorities are primarily concerned with the activities under (*i*) and (*ii*) above; whilst Nos. (*iii*) and (*iv*) are usually the concern of the Provincial Education Department.

[1] The seven provinces are :—Bombay, Madras, Bihar, Orissa, The United Provinces, The Central Provinces and the North-West Frontier Province.

[2] The four provinces are :—Bengal, Assam, Sindh and the Punjab.

As long ago as 1882, the Government of India adopted as a general principle of policy that the object of local government is "to train the people in the management of their own local affairs and that political education of this sort must in the main take precedence of considerations of departmental efficiency; that local bodies should not be subjected to unnecessary control but should learn by making mistakes and profiting by them."[1] Since then a very considerable devolution of the management of primary schools upon municipalities and district boards has been effected. About 36 per cent of the total number of primary schools in British India are now managed by local bodies only 1·2 per cent by Government, about 55·8 per cent by private bodies which are in receipt of grants-in-aid from Government and local bodies and about 7 per cent by private bodies not receiving any grant from public funds. Excluding Bengal which has about 78 per cent of its primary schools controlled by private bodies, British India has nearly 50 per cent of its primary schools administered by municipalities and district boards.

In their resolution, dated the 21st February 1913, the Government of India again asserted that the support and enthusiasm of local bodies in the expansion and improvement of primary education must be utilised to the full. The authors of the

[1] The 10th Quinquennial Review on Education in India, page 41.

Report on Indian Constitutional Reforms, 1918, recognised the defects of the system of primary education, the control of which was even then practically in the hands of local bodies. But they declared that "there should be as far as possible complete popular control in local bodies and largest possible independence for them of outside control" and that "the accepted policy must be to allow the boards to profit by their own mistakes." The same policy has been followed even after the Legislatures in the provinces have been demo-crtised by the passing of the Government of India Acts of 1919 and 1935.

In most provinces, under Local or Self-Government or similar Acts, the District Boards, Municipalities, District School Boards or other statutory bodies exercise almost full control over primary and vernacular education in their respective areas. These Acts have removed from the Provincial Governments and their officers many powers which they formerly exercised. In this connection some provinces have gone much further than others, for example, the Bombay Government retain very few powers indeed, whilst the Government of the North-West Frontier Province indirectly retain control by nominating members to the District Board, the chairman of which is invariably the Deputy Commissioner of the District.

The following paragraphs summarize the powers retained by the Provincial Governments in regard to the administration of primary education.

(A) *The Bengal Presidency.*

(1) In Bengal, primary education is administered in urban areas partly by Government and partly by Municipalities, and in 16 districts of rural areas by District School Boards established under the Bengal (Rural) Primary Education Act, 1930, and in other districts by District Boards. The School Boards are constituted in accordance with the rules prescribed by Government. The Education Committee of the District Board is also formed in accordance with the rules prescribed by Government.

(2) The Government may appoint any persn to the District School Board, or to the Central Primary Education Committee formed under the provisions of the Bengal (Rural) Primary Education Act of 1930, if the electional bodies fail to elect a person by a fixed date.

(3) The Government may refer any matter to the Central Primary Education Committee for its opinion.

(4) The Government may remove a President, Vice-President, or member of the District School Board under certain conditions, and may declare that such person or persons shall not be eligible for re-appointment or re-election for a fixed period.

(5) The Government may fix a period for the performance of a duty by a Board or its President in respect of which they have made a default.

(6) If the duty is not performed within the

fixed period, Government may appoint any person to do so, and the cost shall be borne by the Board.

(7) The Government may pass such orders as they like in respect of the budget of the Board which must be submitted to Government before a prescribed date.

(8) The accounts of the Board shall be audited by an auditor appointed by the Government.

(9) The Government may disband the Board if it is not functioning properly.

(10) The Government may make rules in respect of certain matters, the following among which are important:—

(*a*) the subjects and standards, and the circumstances in which such subjects may vary in different schools,

(*b*) the appointment of the staff of officers and servants of the Committee and the Board, and the pay and allowances of such staff,

(*c*) the appointment of a President of the Committee and the method of conducting business of the Committee, and

(*d*) the manner of opening additional primary schools.

(B) *The Madras Presidency.*

(1) In Madras Presidency, primary education is administered by District Educational Councils elected by local bodies.

(2) The Government may remove the President, Vice-President or members of a District Educational Council under certain conditions.

(3) The Government may suspend, modify or cancel any resolution or order passed by the District Educational Council.

(4) The Government may fix a period within which the District Educational Council or its President must perform a duty in respect of which they have made a default.

(5) The Government may disband a District Educational Council if it is not properly performing its duties under the Madras Elementary Education Act, 1920.

(5) The Government may pass such orders as they like in respect of the budget of the District Educational Council which must be submitted to them before a prescribed date.

(7) The Government may appoint an audit officer to audit the accounts of the council which must carry out the orders issued by the Government on the audit report.

(8) The Government may refuse recognition or grants-in-aid if schools are not accessible to all classes of population, and public are not actually admitted into them irrespective of caste or community.

(C) *The Bombay Presidency and Sindh.*

(1) In Bombay Presidency, both in urban and rural areas, primary education is administered by

School Boards elected by Local Authorities. Government's control of primary education is limited to seeing that the Local Authorities carry out their duties in accordance with the provisions of the Primary Education Acts and to checking the accounts of the Local Authorities. Although Sindh has been made into a new province under the Government of India Act of 1935, it follows the provisions of the Bombay Primary Education Acts. The powers retained by the two provincial governments are identical.

(2) The sanction of the Government is necessary to alter the scales of pay, etc., of teachers whom a local authority has taken over for service under it from the Education Department of the Government.

(3) The sanction of the Government is necessary to fix the pay, powers and duties of the chief executive officer of a school board.

(4) A local authority shall submit a scheme for compulsory primary education to Government, which may sanction it with or without modification.

(5) The Government may call for an explanation for any misuse or misapplication of the educational fund of any local authority.

(6) The subjects, curricula, books and standards of teaching cannot be altered without the sanction of the Government.

(7) Only the Government can exempt children from the operation of compulsion.

(8) If a sanctioned scheme of compulsion has not been brought into operation by a local authority, the Government may empower any person to do so and the cost thereof shall be borne by the local authority.

(9) The Government may make rules in respect of certain matters among which the following are important:—

(*a*) Physical and moral training of children.

(*b*) Pay and terms of employment of the teaching, inspecting and supervising staff.

(*c*) Curriculum.

(*d*) Powers and duties of local authorities.

(10) In extreme cases, the Government have power to reduce or withhold grant under certain conditions.

(D) *The Punjab.*

(1) Primary education in the Punjab is administered in urban areas by Municipal Committees and in rural areas by District Boards.

(2) The Government may sanction or reject the proposals of a local authority regarding compulsory primary education.

(3) A local authority shall obey the rules made by the Government in imposing additional taxation towards meeting the cost of compulsion.

(4) The Government may exempt particular classes or communities from the operation of compulsion.

(5) The Government may direct that the additional taxation shall be reduced or discontinued from a fixed date.

(6) The sanction of the Government is necessay to make alteration in the compulsory age limits.

(7) The previous sanction of the Government is necessary to make bye-laws.

(8) The local authority shall provide and maintain such school accommodation and equipment, and shall employ such educational staff as the Director of Public Instruction may consider necessary.

(9) The Government may make rules for carrying out the provisions of the Punjab Primary Education Act, 1919.

(10) The previous sanction of the Government is necessary to fix or levy school fees.

(11) The Deputy Commissioner is the Chairman of the District Board except in three districts.

(12) The District Board Act provides for the delegation of powers to the District Inspector of Schools. But the Boards are becoming more and more reluctant to delegate their powers.

(E) *The United Provinces.*

(1) In the United Provinces, primary education is administered in urban areas by municipal boards and in rural areas by specially elected education committees of district boards. The Government have little control under the consti-

tution of the Board in matters relating to primary education except in regard to the following.

(2) The Government may exempt any particular class of community from the operation of the United Provinces Primary Education Act, 1926.

(3) In case of default by a Board in its duties, the Government may cancel the notification regarding compulsory primary education.

(4) The Government may make rules affecting the range of instruction.

(5) No member of a Board can get any remuneration except with the sanction of the Government.

(6) The Government may remove from a Board or Education Committee any member or its Chairman under certain conditions.

(7) If a Board fails to elect its own chairman, the Government shall nominate a chairman.

(8) The Government may authorize the Board to appoint its secretary and any of the officers or servants required to be appointed. If the Board fails to do so within the prescribed period, the Government may appoint any person, and fix his salary, etc.

(9) The sanction of the Government is necessary to dismiss or punish the Secretary of the Board.

(10) The Government shall be the appealing authorities against the orders of dismissal in the case of certain officers.

(11) The Government may pass any orders on the budget of the Board submitted to them.

(12) The Government may call upon a Board to submit a scheme of compulsory primary education within a specified time. If the Board does not do so, the Government may appoint any person for the purpose, the Board bearing the whole cost of the scheme.

(13) The Government may dissolve the Board or suspend it under certain conditions.

(14) The Government shall make rules for the appointment of persons, not members of the Board, to education committees of the Board.

(F) *The Provinces of Bihar and Orissa.*

(1) In both Bihar and Orissa, primary education is administered by Municial Board or Council in urban areas and by District Boards and subsidiary local boards in rural areas. The Government are not represented on the Boards. Although Orissa has been separated from Bihar and made into a new province under the Government of India Act of 1935, it follows the provisions of the Bihar and Orissa Primary Education Act of 1919. The powers retained by the two provincial governments are identical.

(2) The Government may exempt a child of any class or community from the operation of the Bihar and Orissa Primary Education Act, 1919.

(3) A local authority can impose an Educa-

tion Cess with the sanction of the Government only.

(4) The Government may take such action as they like if a local authority makes default in any of the requirements of the Bihar and Orissa Primary Education Act.

(5) The Government may prescribe any rules they like regarding the constitution, etc., of a school committee.

(6) The Government may remove any member of a District Board, Local Board or Union Committee under certain conditions.

(7) A local authority shall submit its budget to the Government which may return it to the local authority for necessary changes.

(8) If any municipality makes default in the exercise of powers or performance of its duties conferred on it, the Government may appoint any officer to do such duties.

(G) *The Central Provinces.*

(1) In the Central Provinces and Berar, primary education for boys is administered almost entirely either by Local bodies or by Cantonment Boards, but *primary education for girls is administered entirely by Government.* But a few areas have independent boards which manage primary education.

(2) The chairman of an Independent Board is generally the Deputy Commissioner or his official nominee.

(3) The Government exercise only a general supervisory and financial control. It has no control in the actual commission of the local bodies.

(4) The Government retain the right of recognition and inspection of schools and examinations for the Primary Certificate.

(5) A Local Authority, if called upon by the Government, shall submit a scheme of compulsory primary education, which they may sanction, refuse to sanction or return it to the local authority for further consideration.

(6) If a Local Authority, when called upon to do so, fails to prepare a scheme, or does not bring into operation any sanctioned scheme, the Government may appoint any person to do so and the expense thereof shall be borne by the Local Authority.

(7) The Government may exempt any particular class or community from the operation of the Central Provinces Primary Education Act.

(8) The Government may make rules for the purpose of carrying out the provisions of the Central Provinces Primary Education Act.

(9) The previous sanction of the Government is necessary to make bye-laws prescribing the powers and procedure of the school attendance authority.

(10) The previous sanction of the Government is necessary to impose an additional cess for the maintenance of schools.

(H) *The Province of Assam.*

(1) In Assam, primary education is administered by Municipal Boards in urban areas and by District Boards in rural areas. The constitution of the District and Municipal Boards must have the approval of the Divisional Commissioner, and both the Deputy Commissioner and the Commissioner exercise control over the Boards.

(2) The Government indirectly exercise some control over the Boards as in a few cases, the Deputy Commissioner or the Sub-divisional Officer concerned is appointed as chairman of the Board.

(3) In all educational matters the Boards shall on all occasions take into consideration the advice given by the Director of Public Instruction and the Inspectors of Schools.

(4) In matters of disagreement between the Director of Public Instruction and the Board, the decision of the Government shall be final.

(5) The Boards cannot reduce the number of primary schools without previously ascertaining and considering the opinion of the Divisional Inspector of Schools.

(6) The budget estimates of the Boards are required to be passed by the Government and the accounts of the Boards are audited by the Government audit staff.

(I) *The North-West Frontier Province.*

(1) In the North-West Frontier Province, primary education in urban areas is administered

by the Municipal Committees and in rural areas, theoretically by the District Boards and actually by the Government. The control has never been surrendered to the District Boards.

(2) The Deputy Commissioners are the ex-officio Presidents of the District Boards and the Municipal Committees. The Government exercise control by nominating a high proportion of the members of the Boards and Committees.

(4) The appointments, transfers, etc., of all primary school teachers in rural areas are made by officers of the Government.

(4) The expenditure on primary education under the District Boards is entirely controlled by the Government.

Section II.—The Curriculum of Studies and Examination, The Medium of Instruction, and the Wardha Scheme of Education.

(A) *Curriculum of Studies.*

The curriculum of studies in primary schools and the detailed syllabuses of the subjects taught vary in different provinces. In the following paragraphs an attempt has been made to show how widely they vary in some of the important provinces in India.

Assam.

Reading, Writing, Arithmetic, General knowledge (including Hygiene, Sanitation and Temperance) and any four of the following subjects, *viz.*, *Geography, History, Drawing, Hand Work (including sewing, knitting, spinning and weaving)*, Physical Exercise and any other subjects desired by the local authority and approved by the Education Department may be taught. The four compulsory subjects and any four of the selective subjects constitute the *full course* for primary schools. But some schools with the approval of the Inspector of Schools may offer instruction in a second language, e.g., English, Urdu or Hindi or a vocational subject. The time required for the teaching of the extra subjects (entirely optional) must be found by an extension of the ordinary school day.

Bombay.

In the elementary stage Reading, Writing and Aritmmetic form the basis of the course of instruction. In addition Drawing and some form of Hand Work, and Nature Study and Gardening are included. A beginning is also made in Geography and History. In the higher elementary stage, the same subjects are continued.

In 1935, the Municipal Corporation of Bombay submitted a proposal to Government for reduction of the curriculum of studies of primary schools in Bombay from five years to four years. The Government of Bombay refused to accede to the request of the Municipal Corporation. The reasons given by the Secretary to the Government of Bombay were as follows:—

(*i*) The Government consider that there are serious objections to a primary course being reduced to four years and that if literacy is to become a permanent possession of the child, a course of at least five years is essential.

(*ii*) It may be possible for children of advanced communities to complete the primary course in a shorter time, but the course prescribed is meant for the average child and it will not be in the interests of the intermediate and backward classes to shorten it.

(*iii*) The revised curriculum limits the work in primary schools to the teaching of Reading, Writing and Arithmetic only, and omits a number of subjects such as nature-study, drawing, handwork and sewing. There are strong objections to the omission of these subjects from the course. The three R's are only a means to an end. To attempt nothing more than reading, writing and reckoning would create a dislike in the mind of the child for other work which would be difficult to combat in later years.

(*iv*) The revised course of studies does not appear to have been correlated with the secondary course and would, if adopted, make it difficult for pupils passing Class IV to continue their studies in secondary schools.

Bengal.

The following subjects are taught in the Infant Class—Reading, Writing, Arithmetic, Observation

Lessons, Drawing and Physical Drill. In Class I—Reading, Writing, Arithmetic, Hygiene and Observation lessons for boys or Hygiene and Domestic Economy for girls, Physical Drill for boys or Needle work for girls, Manual work for boys and Drawing for boys and girls. In Class II—the same subjects as in Class I and in addition Geography is introduced. In Classes III and IV—Reading, Writing, Arithmetic, History, Geography, Hygiene for boys or Hygiene and Domestic Economy for girls, Drill for boys or Needlework for girls, Nature Study based on school gardening for rural schools or Elementary Science for urban schools, Manual work for boys, Mahajani Account, Drawing and English.

In Bengal the syllabus in each of the subjects is also heavy. The History syllabus is particularly heavy. The primary boys are expected to finish practically the whole of Indian History in the course of two years, viz., in Classes III and IV. No wonder then that there is a heavy falling off in enrolment at the end of Class III.

The above course extending over five years is taught in primary schools located in municipal areas and in district board areas where the School Boards have not been set up under the Bengal Rural Primary Education Act. It has already been mentioned in Section I of Chapter VI that in March 1936, the Government of Bengal appointed a committee to consider the curricula suitable to the needs of primary schools and maktabs and the question of religious instruction in those institutions. The Committee decided at an early stage that the primary school course should extend over a period of five years and on that assumption the detailed syllabuses were drawn up. At a later stage, however, the difficulties of financing a scheme of a five years' primary course were fully discussed, and with a view to avoid financial difficulties the Committee, though feeling that a five years' course was educationally very desirable, resolved to adopt a four years' course.

The question of the inclusion of History in the primary course evoked long discussions in the Committee, and it was ultimately decided that the subject would be treated mainly in the form of historical tales and pages not exceeding one-third of the total number of pages of the Vernacular Reader, in the top two classes, should be devoted to such tales.

As regards teaching of English in primary schools, the Committee were of opinion that English should not be taught in primary schools or in primary departments of secondary schools (high and middle). If, however, Government did not agree to abolish the teaching of English in the primary department of secondary schools, it should be taught as an additional subject in the top two classes of primary schools. It was, however, felt that the teaching of English in primary schools could only be allowed in those schools where qualified teachers were available.

In respect of religious instruction, there was general agreement that religious instruction should be provided in the curricula for primary schools. There should, however, be no examination in the subject.

The Committee did not feel it necessary to make any differentiation between the curricula for boys' and girls' schools respectively, nor was it necessary, according to them, to make any distinction between the rural and urban schools so far as primary curricula were concerned. The Committee, however, suggested different types of Handwork and Physical Exercises for boys and girls in primary schools.

The recommendations of the Committee were carefully considered by the Government of Bengal in the Ministry of Education* and in their Resolution of March 1937, they generally approved of them and ordered—

* From the middle of 1934 till the end of March 1937, the Hon'ble Mr. (now Sir) Muhammad Azizul Huque was the Minister of Education Bengal. The Government Resolutions of 1935 and 1937 were issued during his tenure of office. Since the 1st of April 1937, the Hon'ble Chief Minister, Mr. A. K. Fazlul Huq, himself has been in charge of the education portfolio of the Government of Bengal.

In this connection it should be mentioned that with the levy of the education cess by some of the District School Boards there has been a progressive increase in the total amount spent by the Government of Bengal from Provincial Revenues (i) as grants to Local Bodies for primary education for boys and girls and (ii) as direct grants to non-Government primary schools. During 1930-40 the total grants for the above purposes from the provincial revenues were Rs. 33,00,000 and during 1940-41 the grants according to the revised budget estimate amounted to Rs. 41,00,000. The budget for 1941-42 provides for an expenditure of Rs. 49,00,000.

(*i*) that a four years' course should be adopted in view of the difficulty of financing a scheme involving a five years' course;

(*ii*) that religious instruction should be provided in the curricula of primary schools;

(*iii*) that the following subjects should be compulsorily taught:—

Examination subjects—

(1) Vernacular Reading and Writing.

(2) Arithmetic.

(3) Geography and Rural Civics.

(4) Elements of Science.

Non-examination subjects—

(1) Games and Physical Exercises.

(2) Handwork, *or* work in farms or in the school garden.

(3) Religious instruction.

(*iv*) that some of the schools may be allowed to teach English on their satisfying certain conditions: when taken up English should be treated as an examination subject;

(*v*) that a departmental public examination should be held at the end of the four years of the primary course: this examination should be open to boys and girls;

(*vi*) that scholarships should be awarded on the results of the Primary Final Examination, provided that marks obtained in English would not be taken into account for this purpose.

The curricula for a four years' course as approved by Government in 1937, at first came into operation in 1940 in schools under the District School Board of Mymensingh and subsequently in schools in such other districts as had levied the primary education cess. By the end of the year 1941-42, the education cess will have been levied in more than half the number of districts in Bengal. The new curricula will also be operative in all these districts.

The Punjab.

In the Punjab, as has already been mentioned, the primary school has only four classes. The following subjects are taught in them:—In Classes I and II—Reading, Writing, Arithmetic, Games and Drill; in Classes III and IV—Reading, Writing, Composition, Arithmetic, Geography, Drawing, Gardeneing, Games and Drill.

The United Provinces of Agra and Oudh.

The following subjects are taught:—In the Infant Class and Class I—Reading, Writing, Arithmetic, Object lessons, Drawing and Physical Exercises. In Class II—the same subjects as in the two previous classes; but Geography is introduced for the first time in this class. In Classes III and IV—Reading, Writing, Grammar, Arithmetic, Geography, Object lessons, Drawing and Physical exercises.

(B) *The Primary Final Examinations.*

In Bengal a public examination called the Primary Final Examination is held at the end of Class IV of primary schools and maktabs for boys. The examination is held in the following subjects:—*Compulsory Subjects*—(1) Vernacular, (2) Writing, (3) Arithmetic, (4) Geography, (5) History, and (6) Hygiene. In addition to these subjects the primary school boys are examined in *any two* of the following subjects—(7) Drawing, (8) Manual Work, (9) Nature Study, (10) English, and (11) Mahajani and Zamindari accounts. The maktab boys are examined in the first five subjects mentioned above and in addition are examined in (6) Urdu and Ritual of Islam and in *any two* of the following subjects—(7) Hygiene, (8) Manual Work, (9) English, and (10) Mahajani and Zamindari Accounts. The Primary (Maktab) Final Examination in Bengal is a stiff test for admission into the secondary (middle and high schools.

The Primary Final Examination under the new scheme of studies for a four years' course has not yet been held. But it has been decided that a departmental public examination, open to boys and girls, shall be held in the following subjects:—

(1) Vernacular Reading and Writing.
(2) Arithmetic.
(3) Geography and Rural Civis.
(4) Elements of Science.

(5) English (where it is taught as an optional subject).

The examination under the new scheme is intended for those pupils who are reading in primary schools in such districts as have levied the primary education cess.

It has already been mentioned that in the Punjab the primary course covers a period of four years. The old five years' course was overburdened with such subjects as Nature Study, Kindergarten, Manual Training, Drawing, History, Geography, etc., and resulted in a decreased efficiency in the three R's. It frustrated the main object of the primary course which was to enable boys to carry on ordinary correspondence and to keep accounts. The scheme of studies was therefore revised to make it suited to the four-class school.

It has also been mentioned that in Bengal a primary final examination is held by the Education Department at the end of the Class IV. In the Punjab and in the United Provinces of Agra and Oudh no such public examination is held. In the Punjab, an examination principally in the three R's is conducted by the District Inspectors and Assistant District Inspectors on completion by the boys of their primary course. Besides this examination by the Inspecting officers, a special scholarship examination is held for the award of scholarships to meritorious boys. A departmental examination is held at the end of the Upper

Middle Course and scholarships are awarded on the results of this examination.

In the United Provinces the primary examination is not conducted by the Inspector of the District. It is conducted by the headmaster of the primary school concerned except in one-teacher schools where the Deputy or Sub-deputy Inspector of Schools holds it. In order to secure uniformity the Deputy Inspector of the district arranges each year for a systematic inquiry into the standard of the examination. Head-masters who are found not to maintain a satisfactory standard are placed on a black list of headmasters whose schools are then examined by the district inspecting staff for such period as the Deputy Inspector considers necessary. Each year the Deputy Inspector is expected to submit a special report to the Divisional Inspector on the result of his inquiry. The system of examination in the United Provinces has added to the dignity and authority of the primary school head master.

(C) *The Medium of Instruction.*

Since 1883 primary education in India has been recognised as the instruction of the masses through the vernacular dialects of the country in such subjects as will fit them for their position in life. In such schools the problem of the medium of instruction does not arise now. But for years since 1835, when Macaulay penned his famous minute, the teaching of vernaculars was relegated to a very low place. From 1835 to 1854 the vernacular teaching was almost completely lost sight of in secondary schools, and even occasionally was banished from primary schools. It was neither the aim nor desire of the great Despatch of 1854 to substitute the English language for the vernacular languages of India. The intention of the Despatch was that English and the vernaculars together should be the media for the diffusion of European knowledge. Though it desired to cultivate a bilingual system it asked that the vernacular schools should gradually be raised to the level of English schools. When the three universities at Calcutta, Bombay and Madras were opened in 1857 the intention of the authors of the Despatch was lost sight of, and English became the sole medium of instruction not only in the colleges but also in secondary schools. Even in the higher forms of elementary schools English began to be taught. The Universities Commission of 1902 discouraged the use of English as a medium, and even the study of the language, till a boy could be expected to understand what he was being taught in that language. "The line of division between the use of the vernacular and of English as a medium of instruction would, broadly speaking, be drawn at a minimum age of thirteen."[1] Moreover the Government of India Resolution of 1913 on the

[1] Resolution on the Indian Educational Policy of 1904.

Educational Policy states that "there is much evidence to the effect that scholars who have been through a complete vernacular course are exceptionally efficient mentally." Hence on the face of such pronouncements no question arises as to what shall be the medium of instruction in primary schools if we consider eleven years as the upper limit of elementary school age. It must be the mother tongue.

Now the question is whether English should be taught as a second language in the primary schools, and if so, at what stage. When it is said that primary education is education in the vernacular, it must be made clear that this statement does not apply to such education when imparted in the primary stages of secondary schools. And in all the provinces except Bombay most of the secondary schools have primary classes attached to them, and take in pupils at the age of six and even at five. English is taught in some of these primary classes; sometimes it is also used as a medium of instruction in History, Geography, etc. Besides these about two per cent of the pupils of both sexes studying in the recognized primary schools learn English. Two-thirds of these English learners in primary schools are to be found in the Madras Presidency. No English is taught in primary schools in the Bombay presidency. Hence the remaining one-third is distributed all over Northern India and the number of students in the primary schools keen on learning

English is increasing every year. No English need however be taught in primary schools to pupils below ten years of age. If we consider eleven years as the upper limit of primary school age, only in the two highest classes some English may be taught as an optional subject. With the introduction of compulsory primary education a number of students of primary schools might be expected to prosecute their studies in secondary schools. Such students should be asked and encouraged to take up English in the two highe classes in the primary schools. To allow a pri-mary school boy to take full advantage of education provided in a secondary school immediately on entering it on completion of 10 or 11 years of age, it is desirable that those secondary schools which have primary classes attached to them must give up teaching English in such classes. As a matter of fact the teaching of English in the lower forms of secondary schools is slowly being given up. Of late this has received a great stimulus since the publication of the Report of the Calcutta University Commission (1917-19). The Commission recommended that English should be used in high schools only in the teaching of English and of Mathematics in the four highest classes.[1] Assuming that a pupil matriculates at the age of 15, he can safely

[1] Report of the Calcutta University Commission (1917-19), Vol. V, page 33.

begin learning in English at the age of ten.[1] The Commission further recommended that at the Matriculation or High School Examination English should be compulsory medium only for English and Mathematics. The other subjects should be examined in the vernaculars. Up till now the medium of examination, even at the Matriculation stage, for all subjects in several of the Indian Universities has been English. But Calcutta, Patna and a few of the other Universities have already started conducting their Matriculation Examination through the medium of the major Indian languages. It is hoped that the other universities will also do so in the near future. When this is carried out in all the Indian Universities the teaching of English in secondary schools should begin at the age of ten, i.e. from Class V. Therefore, those pupils who will join secondary schools, after finishing their course in the primary, will be under no disadvantage in following the courses there.

(D) *The Wardha Scheme of Education.*

The curricula of studies in primary schools of some of the important provinces have been given in paragraphs under (A) of Section II. It would be worthwhile noting at this stage the salient features of the Basic National Education Scheme, commonly known as the Wardha Scheme

[1] Class V of a secondary school.

of Education. The idea behind the scheme was originally propounded by Mahatma Gandhi in a series of articles in "Harijan," during the months of July, August and September 1937. His proposals caused considerable controversy in the country. In connection with the silver jubilee celebration of the Navabharat Vidyalaya its managers conceived the idea of calling a small conference of nationally minded educationists to discuss the plan of education which Mahatma Gandhi had been endeavouring to propound in the columns of "Harijan". Gandhiji approved of the proposal to hold a National Education Conference at Wardha on the 22nd and 23rd October 1937, and agreed to preside over it.

The agenda for the Conference was prepared by Gandhiji himself and consisted among others of a consideration of the following propositions:—

1. "The present system of education does not meet the requirements of the country in any shape or form. English, having been made the medium of instruction in all the higher branches of learning, has created a permanent bar between the highly educated few and the uneducated many. It has prevented knowledge from percolating to the masses. The excessive importance given to English has cast upon the educated class a burden which has maimed them mentally for life and made them strangers in their own land. Absence of vocational training has made the educated class almost unfit for productive work and harmed them physically.

Money spent on primary education is a waste of expenditure inasmuch as what little is taught is soon forgotten and has little or no value in terms of the villages or cities. Such advantage as is gained by the existing system of education is not gained by the chief taxpayer, his children getting the least."

2. "The course of primary education should be extended at least to seven years and should include the general knowledge gained up to the matriculation standard less English and plus a substantial vocation."

3. (*a*) "For the all-round development of boys and girls all training should so far as possible be given through a profit-yielding vocation. In other words vocations should serve a double purpose—to enable the pupil to pay for his tuition through the products of his labour and at the same time to develop the whole man or woman in him or her through the vocation learnt at school."

(*b*) Land, buildings and equipment are not intended to be covered by the proceeds of the pupil's labour."

(*c*) All the processes of cotton, wool and silk commencing from gathering, cleaning, ginning (in the case of cotton), carding, spinning, dyeing, sizing, warpmaking, double twisting, designing and weaving, embroidery, tailoring, paper making, *gur* making are undoubted occupations that can easily be learnt and handled without much capital outlay."

(*d*) This primary education should equip

boys and girls to earn their bread by the State guaranteeing employment in the vocations learnt or by buying their manufactures at prices fixed by the State."[1]

The conference was attended by some select educationists from all over India, as well as by all the Ministers for education in the seven Congress Provinces. After the first day's proceedings the Conference converted itself into a committee under the chairmanship of Dr. Zakir Hussain, Principal, Jamia Milia, Delhi, to express its opinion on the propositions originally formulated by Gandhiji. On the second day (23rd October 1937) the Conference met again when Dr. Zakir Hussain submitted the following four resolutions for its consideration:—

"(1) That in the opinion of this Conference free and compulsory education be provided for seven years on a nation-wide scale."

"(2) That the medium of instruction be the mother tongue."

"(3) That the Conference endorses the proposal made by Mahatma Gandhi that the process of education throughout this period should centre round some form of manual and productive work, and that all the other abilities to be developed or training to be given should, as far as possible, be integrally related to the central handicraft

[1] *Vide* Harijan, 2nd October 1937. The items relating to higher education have not been quoted as they are outside the scope of this book.

chosen with due regard to the environment of the child."

"(4) That the Conference expects that this system of education will be gradually able to cover the remuneration of the teachers."[1]

After some discussion the resolutions were passed. Thereafter a Committee composed of ten persons with Dr. Zakir Hussain as President and Mr. E. W. Aryanayakam as Convener, was appointed to prepare a curriculum of studies and detailed syllabus on each subject on the basis of the above resolutions. The report of the Committee was to be submitted to the Chairman of the Conference within a month.[2]

The Committee submitted two reports to Gandhiji. The first report submitted in December 1937, contained (i) an exposition of the scheme as outlined in the four resolutions of the Conference, (ii) a detailed plan of a course of studies for seven years, (iii) two courses of training for teachers—a complete course of three years and a short course of one year and (iv) proposals regarding administration, supervision and examination. The second report was submitted in April 1938, and contained an elaborate exposition of the syllabuses in different subjects and of the method of correlating these subjects with the basic craft taught to the pupils. Further the

---

[1] *Vide* Proceedings of the Conference published in Harijan, 30th October 1937.

[2] *Ibid.*

second report attempted to meet the criticisms which were levelled against the scheme outlined in the first report.

The main principles of the new scheme may be summed up as follows[1] :—

(1) Education up to a particular minimum standard should be universal for all citizens, men and women. It may not be compulsory to begin with, but as facilities are available it is to be compulsory. The universal minimum is therefore called the Basic National Education.

(2) The courses of this education is to run for seven years, beginning from the age of seven.

(3) Basic National Education does not concern itself, for the present, with the pre-school stage or the post-basic stage.

(4) Basic National Education must be imparted through the mother-tongue.

(5) In its method it must be woven round some art or handicraft. All intellectual instruction must be imparted through the instrumentality of the craft chosen.

(6) The craft chosen must be learnt systematically and scientifically with a view to efficiency and practical results.* It must not be learnt

[1] *Vide*—J. B. Kripalini—"The Latest Fad (Basic Education')', pp. 72 and 73.

* Gandhiji's own views are quoted below from Harijan (11-9-37). "Manual work will have to be the centre of the whole thing. I am told that Messrs Abbott and Wood recognise the value of manual work as an important part of rural education. But I do not suppose they place on manual work the kind of emphasis I place. The

merely as a means either for intellectual work or for economic self-sufficiency. It must be both a means and an end.

(7) The product of the craft must be economically paying.

(8) Efforts should be made to see that the money value of the work done covers the pay of the teacher.

(9) The State should provide the rest of the expenses, of school buildings, furniture, books, maps and the whole of the apparatus including tools, etc. for the craft taught.

(10) The State should undertake to utilise the produce of the craft by which it may meet its own requirements or those of the local bodies where the school is established. For any excess of goods produced the State should provide marketing facilities.

(11) The proper training of teachers is the most important condition for the success of the scheme. It is essential that teachers should have some training in formulating projects and schemes of correlated studies, and thus link up life, learning and activity. Since they are to teach not only certain academic subjects, but also crafts, their training should include a reasonably thorough

development of the mind should come through manual training. The manual training will not consist in producing articles for a school museum or toys which have no value. It should produce marketable articles."

mastery of the processes and technique of certain basic crafts.

(12) The object of the training to be given to the teachers should be not to produce academically perfect scholars, but to produce skilled, intelligent, educated craftsman with the right mental orientation who should be desirous of serving the community and anxious to help the coming generation to realise and understand the standard of values implicit in this educational scheme.

The main outlines of the Seven Years' Course of Basic Education as given in the Committee's first report submitted to the President, National Education Conference, on the 2nd December 1937, and published in the Harijan of December 11, 1937, are quoted below *in extenso* for the purpose of understanding the scheme.

I. *The Basic Craft.*

Such reasonable skill should be attained in the handicraft chosen, as would enable the pupil to pursue it as an occupation after finishing his full course. The following may be chosen as basic crafts in various schools:—(*a*) Spinning and weaving. (*b*) Carpentry. (*c*) Agriculture. (*d*) Fruit and vegetable gardening. (*e*) Leather work. (*f*) Any other craft for which local and geographical conditions are favourable.

Even where an industry other than spinning and weaving or agriculture is the basic craft, the pupils will be expected to attain a minimum knowledge of carding and spinning with takli, and a practical acquaintance of easy agricultural work in the local area.

II. *Mother Tongue.*

The proper teaching of the mother tongue is the foundation of all education. Without the capacity to speak effectively and to read and write correctly and lucidly, no one can develop precision of thought or clarity of ideas. Moreover, it is a means of introducing the child to the rich heritage of his people's ideas, emotions and aspirations, and can therefore be made a valuable means of social education, whilst also instilling right ethical and values. Also it is a natural outlet for the expression of the child's aesthetic sense and appreciation, and if the proper approach is adopted, the study of literature becomes a source of joy and creative appreciation. More specifically, by the end of the seven years' course, the following objectives should be achieved:—

(*i*) The capacity to converse freely, naturally and confidently about the objects, people, and happenings within the child's environment.

(*ii*) The above capacity should gradually develop into the capacity to speak lucidly, coherently and relevantly on any given topic of every day interest.

(*iii*) The capacity to read silently, intelligently and with speed, written passages of average difficulty. (This capacity should be developed at least to such an extent that the student may read news papers and magazines of every day interest.)

(*iv*) The capacity to read aloud—clearly, expressively and with enjoyment—both prose and poetry. (The student should be able to discard the usual lifeless, monotonous and bored style of reading.)

(*v*) The capacity to use the list of contents and the index and to consult dictionaries and reference books, and generally to utilise the library as a source of information and enjoyment.

(*vi*) The capacity to write legibly, correctly, and with reasonable speed.

(*vii*) The capacity to describe in writing, in a simple and clear style, everyday happenings and occurrences; and the capacity to write personal letters and business communications of a simple kind.

(*viii*) An acquaintance with, and interest in, the writings of standard authors, through a study of their writings or extracts from them.

III. *Mathematics.*

The objective is to develop in the pupil the capacity to solve speedily the ordinary number and geometrical problems arising in connection with his craft and with his home and community life. Pupils should also gain a knowledge of business practice and book-keeping. The above objectives can be attained by a knowledge of and adequate practice in the four simple rules: the four compound rules: fractions: decimals: the rule of three: the use of the unitary method: interest; elements of mensuration: practical geometry: the rudiments of book-keeping.

The teaching should not be confined merely to the facts and operations of number. It should be closely co-ordinated with life situations arising out of the basic handicraft and out of the great variety of actual problems in the life of the school and the community. Measurements of quantities and values in these connections would supply ample opportunity for the development of the reasoning capacities of the pupils.

IV. *Social Studies.*

The objectives are:

(*i*) To develop a broad human interest in the progress of mankind in general and of India in particular.

(*ii*) To develop in the pupil a proper understanding of his social and geographical environment, and to awaken the urge to improve it.

(*iii*) To inculcate the love of the mother land, reverence for its past, and a belief in its future destiny as the home of a united co-operative society based on love, truth and justice.

(*iv*) To develop a sense of the rights and responsibilities of citizenship.

(*v*) To develop the individual and social virtues which make a man a reliable associate and trusted neighbour.

(*vi*) To develop mutual respect for the world religions.

A course in history, in geography, in civics and in current events, combined with *a reverential study of the different religions of the world showing how in essentials they meet in perfect harmony*, will help to achieve these objectives. The study should begin with the child's own environment and its problems. His interest should be awakened in the manifold ways in which men supply their different wants. This should be made a starting point to arouse their curiosity about the life and work of men and women.

(A) *History.*—A simple outline of Indian history should be given. The chief land marks in the development of the social and cultural life of the people should be stressed, and the gradual movement towards greater political and cultural unity be shown. Emphasis should be laid on the ideals of love, truth and justice, of co-operative endeavour, national solidarity, and the equality and brotherhood of man. The treatment of the subject should be chiefly biographical in the lower, and cultural and social in the upper grades. Care should be taken to prevent pride in the past from degenerating into an arrogant and exclusive nationalism. Stories of the great liberators of mankind and their victories of peace should find a prominent place in the curriculam.

(B) *Civics.*—The pupils should become acquainted with the public utility services, the working of the panchayat and the co-operative society, the duties of the public servants, the constitution of the District Board and Municipality, the use and significance of the vote, and with the growth and significance of representative institutions. Training under this head should be as realistic as possible and should be brought into close relationship with actual life. Self-governing institutions should be introduced in the school. The pupils should be kept in intelligent touch with important current events through the co-operative study of some paper, preferably brought out by the school community.

(C) *Geography.*—The course in social studies should also include a study of world geography in out line, with a fuller knowledge of India and its relations with other lands. It should consist of:— (*a*) Study of the plant, animal and human life in the home region and in other lands as controlled by geographical environment (stories, description, picture-study, practical observation and discussion, with constant reference to local facts and phenomena). (*b*) Study and representation of weather phenomena; [mainly out door work, e.g., direct observation of the sun; changes in the height of the noonday sun at different times of the year;

readings of the weather vane, thermometer and barometer; methods of recording temperature and pressure; records of rainy and dry days and of the rainfall; prevailing wind directions; duration of day and night in different months; etc.]. (*c*) Map-study and map-making; the world a globe; study of local topography; making of and study of plans of the neighbourhood; recognition of conventional signs; use of the atlas and its index. (*d*) Study of the means of transport and communication correlated with industries and life. (*e*) Study of occupations; local agriculture and industry; economic self-sufficiency and interdependence of different regions; types of agriculture and industry favoured by geographical environment; the principal industries of India.

V. *General Science.*

The objectives are:

(i) To give pupils an intelligent and appreciative outlook on nature.

(ii) To form in the pupils habits of accurate observation and of testing experience by experiments.

(iii) To enable them to understand the important scientific principles exemplified in the natural phenomena around, and in the application of science to the service of man.

(iv) To introduce them to the more important incidents in the lives of the great scientists whose sacrifices in the cause of truth make a powerful appeal to the growing mind.

The curriculum should include the following topics from various sciences:—

(A) *Nature Study.*—(*a*) A knowledge of plants, crops, animals and birds in the environment. (*b*) A knowledge of the changes of seasons and their effect on the activity of plants, animals, birds and man. (*c*) A knowledge of crops in different seasons.

(B) *Botany.*—(*a*) Different parts of plants and their functions. (*b*) Processes of germination, growth and propagation. (*c*) Work on the school garden and the fields around to give the pupils an understanding of the effects of differing conditions of moisture, heat and light, and of the different qualities of seeds and manures.

(C) *Zoology.*—A study of germs, insects, reptiles and birds as friends and foes of man.

(D) *Physiology.*—The human body, its organs and functions.

(E) *Hygiene.*—(*a*) Personal Hygiene; cleanliness of teeth, tongue, nails, eyes, hair, nose, skin and clothes. (*b*) Cleanliness of the home and village; sanitation; disposal of night-soil. (*c*) Purewater; the village well. (*d*) Pure air; the function of trees in its purification; proper breathing. (*e*) Food, hygienic and unhygienic; balanced diets. (*f*) First aid and simple remedies. (*g*) Common infections; contagious diseases; how to safeguard against them. (*h*) Purity of conduct as a preservative of health.

(F) *Chemistry*—of air, water, acids, alkalis and salts.

(G) *Astronomy*—A knowledge of the Stars showing direction and time at night.

(H) *Physical Culture*—Games, Atheltics, drill (Deshi games to be encouraged).

(I) *Stories* of the great scientists and explorers and of their contributions to human well being.

VI. *Drawing.*

The objectives are—

(*i*) To train the eye in the observation and discrimination of forms and colours.

(*ii*) To develop the memory for forms.

(*iii*) To cultivate a knowledge of and appreciation for the beautiful in nature and in art.

(*iv*) To draw out the capacity for tasteful design and decoration.

(*v*) To develop the capacity to make working drawings of objects to be constructed.

These objectives can be obtained by (*a*) drawing made by children to illustrate read or observed material, (*b*) object and memory drawings, e.g., drawings of plants and of animal and human forms (correlated with work in general science, handicraft, etc.), (*c*) designing, (*d*) scale drawing, graphs and pictorial graphs.

The work in drawing during the first four

years should be correlated chiefly with work in reading and pictorial representation in nature study and the craft. During the last three years emphasis may be laid on design and decoration and mechanical drawing so as to enable pupils to make correct working drawings.

VII. *Music.*

The objective is to teach the pupils a number of beautiful songs and to cultivate in them a love for beautiful music. The child's natural sense of rhythm should be developed by teaching him to keep his own time by beating with the hand. Walking in time to a fixed rhythm can be a great aid in achieving this.

Care should be taken to select only the best and most inspiring songs, artistic interpretation of some healthy and elevating theme. Special emphasis should be placed on group or choral singing.

VIII. *Hindustani.*

The object of including Hindustani as a compulsory subject in the school curriculum is to ensure that all the children educated in these national schools may have a reasonable acquaintance with a common "lingua franca". In Hindustani-speaking areas this language will be the mother-tongue, but the students as well as the teachers will be required to learn both the scripts, so that they may read books written in Urdu as well as in Hindi. In non-Hindustani-speaking areas, where the provincial language will be the mother-tongue, the study of Hindustani will be compulsory during the 5th and 6th years of school life, but the children will have the choice of learning either one or the other script. However, in the case of teachers who have to deal with children of both kinds, knowledge of both the scripts is desirable.

The Committee in their second report submitted in April 1938, gave the detailed syllabus in each subject and indicated the portions and topics to be taught in each of the seven classes or grades. It should also be stated that in their first report the Committee made the following recommendation:—

"In general outlines, the syllabus of studies will be the same for boys and girls up to the 5th Grade (or Class V) of the school. In Grades 4 and 5, the syllabus in general science should be so modified as to include Domestic Science for girls. In Grades 6 and 7, the girls will be allowed to take an advanced course in Domestic Science in place of basic craft." (Harijan, Decr. 11, 1937.)

Several questions on the scheme were asked and many criticisms were made in the press and on the platform during the year 1938. But, perhaps, the best answer to them all was given by Mr. C. J. Varkey (Minister for Education, Government of Madras, in 1939) in the following words:—

"The present system of education is 'book-centred', while the Wardha system is 'child-centred', 'craft-centred' and 'teacher-centred'. *Child-centred,* because all teaching will be through concrete life situations relating to the child's social and physical environment, so that whatever the child learns becomes assimilated into his growing personality instead of, as at present, being a mere collection of unrelated facts having no direct bearings on children's experiences or on social life. *Craft-centred,* because all knowledge is to be learnt through the craft and all the child's powers are to be drawn out and developed through craft work. And *teacher-centred*, because the teacher is to play a more important and active part in the process of education and because the success of the scheme depends considerably in the knowledge, skill, enthusiasm and patriotism of the teacher."[1]

The question of adopting the Wardha scheme for the Congress Provinces[2] was discussed at the Haripura Session of the Indian National Congress in February 1938. The Congress passed the following resolution on the subject:—

"The Congress is of opinion that for the primary and secondary stages a basic education should be imparted in accordance with the following principles:

(*i*) "Free and compulsory education should be provided for seven years on a nation-wide scale."

[1] C. J. Varkey—"The Wardha Scheme of Education", page 166.

[2] During July 1937, to November 1939, the Congress Provinces were- Bombay, Madras, Bihar, Orissa, the United Provinces, the Central Provinces and the North-West Frontier Province.

Assam was also a Congress Province for over a year.

(*ii*) "The medium of instruction must be the mother-tongue."

(*iii*) "Throughout this period education should centre round some form of manual and productive work, and all other activities to be developed and training to be given should, as far as possible, be integrally related to the central handicraft chosen with due regard to the environment of the child."

It should be noted that *in the Congress Resolution there was no reference to the self-supporting character of the scheme.* Obviously the fourth resolution of the Wardha Conference which ran as follow: 'that the Conference expects that this system of education will be gradually able to cover the remuneration of the teachers', was considered as not a practical proposition.

The Central Advisory Board of Education of the Government of India in January 1938 appointed a committee 'to examine the scheme of educational reconstruction incorporated in the Wardha Scheme, in the light of the Wood-Abbott Report on General and Vocational Education and of other relevant documents'. The report of the Committee of the Board was considered by the whole Board in December of the same year. The following recommendations of the Committee were approved by the Central Advisory Board of Education of the Government of India:—

(1) "The scheme of basic education should first be introduced in rural areas."

(2) "The age range for compulsion should be 6 to 14 years but children can be admitted to the 'basic' school at the age of 5."

(3) "Diversion of students from the basic school to other kinds of school should be allowed after Class V or about the age of 11 plus."

(4) "The medium of instruction should be the language of the province."

(5) "A common language for India is desirable. This should be Hindustani with both the Urdu and Hindi scripts. Option should be given to children to choose the script and provision should be made for teaching them in that script. Every teacher should know both scripts, viz., Urdu and Hindi."

(6) "The Wardha Scheme of basic education is in full agreement with the recommendations made in the Wood-Abbott Report so far as the principle of learning by doing is concerned. This activity should be of many kinds in the lower classes and later should lead to a basic craft the produce from which should be saleable and the proceeds applied to the upkeep of the school."

(7) "In the lowest classes education should be carried on through the activities."

(8) "Certain elements of cultural subjects cannot be correlated with the basic craft and must be taught independently."

(9) "The training of teachers should be reorganised and their status raised."

(10) "No teacher should receive less than Rs. 20 per mensem."

(11) "Efforts should be made to recruit more women teachers."

(12) "Basic schools should be started only when suitable trained teachers are available."

(13) "The curriculum will need revision in the light of experience."

(14) "English should not be introduced as an optional subject in basic schools."*

(15) *"The State should provide facilities for every community to give religious teaching."*

(16) "No external examinations need be held. At the end of the basic school course a leaving certificate based on an internal examination should be given."

(17) "Pupils wishing to join other schools at the age of about 11 plus should also be granted a leaving certificate."

(18) "Promotion from class to class will be determined by the school, though the results of the internal examinations should be subject to the supervisors' inspection."[1]

* The Committee's Report to the Board states:—"The Committee agree that the demand for English will be met by the transfer after Class V or about the age of 11 plus to schools where English is taught and that English should not be included in the curriculum of 'basic' Wardha schools."

[1] *Vide* Proceedings of the Central Advisory Board of Education quoted by Mr. C. J. Varkey in his book on the Wardha Scheme of Education, pages 171 and 172.

The above recommendations were not binding on the Provincial Governments. They were in the nature of an advice given by the educational experts of the Government of India. In a few of the provinces, e.g., the United Provinces of Agra and Oudh, the Central Provinces, the Bombay Presidency, the Madras Presidency and Orissa the Congress Ministers before they resigned[2] started a number of teachers training schools in conformity to the programme of the basic education scheme. To each of these training schools were attached at least one demonstration school and several practising schools to impart basic education according to the syllabus and the technique outlined in the report of the Wardha Education Committee. The Ministers for Education in two other provinces, viz., Bihar, and the North-West Frontier Provinces, also prepared schemes for starting such schools before they resigned. But no such schools were actually opened in N.-W. Frontier Province. The Governments of Bengal, Assam, Sindh and the Punjab did not consider the scheme as suitable for introduction in their provinces.

The Government of Orissa in a communique issued on the 6th Febraury 1941, announced their decision to close the Basic schools and the Training School with effect from the 1st March 1941. As the arguments in support of their decision may have a general application they are quoted below:—

[2] The Congress Ministers resigned in November 1939.

"In 1938, Government decided to experiment on a system of education known as the Wardha Scheme of Basic Education.....A training school for teachers for the Basic Schools was started in June 1939, and 15 Basic Schools were opened in February 1940."

"Since the scheme was only an experimental one, Government sanctioned it temporarily for a period of one year which has just expired. They have now examined the progress of the experiment in the light of the report of the Director of Public Instruction and have decided that it is not in the interests of this province to continue it further. Some of the reasons which led to this decision are given below."

"Although the idea behind the scheme is that teaching instead of relying on text-books should be correlated to the exercise of some craft chosen out of a number of different crafts likely to bring about an all-round development of the children, only one craft, i.e., spinning, has actually been adopted in the Basic schools at Bari, and Government are advised that no other useful craft can be substituted or added owing to lack of teachers capable of giving instruction through such crafts,"

"The Wardha scheme provides for 3 hours 20 minutes of every school day of 5½ hours to be spent in the practice of crafts, and there is an obvious likelihood that with no alternative craft to spinning these schools will quickly degenerate into mere spinning schools. Spinning is a sedentary and monotonous occupation and not at all calculated to lead to the all-round development of children in Orissa, where a more stimulating medium of instruction is obviously required. Moreover, as no craft other than spinning can be introduced, this experiment cannot even be given the best chance of success in this province."

"These Basic schools are far more expensive than the ordinary primary schools, and it would be quite impossible for this province to introduce them on a large scale unless they proved to be self-supporting. In this respect also the experiment has not shown any signs of success. The actual receipts of the Basic schools in Orissa are reported to have amounted to 8 annas per head against an estimate of Rs. 3-9 a head for the first year in the original scheme. They have therefore failed in the 'acid test' prescribed by the author of the scheme."

"The cost of continuing the existing 15 schools together with the Training School for a further period of three years would be approximately Rs. 1¼ lakhs, and if the experiment were continued on a seven years' basis, i.e., for the whole course, the cost would be very much greater. In the financial circumstances of this province such a heavy expediture is not justified merely in order to test the merits of the scheme. It is understood that the Government of Madras during the Congress regime decided against the introduction of the system, preferring a revised system of elementary education which is believed to be fundamentally the same as the primary school system already in force in Orissa. The experiment is, however, being carried out in some other provinces and from the results so obtained it will be possible to ascertain the value and practicability of the system without incurring the heavy expenditure required to try it out thoroughly in Orissa,"

"Government have therefore decided to close the Basic schools and Training school with effect from the 1st March, 1941. Attempts will be made to absorb the teachers trained in these schools into the ordinary schools of the province as far as possible."

An account of the progress of the experiment of the Basic system of education introduced in 90 selected schools of the Allahabad District Board is contained in the Board's Annual Report for 1940-41. The Report says that the teachers have been able to assimilate the principles of basic system of education. The children have become engrossed in their task under this new system. The cultivation of artistic talent, almost wholly absent in the past, has made the teachers' work remarkably interesting. The boys show their peculiar taste for self-expression and the work of majority in designing, paper cutting, folding, pottery and marble making, etc., is marvellous. Then can spin on their taklis with sufficient ease and rapidity. The scheme, however, has been partially abandoned in some of the other areas in the United Provinces.

With the closing of the experimental Basic

schools in the Madras Presidency and Orissa, and the partial abandonment of the scheme in the Central Provinces, the United Provinces and the Bombay Presidency the Basic Education Syllabus has now become a matter of history. Perhaps when the present political controversies die out the educational significance of the Wardha scheme will be more fully realised.

SECTION III.—THE EDUCATION OF MUSLIMS AND SPECIAL CLASSES.

For many years the Muslims of India have been backward in the matter of education in general. "The most powerful factors in keeping the majority of Moslems aloof from the educational movement of the day were pride of race, a memory of bygone superiority, religious fears and a not unnatural attachment to the learning of Islam."[1] On the other hand, the Hindus have taken increasing advantage of the benefits of Western Education. Special encouragement therefore should be given to the spread of higher education among Muslims. With reference to primary education however they can now scarcely be said to need any such special help. The Education Commission of 1882-83 recommended that special encouragement of Muslim education was to be regarded as a legitimate charge on Local (District Board), Municipal, and Provincial funds.

[1] Earl of Ronaldshay—'India—A Bird's-Eye View', page 235.

Since then all these authorities have given encouragement to Muslim education by prescribing special standards for Muslim primary schools, by making Urdu the principal medium of instruction, except in Bengal where the mother tongue of the Muslims is Bengali, and by providing special scholarships for them. These encouragements gave a great impetus to Muslim education. The percentage of Muslim pupils to the total of pupils of all classes in all institutions (public and private) in India in 1918 was 23·5.[1] The percentage of the Muslim population in India in the same year was also 23·5. In Bengal, "the proportion of Muslims in primary schools was 51·4 per cent. in 1918-19, so that at this stage of education they have nearly reached their proper percentage according to their proportion of the general population, which is 52·7."[2] In India, the population of school-going age is now reckoned at 12 per cent of the total population. Formerly, the school-going population used to be reckoned at 14 per cent. But for various reasons discussed in the Quinquennial Review on Progress of Education in India during 1932-37, the Educational Commissioner with the Government of India lays down that the approximate number for the school-going population in India is 12 per cent. of the total popula-

[1] Statistics of British India (1917-1918), Vol. V, Education, page X.

[2] Biss—First Report on Primary Education in Bengal, page 31.

tion.* In 1931, after the new census was taken, 11·5 per cent. of the Indian Christian population, 6·1 per cent. of the Sikhs, 5·1 per cent. of the Buddhists, 5·0 per cent. of the Muslims and only 4·4 per cent. of the Hindus in British India were under instruction.[1] In 1937, the percentage of Muslim pupils to Muslim population further increased to 5·5. In British India the percentage of Muslim population to total population was 24·7, according to the Census of 1931 and it is satisfactory to note that the percentage of Muslim pupils to total pupils was 26·1 at the end of the last quinquennium in 1937. Moreover the following figures reveal the situation in some of the important provinces.[2]

* The Educational Commissioner says:—"The total population on which the percentage for 1932 and 1937 have been calculated is that of 1931 census. Recent calculations on the basis of this census have shown that the percentage of children of educable age (*i.e.* between the ages of 6 and 11 years) to the total population is approximately 12 per cent. As stated in the United Provinces Report, at the most only 15 per cent. of the population will under the most favourable conditions be attending *schools of all grades*. In the whole of British India the percentage of pupils attending all types of schools to the total population is 5·2 only. There is thus much leeway to be made up." (*Vide* Quinquennial Review on Progress of Education in India, 1932-37, page 13.)

[1] Education in India in 1930-31 (Government of India Publication), page 3.

[2] Quinquennial Review on Progress of Education in India 1932-37 (Government of India Publication, 1940), page 242.

Province	Percentage of Muslim population to total population.	Percentage of Muslim pupils to Muslim population. (standard to be reached is 12 per cent.)	Percentage of Muslim pupils to total pupils.
N. W. Frontier Province	91·8	3·2	71·0
Punjab ...	56·5	4·7	48·6
Bengal ...	54·9	6·0	51·7
Assam ...	32·0	4·6	27·4
United Provinces	14·8	4·2	18·3
Bihar ...	12·8	3·6	14·9
Bombay ...	8·8	11·6	13·7
Madras ...	7·5	10·8	11·2
Central Provinces...	4·4	7·8	10·7
Orissa ...	1·6	7·5	2·9

In some provinces like Bombay, Madras, United Provinces, Bengal, Bihar and Orissa the percentage of Muslims at school is increasing more rapidly than that of other communities. This is undoubtedly a healthy sign. In Madras, there was a satisfactory increase in the number of Muslim boys and girls under instruction, the increase being 9 per cent in the case of boys and 26 per cent in the case of girls. In Bombay, the educational progress of Muslims has been as satisfactory as could have been expected. There has been an increase of 11·3 per cent. in the number of Muslim pupils in the province. In Bengal, the total number of Muslim pupils is nearly twice what it was in 1922. The number of Muslim pupils in schools in Bengal is now roughly proportionate to the total Muslim population.

The percentage of Anglo-Indian and European pupils to the total Anglo-Indian and European population in British India is 23·5 as against 5·2 for all communities. This high percentage shows that practically all the children of school going age belonging to the community are attending schools and colleges.

The people of the low castes and aboriginal tribes did not make much progress in education; and they formed the bulk of the population in some provinces. No doubt special encouragements were given for the education of these communities by exempting them from payment of fees, by giving them extra allowances under the results-grants system and by liberally assisting many private associations like the Christian Missions, the Society for the Improvement of Backward Classes, etc.. which have been willing to establish schools for them. Yet they are even now far behind the other communities in educational attainments. However, with the enforcement of the compulsory system of education for boys the illiteracy of the male population of all communities will soon disappear.

SECTION IV.—THE EDUCATION OF GIRLS.

So far as literacy in India is concerned its progress among the female population may almost be ignored. No one can possibly determine by actual calculation what has been its reaction on the male population; but it can be pointed out that when the light of knowledge never reaches half the population, the stimulus to education in the other half becomes necessarily very feeble. Such a state of things practically makes 'home education' an impossibility, and the figures of literacy are affected. Education consequently does not bulk as a customary and natural adjunct of home life. In 1931 the percentage of female scholars in public and private institutions to female population of British India was only 1·8. This undoubtedly affected the figures for literacy of the whole population of India. Of course rapid strides were made during 1932 to 1937 to spread education among girls and the percentage of increase in the number of girls receiving education in recognised institutions was 25·9 in March 1937. Still it should be remembered that even in 1937, the percentage of female scholars in all types of institutions to female population was only 2·38.[1] It is to be regretted that the majority of the provinces, when they passed the Compulsory Education Acts, confined their attention to boys. Only the Bombay Acts of 1920 and 1923 provided clauses for compulsory primary education of children of both sexes whose age is not less than six and not more than eleven years. The former Act (for the

[1] Quinquennial Review on Progress of Education in India, 1932-37, Statistical Tables and Appendices (Vol. II), page 3.

City of Bombay) also stated that of the sixteen members of the school committee at least two shall be women, not being municipal councillors, resident in the City of Bombay. The Acts of the Punjab, Bihar and Orissa, and the United Provinces contemplated providing compulsory education for boys only. The Acts of the Central Provinces and Madras laid down clauses to extend the provisions to girls when funds permitted after making arrangements for the compulsory education of the boys. The Bengal and Assam Acts contained provisions for making education of girls compulsory. But nowhere these provisions of the Acts have been enforced. "The exclusion of girls from practically all schemes for the introduction of compulsory education is one of the reasons for the great increase in disparity between the development of education for boys and girls during the last quinquennium and, if the total exclusion of Muslim girls is continued, there is no doubt that this community will fall rapidly behind all others in the matter of education for both boys and girls, since it is impossible to bring boys of uneducated parents to the same standard of education as boys who come from homes in which the women as well as the men are educated."[1]

Household work is considered in India a woman's chief work in life, and as such, her

[1] Report on the Development of Women's Education in the Madras Presidency (Madras Government Press, 1928), page 12.

education is entirely domestic and may even be called vocational. The education of girls in India was and still is a preparation for the duties of the household. In ancient India, however, women had a much higher status than they have occupied from the time the caste system became prevalent. Very early marriage of girls and compulsory widowhood were unknown in Vedic times; and there were instances of marriage taking place by free choice of man and maid. The Sanskrit word *acharyani* which now means the wife of a professor used to mean in ancient times a lady-professor. From the time the early marriage of girls became a custom, the only education thought best for them was that which made them fit to discharge their duties in the homes of their husbands. The Muhammadans also believed in the same kind of instruction for girls as the Hindus did, *viz.*, preparation for household work. The inevitable result was that though their women became very proficient in housewifery they began to grow up in illiteracy. Women in India, therefore, became very conservative and scrupulous in performing their household duties which they considered their religion. They began to believe implicitly what their husbands and priests used to say. G. K. Gokhale more than forty years ago remarked—"A combination of enforced ignorance and overdone religion has not only made women in India willing victims of customs, unjust and hurtful in the highest degree, but it has also made them the most formidable and the most effective opponents of all change or innovation." This is true even now—all social reform programmes as regards removal of untouchability, caste distinction, etc. are made ineffective by the women clinging rigidly to their orthodox ideas. The classic Indian ideal of womanhood with its wonderful vicarious suffering, its selflessness and devotion, is enough to make the world admire such a type of girls, yet it may bring tears to the eyes of those who listen to their past sufferings. Better times have dawned since the days of Rajah Ram Mohan Roy, Pandit Iswar Chandra Vidyasagar, Keshub Chunder Sen, M. G. Ranade and the pioneer Christian missionaries who advocated *zenana* education; but even now one may possibly say that in India it would be better for the husbands themselves if their wives were less soft and good.

The Indian Education Commission of 1882-83 made a special recommendation for the spread of education among the female population. Accordingly the standards of instruction for primary girls' schools were made simpler than those for the boys and were drawn up with special reference to the requirements of home life and to the occupations open to women. Small fees were levied in some schools and a large number of them in different parts of India were free; and no girls' school was debarred from a grant on account of its not levying fees. Special provision was made for girls' scholarships, and with a view to encouraging girls to remain longer at school, a certain proportion of them was reserved for girls above twelve years of age. The establishment of infant schools or classes under schoolmistresses was liberally encouraged. The Commission suggested that an alternative examination in subjects suitable for girls should be instituted, corresponding in standard to the Matriculation examination, but having no relation to any existing University course. This suggestion, however, was not carried out by the Department of Education.

During the last fifty years the social conditions of women in India have undoubtedly changed, and are still changing; but the process has been and is a very slow one. In India any sudden and disastrous dislocation of the social structure will not be tolerated by any community. At the same time the enlightenment of women is necessary for the well-being of a progressive society. This could be brought about by extending the compulsory system of primary education to girls as well. The *purdah* no doubt prevails in Northern India, but even there girls under ten years of age come out of it. Hence, if primary education for girls be made compulsory along with that for the boys, in the first instance, up to the age of ten, there would not be a sudden dislocation of the social structure. Once a taste for learning is acquired it is bound to increase and will eventually pave the way for social amelioration. The widened outlook on life due to the acquirement of knowledge, coupled with the classic Indian ideal of womanhood, will no doubt enable the girls to make their homes sweeter and happier than they could otherwise do.

SECTION V—COST OF COMPULSORY PRIMARY EDUCATION AND CONCLUDING REMARKS.

The average monthly salaries of teachers in boys' and girls' primary schools are almost incredibly low, especially when it is borne in mind that they cover all kinds of schools, viz., the schools managed by Government, District Boards, Municipalities and schools for girls in which salaries are comparatively high, as well as aided schools in which salaries are low. In Madras and Bombay they cover higher elementary schools which carry their pupils up to class VIII, and are obviously not comparable with ordinary village schools with three or four classes. They cover schools in big cities like Calcutta and Bombay (where fairly high scales of pay prevail) as well as in schools in small villages. Taking all these into consideration, the average monthly pay of teachers in boys' and girls' primary schools in 1929 was calculated as follows:—The Bombay Presidency—Rs. 47-0-0; The Punjab—Rs. 25-8-0; The Central Provinces—Rs. 24-8-0; The United Provinces of Agra and Oudh—Rs. 18-8-0; The Madras Presidency—Rs. 15-4-0; Assam—Rs. 14-4-0; Bihar and Orissa—Rs. 11-5-0; and Bengal—Rs. 8-6-0. There has not been much change in the average pay of teachers during the last twelve years. In some of the provinces the figures have gone up slightly. The untrained teacher is naturally paid a lower salary than the trained teacher and there are as many as 162,000 untrained teachers in India in primary schools. In view of the large preponderance of single-teacher schools, of the lax attendance and of the alarming extent of wastage, it is essential that the teachers should both have initial qualifications and be well trained, but it can hardly be expected that any large number of such teachers can be secured in existing conditions of recruitment, training and pay. *The average direct cost of educating a boy in a primary school in 1937 was slightly more than Rs. 7 per year and that of a girl about Rs. 10 per year.* There were nearly 11·5 millions of pupils in primary schools for boys and girls and another 1·9 millions of pupils in other types of educational institutions throughout British India in 1937. The total number represented 7·86 per cent. of the male population and only 2·38 per cent. of the female population according to the Census of 1931. India now spends from all sources (viz., Government funds, District Board funds, Municipal funds, fees and other sources) nearly 86 millions of rupees for the education of nearly 11·5 millions of boys and girls. There are about 9 millions of boys and over 13 millions of girls of school-going age who are not in school and for whom provision must be made. Even assuming that under a system of compulsory education 90 per cent. of the remaining number of boys and girls are brought under instruction provision will have to be made for the education of nearly 8 millions of boys and 12 millions of girls. On the basis of the existing expenditure (viz., Rs. 8 per boy and Rs. 10 per girl), although it is exceedingly low, the additional cost will be 64 millions of rupees for boys and 120 millions of rupees for girls, or in other words the additional cost for introducing compulsory primary education for both boys and girls throughout British India will be 184 millions of rupees. Hence, taking into consideration the existing expenditure on primary schools, the total recurring cost for compulsory education of all boys and girls will be approximately 270 millions of rupees. In addition to this expenditure there will, of course, be a heavy capital expenditure on buildings and equipment.[1]

The Census of 1941 will no doubt show a large increase in population in all the provinces of India. This will also mean an increase of nearly ten per cent. in the total number of school-going children. Therefore the total recurring cost for compulsory education will

[1] This paragraph is based on Chapter IV (Section VI) and Chapter XIV (Section III) of the Review of Growth of Education in British India by the Auxiliary Committee appointed by the Indian Statutory Commission (1928-29), the Government of India Report on Education in India in 1930-31, and the Report on the Progress of Education in India during the Quinquennium 1932-37.

work out to be nearly 300 millions of rupees. The amount estimated is no doubt large. But after all, nations manage to find the money they need for war. A war against illiteracy has long been overdue. *In India even in 1940, the authorities were thinking in terms of the scheme of expansion of education prepared by England in 1870.* The progress of education in India under such a condition was bound to be unsatisfactory. England's important schemes for the development of education were prepared during the Boer War of 1899-1902 and the last Great War of 1914-18. Two most comprehensive Education Acts were passed by Parliament in 1902 and 1918 respectively. The whole outlook in India requires to be changed if a war against illiteracy is to be fought.

In the scheme of compulsory education the village schoolmaster has a great part to play. At present there are over 376,000 teachers (viz., 336,000 men teachers and 40,000 women teachers) serving in all types of primary schools, of whom 214,000 are trained and 162,000 are untrained. A very large proportion of the untrained teachers possess qualifications which are scarcely superior to those of the pupils in the highest class of the primary stage. Moreover nearly 21·5 per cent. of the trained teachers possess very meagre educational qualifications. They did not proceed beyond the primary stage of instruction in their own school days. Strictly speaking, they cannot be classed as trained teachers. If their number be excluded, then the total number of trained teachers possessing qualifications higher than the primary stage comes down to only 168,000. Facilities for training are urgently required if the scheme of compulsory primary education is to succeed in different provinces of India. Mr. F. L. Brayne in his book on the *Village Uplift in India,* considers the schoolmaster as the pivot of the scheme. He says that "there are four things to teach the villager and to teach the worker who is to go to the villager, viz., (*a*) the dignity of labour, (*b*) the dignity of women, (*c*) the dignity of cleanliness, and (*d*) the dignity of service. The village schoolmaster with his school library, his day school, his night school and his scouts must be the centre of uplift and culture, and he must be so trained that he can solve all the simple problems of the villager, whether they are agricultural, public health, social and moral. But a great obstacle is the low rate of wages for all literate labour which encourages and indeed makes necessary all forms of undesirable selfishness. A spirit of service may survive a period of wages pitched below the economic minimum, but it will not be born in such a period, and if we want willing labour we must be ready to pay for it. This is not extravagance, it is the simplest and most obvious form of economy: but it is one of the hardest to learn."

In conclusion, it is to be stated that education should not be merely a means to improving the conditions of life; it should be the life itself. The social spirit must permeate the entire range of education and school itself should form a community. The interest of the pupils should be so awakened that each should feel that he is better for the other; and their activities should be regulated by the common end to do more service to the country and humanity. Each school should feel that it is a social centre and impress upon the minds of every pupil his immense responsibility for the improvement of the sanitary, economic and social conditions of the country. Though exaggerated hopes cannot be placed on schooling and the social millennium cannot be brought about by education alone, yet it can do more than any other agency to remedy the social evils. At the present time the powers of the individual need greater development than before. But he should develop his powers and try to realize himself in society and not outside it. He would thus be able to improve the conditions of society and ultimately the State itself. The State should, therefore, spend larger sums than before in providing opportunities for this purpose through educational agencies. No State in these days can spend too much on an object like education. Throughout the world every civilised Government now accepts it as a sacred obligation resting on it to provide for the free and compulsory education of its people. And the following words of Mr. G. K. Gokhale, uttered in 1910, have assumed a special significance on account of rapid democratization of the machinery of government of the country:—"This question of compulsory and free primary education is now in this country the question of questions. The well-being of millions upon millions of children who are waiting to be brought under the humanising influence of education depends upon it. The increased efficiency of the individual, the higher general level of intelligence, the stiffening of the moral backbone of large sections of the community, none of these things can come without education. In fact, the whole of our future as a nation is inextricably bound up with it." It is, therefore, no exaggeration to say that at the present time education is at the heart of the whole problem of reconstruction in India.

BIBLIOGRAPHY

List of Books, Reports and Documents consulted in the preparation of this book.

Adam, W.—"Reports on Vernacular Education in Bengal, 1835 to 1838" (with a note by Rev. J. Long, and published by the Secretariat Press, Calcutta, 1868).

Banerjea, Sir Gooroo Dass—"The Education Problem in India" (S. K. Lahiri & Co., Calcutta, 1914).

Banerjea, Pramatha Nath—"Public Administration in Ancient India" (Macmillan & Co., 1916).

Basu, B. D., Major—History of Education in India under the Rule of the East India Company (Panini Office, 1923).

Beal, Samuel—"The Life of Hiuentsiang" (translated from Chinese and published in the Trubner's Oriental Series, 1888).

Birdwood, Sir George—"Industrial Arts of India" (South Kensington Museum Art Hand Books Series, 1880).

Cowan, M. G.—"The Education of Women of India" (Oliphant, Henderson & Co., Edinburgh, 1912).

Grierson, Sir George—"Modern Vernacular Literature of Hindústan" (Asiatic Society of Bengal, 1889).

Howell, Arthur—"Education in British India prior to 1854 and in 1870-71" (Supdt. Government Printing, Calcutta, 1872).

Keay, F. E.—"Ancient Indian Education" (Humphrey Milford & Co,. London, 1918).

Keene, H. G.—"The Fall of the Moghul Empire" (W. H. Allen & Co., 1887).

Kripalini, J. B.—"The Latest Fad—Basic Education" (The Hindustani Talimi Sangha, Segaon, Wardha, 1938).

Law, Narendra Nath—"Promotion of Learning in India by Muhammadans" (Longmans, Green & Co., 1916).

Law, Narendra Nath—"Promotion of Learning in India by Early European Settlers" (Longmans, Green & Co., 1915).

Leitner, G. W.—"History of Indigenous Education in the Punjab since annexation and in 1882" (Superintendent, Government Printing, India, 1882).

Lethbridge, Sir Roper—"High Education in India" (W. H. Allen & Co., 1882).

Bibliography—*continued.*

Majumdar, Ramesh Chandra—"Corporate Life in Ancient India" (Calcutta, 1918).

Mazumdar, N. N.—"History of Education in Ancient India" (Macmillan & Co., 1917).

Matthai, John—"Village Government in British India" (T. Fisher Unwin, 1915).

Mayhew, Arthur—"The Education of India" (Faber & Gwyer, Ltd., London, 1926).

Mookerjee, Radhakumud—"Local Government in Ancient India" (Oxford, Clarendon Press, 1920).

Muhammad Azizul Huque—"History and Problems of Moslem Education in Bengal" (Thacker, Spink & Co., 1917).

Satthianadhan, S.—"History of Education in the Madras Presidency" (Madras, 1894).

Stark, H. A.—"Vernacular Education in Bengal from 1813 to 1912" (Calcutta General Publishing Co., 1916).

Taylor & Fergusson—"Architecture at Bijapur" (John Murray, 1866).

Thomas, F. W.—"History and Prospects of British Education in India" (George Bell & Sons, 1891).

Varkey, C. J.—"The Wardha Scheme of Education" (Oxford University Press, 1939).

Zutshi. Monohar Lal—"Education in British India" (The Indian Press, Allahabad, 1910).

B

Annual Reports of the Directors of Public Instruction of different provinces of India.

Annual Reports on Education in India.

Despatches from the Home Government on the subject of Education in India, 1854 to 1868 (published by Superintendent, Govt. Printing, 1870).

Education Acts of different provinces of India.

Proceedings of the Legislative Councils in India.

Quinquennial Reviews of Progress of Education in India.

Reports of the Parliamentary Debates.

Reports of the Indian Education Commission of 1882-83.

Report of the Calcutta University Commission of 1917-19.

Reports on the Expansion and Improvement of Primary Education in Bengal by Evan E. Biss, 1921 and 1922.

Report on the Elementary Education Survey of the Madras Presidency, 1924-25.

Report on the Development of Women's Education in the Madras Presidency, 1928.

Bibliography—*continued.*

Report of the Committee on Primary and Secondary Education in the Bombay Presidency, 1929.

Report of the Punjab University Enquiry Committee, 1932-33.

Report on India prepared for presentation to Parliament every year in accordance with the requirements of the Government of India Act by the Director of the Central Burea of Information, Government of India.

Review of Growth of Education in India (1928-29).

Selections from Educational Records, Part I, 1781 to 1839 (edited by H. Sharp) and Part II, 1840-59 (edited by J. A. Richey) published by the Bureau of Education, India.

Village Education in India—Report of a Commission of Inquiry by the Missionary Societies, 1920.

INDEX.